T0305134

# The Trust Process in Organizations

# The Trust Process in Organizations

Empirical Studies of the Determinants and the Process of Trust Development

*Edited by*

Bart Nooteboom

*Professor of Organizational Dynamics, Rotterdam School of Management, Erasmus University Rotterdam, The Netherlands*

Frédérique Six

*PhD candidate, Rotterdam School of Management, Erasmus University Rotterdam, The Netherlands*

**Edward Elgar**
Cheltenham, UK • Northampton, MA, USA

Published by
Edward Elgar Publishing Limited
Glensanda House
Montpellier Parade
Cheltenham
Glos GL50 1UA
UK

Edward Elgar Publishing, Inc.
136 West Street
Suite 202
Northampton
Massachusetts 01060
USA

A catalogue record for this book
is available from the British Library

**Library of Congress Cataloguing-in-Publication Data**
The trust process in organizations : empirical studies of the determinants and the process of trust development / edited by Bart Nooteboom, Frédérique Six.
   p.  cm.
Includes index.
   1. Organizational behavior. 2. Corporate culture. 3. Psychology, Industrial. 4. Management. 5. Leadership. 6. Trust. I. Nooteboom, B. II. Six, Frédérique, 1962–

HD58.7.T744   2003
302.3′5–dc21                                 2002032055

MIX
Paper | Supporting
responsible forestry
FSC® C013604

ISBN 978-1-843-76078-8

Printed and bound by CPI Group (UK) Ltd, Croydon, CR0 4YY

# Contents

# Figures

# Tables

# Contributors

**Reinhard Bachmann** is Assistant Professor of Organizational Behaviour and Organizational Theory at the Faculty of Economics of the University of Groningen (the Netherlands). His research interests lie in the fields of organization studies, international business and the sociology of science and technology. Among his publications are articles in *Organization Studies*, the *British Journal of Sociology* and the *Cambridge Journal of Economics*. Together with Christel Lane, he edited *Trust Within and Between Organizations* (Oxford University Press). Together with David Knights and Jörg Sydow, he was guest editor of a Special Issue of *Organization Studies*, on 'Trust and Control in Organizational Relations'.

**Ana Cristina Costa** is Assistant Professor of Management and Organization in the department of product innovation and management of the Delft University of Technology (the Netherlands). She received her MSc in Psychology from the ISPA Institute at Lisbon University (Portugal) and her PhD at Tilburg University. Her research interests are organizational change and implications for work processes, trust and team behaviour in organizations and trust within and climate for innovation. She has published in the *European Journal of Work and Organizational Psychology* and the *Revista de Psicologica Social*, as well as writing a number of book chapters.

**Deanne den Hartog** is Professor of Organizational Psychology in the faculty of economics of the Erasmus University Rotterdam (The Netherlands). She received her PhD in Psychology from the Free University of Amsterdam (the Netherlands). A central topic of her research is (inspirational) leadership in organizations. Other interests include trust, commitment, psychological contracts, personality, team reflexivity and human resource management. She has (co-)authored Dutch books on leadership and human resource management. Her work has appeared in the *Journal of Occupational and Organizational Psychology*, the *Leadership Quarterly*, the *Journal of Leadership Studies*, *Handbook of Industrial, Work and Organizational Psychology* (Sage) and the *European Journal of Work and Organizational Psychology*.

**Nathalie Lazaric** is a researcher at CNRS, Latapses IDEFI (France). She holds an MA in Economics from the University of Villetaneuse (France) and a PhD from the University of Technology of Compiègne (France). Her research interests are organizational learning, routines, knowledge in the firm, organizational change, trust and evolutionary theory. She has co-edited books on *Coordination économique et apprentissage des firmes* and *Trust and economic learning* and has recently published in the *European Journal of Economic and Social Systems*, *Economies et Sociétés*, *Revista de Economia Contemporénea* and *Industrial and Corporate Change*.

**Siegwart Lindenberg** is Professor of Theoretical Sociology at the University of Groningen (the Netherlands). He received his PhD from Harvard University (USA). His research interests focus mainly on issues of governance (ranging from the analysis of revolutions to the analysis of intrinsic motivation in organizations) and the development of theories of 'social rationality' (which includes social production function theory of goals and framing theory). His recent publications include the articles, 'It takes both trust and lack of mistrust: The workings of cooperation and relational signalling in contractual relationships', in the *Journal of Management and Governance* and 'Social Rationality Versus Rational Egoism' in J. Turner (ed.), *Handbook of Sociological Theory* (Kluwer Academic/Plenum).

**Bart Nooteboom** is Professor of Organizational Dynamics in the Rotterdam School of Management at the Erasmus University Rotterdam (the Netherlands). His research interests include learning in and between organizations; philosophy of economics and management, with emphasis on theory of knowledge, learning and language; industrial/innovation/ technology policy and innovation systems. He has recently published *Trust: functions, foundations, failures and facts* (Edward Elgar), *The causal structure of long-term supply relationships* (with Gjalt de Jong, Kluwer), *Learning and innovation in organizations and economies* (Oxford University Press) and *Inter-firm alliances; Analysis and design* (Routledge).

**Frédérique Six** is a PhD candidate at the Erasmus University Rotterdam (the Netherlands) with Bart Nooteboom (Erasmus University Rotterdam) and Arndt Sorge (University of Groningen). She has been a management consultant for some 15 years with McKinsey & Company and KPMG. She holds an MBA from INSEAD (France) and an MSc in environmental engineering from the Agricultural University Wageningen (the Netherlands). Her research interests are the dynamics of trust and trouble, creating the conditions for learning, change and innovation in organizations and tackling social challenges with dialogue in issue networks, social entrepreneurship and social partnerships.

**Henk de Vos** is Associate Professor in Theoretical Sociology, department of sociology, University of Groningen (the Netherlands). He holds a PhD in Sociology from the University of Utrecht. His research interests are in human social evolution, simulation, evolutionary sociology, community in contemporary society and sociological policy analysis. He has published articles in *Social Science Information*, *Evolution and Human Behavior*, *Rationality and Society* and the *Journal of Artificial Societies and Social Simulation*, and a number of book chapters.

**Rudi Wielers** is Associate Professor of Labour and Organization at the faculty of management of the Erasmus University Rotterdam (the Netherlands). He holds an MS in Sociology and History and a PhD in Social Sciences from the University of Groningen. His research interests are trust and solidarity, governance of employment relationships and workforce and employment relationships of the future. He has published in *Work, Employment and Society*, *Computational and Mathematical Organization Theory*, *Acta Sociologica*, *Kyklos* and *Rationality and Society*.

**Rafael Wittek** is Professor of Sociology at ICS/department of sociology of the University of Groningen (the Netherlands). He holds an MA in Cultural Anthropology and Sociology from the University of Tübingen (Germany) and a PhD in Sociology from the University of Groningen. His research interests are solidarity at work, informal control and social capital. He has published in the *Journal of Mathematical Sociology*, *Computational and Mathematical Organization Theory*, *Ethik und Sozialwissenschaften* and *Sociale Wetenschappen*.

# 1. Introduction

## Bart Nooteboom and Frédérique Six

## INTRODUCTION

Much has been written about trust (for a survey, see Nooteboom, 2002). However, there is a relative neglect of systematic empirical study. There is also a lack of detailed analysis of trust processes on the micro-micro level of people within organizations. This includes trust in teams or 'communities of practice', and trust between staff and management. This volume addresses the combination of those two gaps: it focuses on trust processes between people, with an emphasis on empirical studies. After four conceptual chapters that lay some conceptual foundations, there are five empirical chapters.

The volume takes an interdisciplinary approach, with contributions from economists, sociologists, social psychologists and business scholars. This is needed to take into account both rational foundations and psychological causes of trust. Trust encompasses rational evaluation, but this is subject to cognitive limitations, and social–psychological phenomena play an important role. In particular, the question is how people attribute motives and competencies to people on the basis of observed behaviour, and how this affects their trust and their conduct. That theme pervades the present volume. In this introductory chapter we summarize some fundamentals about trust and we indicate the content and connections between the chapters. There are different *definitions* of trust in the literature. Trust entails multiple *objects*, or things one can have trust in. One important question concerns the relation between personal and organizational trust. One can have trust in different *aspects* of behaviour, and trust may vary with the *conditions* of behaviour. Trust has a variety of *foundations* and *sources*. The development of trust is related to *learning*, and for this we need a theory of knowledge.

This chapter proceeds as follows. First we sketch a theory of knowledge, and implications for organizations, taken from Nooteboom (1992, 2000). Next, we specify a definition of trust, possible objects of trust, relevant aspects of behaviour, foundations and sources, and conditions for trust. We discuss the notion of reciprocity and give a few comments on the process of trust development. Finally we sketch the content of this volume.

## KNOWLEDGE

For knowledge, we employ a social constructivist, interactionist view. The term 'knowledge' here is a broad one, including perception, understanding, value judgments and even emotions. We adopt the view that it is difficult to separate reason and emotions (Polanyi, 1962; Merleau-Ponty, 1964; Damasio, 1995; Hendriks-Jansen, 1996; Lakoff and Johnson, 1999). Emotions can trigger reason, or reflexes, and reason is often emotion-laden. People perceive, interpret and evaluate the world according to mental categories (or frames or mental models) that they develop in interaction with their physical, social/institutional environment. This entails perception, interpretation and evaluation being contingent upon the institutional environment. Thus people are influenced in their thinking by prevailing norms. Later, we will show that this yields one source of trustworthiness, in 'institutions-based trust'. The constructivist, interactionist view also implies that to some extent knowledge, in the broad sense, is path-dependent and idiosyncratic. Different people see the world differently to the extent that they have developed in different social and physical surroundings and have not interacted with each other. In other words, environment and past experience determine 'absorptive capacity' (Cohen and Levinthal, 1990). As people interact, and share experience, they may develop shared mental frames, which yields a basis for 'identification-based trust'. This will be taken up in more detail by Bart Nooteboom, in Chapter 2.

As discussed in Nooteboom (1992), an implication of this view of knowledge for the theory of the firm is that, in order to achieve a specific joint goal, the categories of thought of the people involved must be aligned to some extent. Different people have a greater or lesser 'cognitive distance' between them (Nooteboom, 1992, 1999). In view of this, organizations need to reduce cognitive distance, that is, achieve a sufficient alignment of mental frames, to understand each other, utilize complementary capabilities, achieve a common goal and have trust. This yields the notion of organization as a 'focusing device'. That connects with the idea, in the organization literature, that the crux of the firm is to serve as a 'sense-making system' (Weick, 1979, 1995), 'system of shared meaning' (Smircich, 1983) or 'interpretation systems' (Choo, 1998). One interpretation of entrepreneurship, which links with Schumpeter's notion of the entrepreneur as a charismatic figure, is that it is his central task to achieve this: to align perceptions, understandings and goals.

Within the wider institutional environment, organizations constitute more specialized institutional arrangements, and develop their own specialized semiotic niches: cognitive frames, language, symbols, metaphors, myths and rituals. This is what we call organizational culture. Organizational culture differs between organizations to the extent that they have accumulated different experiences, in different industries, technologies and markets. Note that alignment of cognitive frames in the firm need not entail full identity. As discussed in Nooteboom (1999), there is a trade-off between cognitive distance, needed for variety and novelty of cognition, and cognitive proximity, needed for mutual understanding. In fact, different people in a firm will to a greater or lesser extent introduce elements of novelty from their outside lives and experience, and this is a source of both innovation and error, of both learning and conflict.

A second implication of this theory of knowledge is that, as a result of the need to achieve a focus, there is a risk of myopia: relevant threats and opportunities to the firm are not perceived. To compensate for this, people and firms need complementary sources of outside intelligence, to utilize 'external economy of cognitive scope' (Nooteboom, 1992). Here again the trade-off arises between cognitive distance, for the sake of novelty, and cognitive proximity, for the sake of understanding and utilization of complementarity.

A large cognitive distance has the merit of novelty but the problem of comprehensibility. Effectiveness of learning by interaction can be construed as the product of the two, which yields an optimal cognitive distance (Nooteboom, 1999). However, one can increase absorptive capacity to deal with larger cognitive distance. For example, if knowledge is codifiable, absorptive capacity can be built and maintained by R&D in the areas of the partner's activity. This explains the empirical phenomenon that, when firms outsource activities, their R&D does not necessarily go down (Granstrand *et al.*, 1997). On the other hand, when knowledge is tacit, one will need prolonged intensive interaction to achieve mutual understanding.

## DEFINITION OF TRUST

A pervasive notion in the literature is that trust is associated with dependence and risk: the trustor depends on something or someone (the trustee or object of trust), and there is a possibility that expectations or hopes will not be satisfied, and that 'things will go wrong'. Yet one expects that 'things will go all right'.

A central issue is whether trust can be based only on power, control or 'deterrence' of the trustee, including legal and hierarchical coercion as well as control by incentives and dependence. Transaction cost economics (TCE) claims this, and denies the viability of trust that goes beyond 'calculative self-interest' (Williamson, 1993). Other authors feel that deterrence is foreign to the notion of trust, and that 'genuine' trust is based on other, more social and personal foundations of trustworthiness. Maguire *et al.* (2001, p. 286) claimed that, if we do not include the latter, we conflate trust and power. Many authors claim that trust can go beyond control, on the basis of 'goodwill' or 'benevolence', resulting from loyalty or altruism, without necessarily becoming blind or unconditional (Das and Teng, 1998; Lane and Bachmann, 2000; Maguire *et al.*, 2001; see also the special issue of *Organization Studies* on 'Trust and control in organizational relations', 22/2, 2001). Therefore trust has been defined as the expectation that a partner will not engage in opportunistic behaviour, even in the face of countervailing short-term opportunities and incentives (Bradach and Eccles, 1984; Chiles and McMackin, 1996; Nooteboom, 1996). Several authors suggest that goodwill does not operate independently from self-interest or control. Bachmann (in Lane and Bachmann, 2000, p. 303) proposed that trust is a hybrid phenomenon, including both calculation and goodwill. In Chapter 4 of this volume, Reinhard Bachmann continues the discussion on the relationship between trust and power.

To clarify the issue of trust and control, we adopt the convention proposed by Nooteboom (2002) of using the term 'reliance' and 'reliability' for trust and trustworthiness in the wide sense, based on all possible sources of trustworthiness, including deterrence on the basis of coercion and self-interested incentives. The term 'assurance' is used for self-interested sources of trustworthiness, and the term 'real' trust, or 'trust in the strong sense', is used for sources that go beyond calculative self-interest. In other words, we trust someone, in the strong sense, if we expect him not to be opportunistic even if he has both the opportunity and the incentive to do so.

That does not imply that real trust is blind and unconditional. There are generally limits to trustworthiness and trust. While trust is not always calculative, it is constrained by possibilities of opportunism (Pettit, 1995). Even the most loyal, committed and dedicated of people may succumb to the temptation of golden opportunities or pressures of survival. Firms may be subject to competitive pressure to such an extent that they cannot afford to accept any sacrifice for the sake of loyalty. Generally, however, there is some limit within which people and firms may be worthy of real trust (Pettit, 1995; Nooteboom, 2002). This is related to the notions of 'exit' and 'voice' (Hirschman, 1970). In an exit stance concerning relations, one will break relations as soon as one is not satisfied and a more profitable alternative is available. In a voice stance, one will not turn away as soon as that is profitable, but announce one's dissatisfaction, and aim to solve problems jointly. However, voice is bounded by the possibility of exit if persistent efforts to discuss and solve problems fail.

One way to model trustworthiness is in terms of a limited resistance to temptation towards opportunism. This may be modelled as a threshold for defection: one does not opportunistically defect until the advantage one can gain with it exceeds the threshold. This threshold may depend on the wider cultural environment, the narrower cultural environment of a firm one works for, personal upbringing and genetic endowment. The threshold is likely to adapt as a function of experience. Trust may then be modelled as based on a perception of such a (limited) constraint of a partner's opportunism. That perception may entail tacit rather than explicit knowledge. It will become routinized, based on experience, and may sink from 'focal' to 'subsidiary awareness' (Polanyi, 1962). Within that limit one can economize on contracting. When temptations are perceived that may be too large, or unexpected behaviour is perceived, trust can make way for calculation. Relational risk is shifted from subsidiary to focal awareness. So even though trust is and should be constrained, since indeed unconditional trust is unwise, within the margin of perceived or assumed trustworthiness it can save on contracting.

Summing up, we generally do not trust different people equally, we may trust a person in some respects, but not in others, and we often trust people in some conditions but not in others. Trust generally has its limits because trustworthiness generally has its limits.

## OBJECTS OF TRUST

One can trust material objects, empirical regularities or laws of nature, people, authorities, organizations, institutions and higher powers. Trust in people or organizations is called 'behavioural trust'. Like people, organizations can be the object of trust, in both their competence and their intentions. We can trust an organization to behave responsibly, regarding its stakeholders and the environment. Of course an organization itself does not have an intention, but it has interests and can try to regulate the intentions of its workers to serve those interests. The perceived interests of the organization are in turn the result of perceptions and communication of the people in the organization. One's trust in an individual may be based on one's trust in the organization he belongs to. Trust in an organization can be based on trust in the people in it. It can be affected by corporate communication, which aims to project a certain image.

Trust in people and trust in organizations are connected by the functions and positions people have and the roles they play in their organizations (Ring and van de Ven, 1994). For personal trust to be transferred to the organization, trustworthy individuals must be backed up by their authority, position and their bosses. Also, vice versa, for organizational trust to be transferred to individuals, the people involved should implement organizational interests and rules of trustworthy conduct. The question is how that works: on the basis of managerial control, incentives, inspirational leadership or intrinsic motivation? In Chapter 7, Deanne den Hartog takes up the effects of different kinds of leadership.

As in the case of people, trustworthiness of organizations depends on survival conditions. For example, to survive it must guard its reputation for quality and its brand names. Such safeguards depend on industry conditions, such as the effectiveness and importance of reputation mechanisms, and the intensity of price competition. The importance of reputation depends on the ability of users to judge quality prior to consumption. Clearly, a firm that is under great pressure to make all the profit it can get and to cut costs where it can, as a matter of sheer survival, can afford less goodwill or benevolence, at the sacrifice of profit, than a firm that is not under such pressure. This yields differences, especially between industries.

Summing up, in dealing with organizations one has to consider the basis for reliability of both the people one is dealing with and the organization. What mix of foundations of trust is there on the different levels, of people and organization, and how consistent are they; that is, to what extent do they support or compensate for each other? Structure of ownership and control, organizational culture and procedures for guiding, supporting, motivating and controlling people in their organizational roles have a crucial mediating role here, and become part of the basis for organizational trust.

## ASPECTS OF TRUST

Behavioural trust, in people and organizations, has a variety of aspects: trust in competence, intentions and honesty or truthfulness. Competence trust refers to technical, cognitive and communicative competencies. At the firm level it includes technological, innovative, commercial, organizational and managerial competence, and access to resources. Intentional trust refers to the intentions of a partner towards the relationship, particularly the absence of opportunism. Opportunism can have a passive and an active form. The passive form entails lack of dedication or effort to perform to the best of one's competence. Dedication entails active participation, attention and abstention from free-riding. In Chapter 7, Deanne den Hartog uses the term 'consistency'. The active form of opportunism entails the 'interest seeking with guile' proposed in TCE, with lying, stealing and cheating to expropriate advantage from a partner. The term 'opportunism' is reserved for the latter. Absence of such opportunism is called 'benevolence' or 'goodwill'. Thus intentional trust has two dimensions: trust in dedication and trust in benevolence.

Trust, being associated with risk of things going wrong, is challenged when things do go wrong, or when 'trouble' arises, as Frédérique Six discusses in Chapter 10. This does not necessarily entail a breakdown of trust. The question to be asked is why things went wrong. This could be due to outside accidents beyond anyone's control, a mistake, lack of competence, lack of effort, or opportunism. How does one assess what is the case? What motive and competence will one infer and attribute to the trustee, and what implications for action will one derive? An opportunistic partner will not admit his opportunistic motive, and will claim 'force majeure', if he can get away with that. This yields an argument for openness in trust relations: it may be better to admit a mistake, and timely so, in order to have the best chance of redressing it, than to run the risk of one's action being seen as a sign of opportunism (Nooteboom, 2002).

Here, in inference, attribution and decision, social psychology plays a crucial role. As argued by Siegwart Lindenberg, in Chapter 3, trust depends on how the situation is mentally 'framed'. As set out also by Lindenberg, and investigated empirically in Chapter 9 by Rafael Wittek, and in Chapter 10 by Frédérique Six, inferences, attributions and response are sensitive to 'relational signalling'. When people encounter trouble, they give cues and generate responses by the way in which they enact and express their discontent. Is it aimed directly at the trustee, indirectly at colleagues or the boss, and is it done publicly or in private?

## CONDITIONS OF TRUST

Trust is contingent upon both the trustee and conditions. In other words, one will trust different trustees differently, and a given trustee according to conditions: trust is a four-place predicate: someone (trustor) trusts something or someone (trustee) with respect to something (competence, intentions), depending on the conditions (Nooteboom, 2002). All chapters in this volume consider the identity of the trustor, differentiation between trustees, aspects of both competence and intentions, and the conditions for trust, such as task and organizational context.

Trust depends on outside conditions and on inside conditions. In evolutionary terms, outside institutions constitute the selection environment of firms. That includes markets, legal systems, customs and norms of conduct. In Chapter 5, Henk de Vos and Rudi Wielers look at the viability of trustworthiness in terms of its survival in competition with a cheating strategy.

The main focus of this volume is on inside conditions. The evolutionary approach of Chapter 5 may apply also here, to the extent that we can see the organization as an arena of survival for its members, in a struggle between trust and cheating. Other inside conditions are the type of tasks, organizational structure (such as team structure), type of leadership, culture, processes of interaction and patterns of communication. In Chapter 6, Ana Cristina Costa looks at the effects of team composition, task characteristics and organizational context on trust within teams. In Chapter 7, Deanne den Hartog's examination of different types of leadership includes a study on trust that people have in specific others, generalized others and leaders in the organization. In Chapter 8, Nathalie Lazaric looks at the need for trust in the elicitation of knowledge in expert systems. In Chapter 9, Rafael Wittek looks at the relationship between norm violations (including trust violations) and sanctioning behaviour, which includes patterns and types of communication ('relational signalling'). Related to this, in Chapter 10, Frédérique Six looks at the way in which people deal with trust and trouble, depending on the type of trouble, sanctioning behaviour and organizational conditions such as socialization during entry to the firm.

## FOUNDATIONS AND SOURCES OF TRUST

The difference between foundations and sources of trust intended here is that the first refers to rational reasons for trust and the latter to psychological causes. All chapters in this volume allow for both the rational foundations and the psychological sources of trust. Rational trust entails an assessment of a partner's trustworthiness, based on direct evidence or reputation, with an attribution of his competence and his intentions to conform to agreements, depending on conditions. In 'calculus-based' trust, trustworthiness is based on calculated self-interest, and trust is based on control or 'deterrence' of unreliable behaviour by enforcement of authority or contract, or incentives of self-interest.

The literature recognizes the notion of 'identification-based trust' (Lewicki and Bunker, 1996). It entails mutual assimilation of mental categories. Short of identification, there may be empathy: the ability to place oneself in a partner's position, without sharing his cognitive framework. There is also a notion of 'affect- or emotion-based trust'. This seems closely related to identification-based trust and, to a lesser extent, empathy. Identification may go so far that one is not able or willing to consider the possibility of untrustworthiness. This may include cognitive dissonance: one does not want to face evidence of untrustworthiness because it conflicts with deep-seated convictions or feelings.

There is also a notion of 'routinized trust' (Nooteboom, 1996, 2002). This is a combination of rational foundation and psychological cause. Here one assumes trustworthiness, often tacitly, because that assumption never yielded adverse effects (concerning a certain trustee, under certain conditions). That is the rational part. Long ago, Herbert Simon indicated that routines are rational in view of bounded cognitive capacity, to make attention free for new conditions that require attention. Here the possibility of untrustworthiness has subsided to 'subsidiary awareness' (Polanyi, 1962). Extraordinary events may trigger a shift back from subsidiary to 'focal' awareness, where calculation may set in. Emotions of fear or indignation serve to yield such a trigger (Simon, 1983). That is the psychological part. In empathy-based, identification-based and routinized trust, trust often has not only extrinsic, instrumental value, but also intrinsic value: one prefers to act on the basis of trust.

*Table 1.1    Sources of intentional reliability*

|  | Macro | Micro |
|---|---|---|
| Egotistic | sanctions from some authority (the law, god, Leviathan, dictator, patriarch, organization), contractual obligation | material advantage or self-interest: shadow of the future, reputation, hostages |
| Altruistic | ethics: values, social norms of proper conduct, moral obligation, sense of duty | bonds of friendship, kinship; routines, habituation |

*Source:*    Nooteboom (2002), adapted from Williams (1988).

Table 1.1 gives a survey of different sources of intentional reliability, including self-interest as well as sources going beyond that. It is taken from Nooteboom (2002), where it was in turn adapted from Williams (1988). Williams distinguished between 'macro' sources, which apply generally and impersonally, apart from any specific exchange relation. They arise from the 'institutional environment' of laws, norms, values, standards and agencies for their enforcement. They are also called sources of 'thin' trust. The 'micro' sources arise in specific relations, and are therefore personalized. They are also called sources of 'thick' trust. Williams further distinguished between self-interest and altruism as a source of cooperation. Taken together, in a two-by-two matrix, this yields four sources of intentional reliability. The 'altruistic' sources go beyond self-interested behaviour, in the form of established, socially inculcated norms and values (macro), and identification, affect and routines developed in specific relations (micro). These 'altruistic' sources provide the basis for trust in the strong sense, or 'real' trust. In other words, Table 1.1 reflects the widespread view, discussed earlier, that trust in the wide sense of reliance includes elements of control, here along the row of self-interest, including both legal coercion and control by incentives and dependence, as well as elements that go beyond control, as a basis for 'goodwill' or 'benevolence'. The distinction between egotistic and altruistic sources is related to the distinction between what Lindenberg (2000) called a 'gain frame' and a 'normative' frame.

The table recognizes institutional systems as a basis for reliance, in the form of hierarchy and legal systems supporting laws and litigation (first row, first column), and norms of behaviour (second row, first column). This is 'institutions-based trust', which requires that we trust those institutions to support sources of trustworthiness of people and organizations. In the second row, right column we go beyond 'macro' norms of behaviour that are imposed or absorbed in socialization from the institutional environment, to include 'micro' empathy, identification, affect and routinization, embedded and developed in specific relations. In other words, next to an institutional level there is an interpersonal level (Bachmann, 2000, p. 307). The distinction between macro and micro sources is also known as the distinction between 'universalistic' or 'generalized' sources and 'particularistic' sources, made by Deutsch (1973, p. 55), and between impersonal and personalized sources, made by Shapiro (1987). This distinction goes back to the work of Parsons. Social norms and moral obligations, including a sense of duty, following Parsons and Durkheim, were proposed more recently by Bradach and Eccles (1984), Zucker (1986) and Dore (1983), among others. Fukuyama (1995) employed the term 'spontaneous sociability'. Calculation of self-interest includes reputation (Weigelt and Camerer, 1988) and the assessment of future benefits of present cooperativeness ('shadow of the future'), as has been recognized by many (Telser, 1980; Axelrod, 1984; Hill, 1990; Heide and Meiner, 1992; Parkhe, 1993). A taxonomy that is similar in some respects to that of Williams was later proposed by Chiles and McMackin (1996). It included social norms, moral obligations, social embeddedness, sense of duty, rational self-interest and reputation. Some of these elements were added to the original taxonomy proposed by Williams.

Related to the sources of reliability there are sources of reliance. These are specified in Table 1.2. Rational foundations of reliance entail an assessment of the sources of reliability. Here we find the duality of (formal) control, in creating reliability on the basis of contracts, supervision, rewards and incentives, and trust that goes beyond that, on the basis of norms, values or bonding that arise within a relation.

An important condition for reliance to arise is of course the need for it. That increases with the need to collaborate: the more people are indispensable to each other, the more urgent it is to trust each other and find or

*Table 1.2   Sources of reliance*

|  | Macro | Micro |
|---|---|---|
| Control | contracts, supervision | partner's dependence on value, hostages, reputation |
| Trust (in strong sense) | norms, values, habits | routinization, empathy, identification, friendship |

*Source:*   Nooteboom (2002).

develop a basis for doing so. Ana Cristina Costa, in Chapter 6, takes up this and other aspects of tasks and team composition, and their influence on trust. In Chapter 7, Deanne den Hartog establishes a link between styles of leadership and calculus-based versus identification-based trust. However, she finds that different styles of leadership may include both elements, of incentives and intrinsic motivation, with different emphases.

## RECIPROCITY

The matrix in Table 1.1 may suggest a hard, clear separation between the cells, while this is not in fact there. As Bachmann (2000, p. 307) phrased it, they are loosely coupled. There are connections between them, with inter-mediate, mixed forms. The observance of social norms of behaviour may be part of a pursuit of social recognition, which may be seen as part of self-interest. The intrinsic value of trust-based relations may be seen as part of self-interest, and it may be connected with both the social recognition just indicated, and the disposition to be loyal to friends, which is here rendered as part of affect-based altruistic motives.

In sociology, there is an extensive literature on reciprocity and the giving of gifts. For a recent discussion, see Vandevelde (2000). Reciprocity may be seen as an intermediate form between self-interest and altruism. It has been characterized as short-term altruism for long-term self-interest (Putnam, 2000, p. 134). In economic exchange, there is a principle of strict 'quid pro quo', where reciprocity in exchange is either immediate or contractually guaranteed, with an attempt to specify future conditions and procedures. In the social giving of gifts, reciprocity is not immediate, not specified or guaranteed, and cannot be demanded. Such demand would invalidate its social function, which is to bond a relationship. Immediate reciprocation would signal that the recipient declines to engage in a relationship. Nevertheless, the gift establishes an informal, non-strict obligation to reciprocate, in due

time and measure. In view of this, the giver is expected to soften the obligation, by belittling his gift when he is thanked ('you are welcome', 'my plea-
sure', 'pas de quoi'). It is important to maintain reciprocation as a free
choice, and avoid any impression of manipulation, compulsion or intent to
purchase obligation. In social reciprocity, giving must remain spontaneous,
surprising and imperfectly predictable. Nevertheless, gift giving with this
type of reciprocity often serves our self-interest. It fosters good reputation,
gratitude and return gifts. As Vandevelde (2000, p. 15) formulated it: 'The
logic of the gift thus can be reduced neither to disinterestedness or altruism,
nor to strict, calculative egotism. Something of both motivations inheres,
or even better: the logic of the gift is situated beyond the opposition between
egotism and altruism.'

In Table 1.1, social reciprocity may be situated in between the rows of
self-interest and altruism. Gift giving can be used for manipulation, imposing a claim for something in return. However, though unusual, gifts or
sacrifices *can* be completely disinterested or altruistic, without an expectation of or even wish for reciprocity. Then they fall squarely in the lower row.
A form of extreme altruism is friendly reciprocation to a hostile action
('turn the other cheek'; cf. Vandevelde, 2000). In Chapter 5, Henk de Vos
and Rudi Wielers take up the notion of reciprocity as a basis for relationships, in competition with a cheating strategy.

## THE PROCESS OF TRUST

As suggested at the beginning, more research is needed on the process of
trust: how it builds up and breaks down in interaction between people. That
is the focus of this volume. In Chapter 2, Bart Nooteboom gives a survey
of the literature on the trust process. There are important links between
trust and learning. As suggested before, trust is subject to learning, in the
sense that one needs time and experience to understand people's competencies and intentions and to identify with them. Also, vice versa, learning
requires trust. This is reflected indirectly in Chapter 6, where Ana Cristina
Costa finds that within teams uncertainty in the form of task ambiguity
does not have a negative effect on trust, as predicted by transaction cost
economics, but a positive one. This is in accordance with the theoretical
claim that under uncertainty there is increased need for others, who offer
complementary competence and knowledge (Nooteboom, 1992).

Trust and trustworthiness can go too far. Unlimited loyalty might yield
rigidities ('inertia') in innovation. Relations need to last sufficiently long for
investments that are dedicated to the relation to be recouped, including the
build-up of mutual understanding and trust. But if they last too long and

become too exclusive, this may yield an obstacle to learning and innovation, which require a variety of experience. This point also comes up indirectly in Chapter 8, where Nathalie Lazaric finds that, after the codification of expert knowledge in an expert system, measures have to be taken to keep the system open to new experience from practice. That is also needed to maintain the motivation of practitioners.

Thus, for the sake of innovation and learning, conflicts may be needed and relationships may have to end. Conflicts *per se* need not indicate or cause a breakdown of trust. Much depends on what sanctioning mechanisms are used in cases of norm violation. This includes the 'relational signalling' related to the choice of how and to whom to voice the conflict and its relation to the severity of the violation. Rafael Wittek, in Chapter 9, studies this. When relationships have to end, to prevent inertia or deadlock, there is a voice mode of ending the relationships, by announcing the intention to exit and offer help to other partners to prepare for it and find alternatives (Nooteboom, 1999). The possibility that conflict can yield learning and deepen trust, and that there can be collaboration even in conflict, arises empirically in the work of Frédérique Six, in Chapter 10.

## ACKNOWLEDGMENTS

We would like to thank all the participants in the seminar 'trust and trouble', held in May 2001 at the Erasmus University in Rotterdam, for their useful comments and suggestions to the papers which have nearly all found their way into this volume. They also made significant contributions to the discussion of avenues for further research as presented in the final chapter.

## REFERENCES

Axelrod, R. (1984), *The Evolution of Cooperation*, New York: Basic Books.

Bachmann, R. (2000), 'Conclusion: trust – conceptual aspects of a complex phenomenon', in C. Lane and R. Bachmann (eds), *Trust Within and Between Organizations*, paperback edn, Oxford: Oxford University Press, pp. 298–322.

Bradach, J.L. and R.G. Eccles (1984), 'Markets versus hierarchies: from ideal types to plural forms', *Annual Review of Sociology*, 15, 97–118.

Chiles, T.H. and J.F. McMackin (1996), 'Integrating variable risk preferences, trust and transaction cost economics', *Academy of Management Review*, 21 (7), 73–99.

Choo, C.W. (1998), *The Knowing Organization*, Oxford: Oxford University Press.

Cohen, M.D. and D.A. Levinthal (1990), 'Absorptive capacity: a new perspective on learning and innovation', *Administrative Science Quarterly*, 35, 128–52.

Damasio, A.R. (1995), *Descartes' Error: Emotion, Reason and the Human Brain*, London: Picador.

Das, T.K. and B.S. Teng (1998), 'Between trust and control: developing confidence in partner cooperation in alliances', *Academy of Management Review*, **23** (3), 491–512.

Deutsch, M. (1973), *The Resolution of Conflict: Constructive and Destructive Processes*, New Haven: Yale University Press.

Dore, R. (1983), 'Goodwill and the spirit of market capitalism', *British Journal of Sociology*, **34**, 459–82.

Fukuyama, F. (1995), *Trust, the Social Virtues and the Creation of Prosperity*, New York: Free Press.

Granstrand, O., P. Patel and K. Pavitt (1997), 'Multi-technology corporations: why they have distributed rather than distinctive core competencies', *California Management Review*, **39** (4), 8–25.

Heide, J.B. and A.S. Meiner (1992), 'The shadow of the future: effects of anticipated interaction and frequency of contact on buyer–seller cooperation', *Academy of Management Journal*, **35**, 265–91.

Hendriks-Jansen, H. (1996), *Catching Ourselves in the Act: Situated Activity, Interactive Emergence, Evolution and Human Thought*, Cambridge, MA: The MIT press.

Hill, C.W.L. (1990), 'Cooperation, opportunism and the invisible hand: implications for transaction cost theory', *Academy of Management Review*, **15** (3), 500–513.

Hirschman, A.O. (1970), *Exit, Voice and Loyalty: Responses to Decline in Firms, Organizations and States*, Cambridge, MA: Harvard University Press.

Lakoff, G. and M. Johnson (1999), *Philosophy in the Flesh*, New York: Basic Books.

Lane, C. and R. Bachmann (eds) (2000), *Trust Within and Between Organizations*, paperback edn, Oxford: Oxford University Press.

Lewicki, R.J. and B.B. Bunker (1996), 'Developing and maintaining trust in work relationships', in R.M. Kramer and T.R. Tyler (eds), *Trust in Organizations: Frontiers of Theory and Research*, Thousand Oaks: Sage Publications, pp. 114–39.

Lindenberg, S. (2000), 'It takes both trust and lack of mistrust: the workings of cooperation and relational signalling in contractual relationships', *Journal of Management and Governance*, **4**, 11–33.

Maguire, S., N. Philips and C. Hardy (2001), 'When "silence = death", keep talking: trust, control and the discursive construction of identity in the Canadian HIV/AIDS treatment domain', *Organization Studies*, **22** (2), 285–310.

Merleau-Ponty, M. (1964), *Le visible et l'invisible*, Paris: Gallimard.

Nooteboom, B. (1992), 'Towards a dynamic theory of transactions', *Journal of Evolutionary Economics*, **2**, 281–99.

Nooteboom, B. (1996), 'Trust, opportunism and governance: a process and control model', *Organization Studies*, **17** (6), 985–1010.

Nooteboom, B. (1999), *Inter-firm Alliances, Analysis and Design*, London: Routledge.

Nooteboom, B. (2000), *Learning and Innovation in Organizations and Economies*, Oxford: Oxford University Press.

Nooteboom, B. (2002), *Trust: Forms, Foundations, Functions, Failures and Figures*, Cheltenham, UK and Northampton, MA, USA: Edward Elgar.

Parkhe, A. (1993), 'Strategic alliance structuring: a game-theoretic and transaction cost examination of inter-firm cooperation', *Academy of Management Journal*, **36**, 794–829.

Pettit, Ph. (1995), 'The virtual reality of homo economicus', *The Monist*, **78** (3), 308–29.

Polanyi, M. (1962), *Personal Knowledge*, London: Routledge.

Putnam, R.D. (2000), *Bowling Alone: The Collapse and Revival of American Community*, New York: Simon & Schuster.

Ring, P. and A. van de Ven (1994), 'Developmental processes of cooperative inter-organizational relationships', *Academy of Management Review*, **19** (1), 90–118.

Shapiro, S.P. (1987), 'The social control of impersonal trust', *American Journal of Sociology*, **93**, 623–58.

Simon, H.A. (1983), *Reason in Human Affairs,* Oxford: Basil Blackwell.

Smircich, L. (1983), 'Organization as shared meaning', in L.R. Pondy, P.J. Frost, G. Morgan and T.C. Dandridge (eds), *Organizational Symbolism*, Greenwich, Conn: JAI Press, pp. 55–65.

Telser, L.G. (1980), 'A theory of self-enforcing agreements', *Journal of Business*, **53**, 27–44.

Vandevelde, A. (2000), 'Reciprocity and trust as social capital' (in Flemish), in A. Vandevelde (ed.), *Over vertrouwen en bedrijf*, Louvain: Acco, pp. 13–26.

Weick, K.F. (1979), *The Social Psychology of Organizing*, Reading, MA: Addison-Wesley.

Weick, K.F. (1995), *Sensemaking in Organizations*, Thousand Oaks, CA: Sage.

Weigelt, K. and C. Camerer (1988), 'Reputation and corporate strategy: a review of recent theory and applications', *Strategic Management Journal*, **9**, 443–54.

Williams, B. (1988), 'Formal structures and social reality', in D. Gambetta (ed.), *Trust: Making and Breaking of Cooperative Relations*, Oxford: Blackwell, pp. 3–13.

Williamson. O.E. (1993), 'Calculativeness, trust and economic organization', *Journal of Law and Economics*, **36**, 453–86.

Zucker, L.G. (1986), 'Production of trust: Institutional sources of economic structure 1840–1920', *Research in organizational behaviour*, **8**, 53–111.

# 2. The trust process

## Bart Nooteboom

---

## INTRODUCTION

As indicated in Chapter 1, this volume focuses on processes of trust, in interaction between people in organizations. To deal with such processes we need to take economic, social and psychological phenomena and considerations into account. There are rational reasons for trust, based on an inference and attribution of trustworthiness. Here, the analysis is normative, indicating what would be rational to do. In a more descriptive account, trust is also based on psychological causes of affect, routine, lack of awareness or neglect of relational risk and psychological phenomena such as cognitive dissonance and decision heuristics. Much work remains to be done in that area and this book hopes to make a contribution. However, some studies on the process of trust are available from the literature and we can build on them. The purpose of this chapter is to survey that work. The focus is on behavioural trust, that is, trust with regard to people, individually and in organizations and particularly intentional trust: what will make people dedicate themselves and refrain from opportunism? However, some attention will also be paid to competence trust.

Use is made here of the convention, adopted in Chapter 1, of using the term 'reliance' for trust which includes all sources, including both deterrence or control and sources that go beyond calculative self-interest. The term 'trust' or 'real trust' is reserved for the latter, where one has trust even if the partner has both opportunities and incentives for opportunism.

This chapter proceeds as follows. It begins with a survey of the psychological sources of trust, before proceeding to a more detailed analysis of phenomena in the process of trust that are taken from psychology and sociology. Several blocks of text are taken from Nooteboom (2002).

## PSYCHOLOGICAL SOURCES OF TRUST[1]

Sources of trust are not always rational: as a result of psychological mechanisms, one may trust an opportunist. Psychological sources include cognitive heuristics for assessing the probability of events, for attributing causes, motives and characteristics to partners, for assigning blame, to others and oneself, and for taking action. These heuristics can yield error, in the sense that in retrospect their outcomes are not rational in some specific situation. However, they may be rational, at least in part, in the sense of being adaptive, that is, contributing to survival, in view of uncertainty, bounded rationality and the need to make quick decisions and act fast.

Evolutionary psychology suggests that a tendency towards reciprocity is 'in our genes', since it was conducive to survival in the ancient hunter–gatherer societies in which humanity evolved. The variance of yields, in gathering edible plants, roots, nuts and so on and the even greater variance in individual success with hunting, together with problems of durable storage, entails an evolutionary advantage of the willingness to surrender part of one's yield to others in need, in the expectation of receiving from them when they are successful (Cosmides and Tooby, 1992, p. 212). This would solve the problem, often noted in the literature, of how in a sequential game of give and take the first move of giving, and thereby making a risky pre-commitment, is made (Simmel, 1978; Luhmann, 1979, quoted in Lane and Bachmann, 2000, p. 3). The evolutionary argument suggests that we do this instinctively. However, psychological mechanisms that were conducive to survival in evolution do entail biases that can lead to serious error (Bazerman, 1998).

Here we should no longer talk of reasons but of causes of trust. However, the distinction being made here may suggest a greater cleavage between rationality and emotion than is valid. As suggested in Chapter 1, rationality and emotions are intertwined. As also indicated in Chapter 1, we include in cognition not only perception and interpretation but also evaluation; that is, value judgments. Not only value judgments but also interpretations and even perceptions are emotion-laden. Nevertheless, we can distinguish more or less rational inference of trustworthiness from less reflective causes of trust, such as empathy, identification, friendship or kinship. In Chapter 1, we recognized the role of routines and the role of emotions, to shift routinized behaviour from subsidiary to focal awareness. Emotions are rational in triggering reflexes or attention when survival requires it. However, they can yield error. They may lead us to jump to erroneous conclusions and may produce prejudice. Evidence of untrustworthiness may be ignored as a result of cognitive dissonance. As Deutsch (1973, p. 159) put it:

> A person's perceptions of another will be determined not only by the information he receives from his direct experiences or from what others tell him, but also by his need to absorb this information in such a way as to prevent disruption of existing perceptions, cognitions, or evaluations to which he is strongly committed.

## DECISION HEURISTICS

Social psychology offers a number of insights into the decision heuristics that people use. In a survey, Bazerman (1998) mentions the following heuristics:

- Availability heuristic: people assess the probability and likely causes of an event by the degree to which instances of it are 'readily available' in memory, that is, are vivid, laden with emotion, recent and recognizable. Less available events and causes are neglected.
- Representativeness heuristic: the likelihood of an event is assessed by its similarity to stereotypes of similar occurrences. We recognize something according to the likeness of some focal features to those of a prototype, which may be a stereotype and on the basis of that attribute other features from the stereotype that are not in fact present. This can easily yield prejudice.
- Anchoring and adjustment: judgment is based on some initial or base value ('anchor') from previous experience or social comparison, plus incremental adjustment from that value. People have been shown to stay close even to random anchors that bear no systematic relation to the issue at hand. First impressions can influence the development of a relation for a long time.

Deutsch (1973) suggested that there is circular causation between characteristics of participants and the results of interaction. He offered his 'crude law of social relations': 'The characteristic processes and effects elicited by a given type of social relationship (cooperative or competitive) tend also to elicit that type of social relationship.' This is consistent with the decision heuristics of availability, representativeness and anchoring. If this is true, then one must be very careful how to start a relationship, because it may be difficult to get out of the initial mode of interaction. To say, as Deutsch did, that the type of relationship tends to reinforce itself of course does not mean that this is inevitable. A mistrustful, rivalrous relationship may develop into a trustful, cooperative one and vice versa. The latter is more probable than the former, as is expressed in the saying that 'trust comes on foot and departs on horseback'.

One cannot say that these heuristics are irrational. In view of uncertainty and bounded rationality, they may well be adaptive, that is, they may contribute to survival. Concerning the availability heuristic, in the discussion of routines we noted the importance of an emotional trigger attached to a suspicious event, to generate awareness of the routine and subject it to scrutiny, in focal awareness. Perhaps this is connected with the availability heuristic: we pay attention only when triggers are emotionally laden. If we did not apply such filters our consciousness would likely be overloaded.

The representativeness heuristic is related to the role of prototypes in language and categorization. Since definitions can seldom offer necessary and sufficient conditions for categorization, and meaning is context-dependent and open-ended, allowing for variation and change, we need prototypes (Rosch, 1977). A prototype represents an exemplar of a class that connects others in the class. Class membership is decided on the basis of resemblance to a salient case, or a typical case, which serves as a prototype. A prototype may turn into a shallow stereotype. However, the mechanism of attributing unobserved characteristics upon recognition of observed ones enables pattern recognition that is conducive to survival.

Concerning anchoring and adjustment, under uncertainty we need such an anchor and taking the most recent value of a variable, or a value observed in behaviour of people in similar conditions, with whom one can empathize, may well be rational. Trust can be seen as a default, in the sense that, on the basis of past experience, we assume trustworthiness unless we find new evidence that contradicts it. We adapt past guidelines for behaviour on the basis of new evidence. Incremental adjustment can be inadequate, but so can fast adjustment. Studies of learning and adjustment have shown that hasty and large departures from existing practices can yield chaotic behaviour (Lounamaa and March, 1987; March, 1991). Thus anchoring and adaptation may also be a useful and justified heuristic, in view of uncertainty. Nevertheless, these heuristics can yield errors.

The relevance of these heuristics to trust is clear, because they affect, or enable, expectation and attribution of trustworthiness. According to the heuristics, one would develop expectations, explain broken expectations and attribute trustworthiness according to what is 'available' in the mind, stereotypes, existing norms or recent experience.

Another psychological phenomenon is that people are found to have difficulty in choosing between immediate gratification and long-term benefit, yielding a problem of 'the weakness of the will'. This has been explained in terms of people having multiple selves that are at odds with each other, or as a visceral drive competing with a rational inclination. Another interpretation follows the availability heuristic: immediate gratification is more 'available'. Studies of behaviour under uncertainty have shown that people may assess delay in gratification differently when it is near than when it is far ahead and that sometimes discounting seems to take place, not according to an exponential function, but according to a hyperbolic function. According to that function, the negative utility of a delay of gratification increases as the decision moves to the present. As a result, preferences may reverse at some point in time. The relevance of this phenomenon to collaborative relations is also clear, in the trade-off between loyalty to a partner, which may be in one's long-term interest and the temptation to defect to another partner who offers more advantage in the short term. One may honestly think one is able to withstand that temptation in the future and succumb to it when it nears. Again, we cannot unequivocally judge that this psychological mechanism is maladaptive. As noted also by Bazerman (1998), the impulse of temptation may also entail the vision of entrepreneurial opportunity and too much repression of it may suppress innovation.

## PROSPECT THEORY

'Prospect theory' (Kahneman *et al.*, 1982) has demonstrated that people are not risk-neutral, but can be risk-taking when a decision is framed in terms of loss and risk-averse when it is framed in terms of gain. In this volume, Siegwart Lindenberg takes up the subject of framing in much more detail. Framing entails, among other things, that in a relationship people will accept a greater risk of conflict when they stand to incur a loss than when they stand to obtain a benefit. Related to this effect is the 'endowment effect': people often demand more money to sell what they have than they would be prepared to pay to get it. In the first case one wants to cover for loss. This may contribute to loyalty and stable relations, as follows. Relations typically end when one of the partners encounters a more attractive alternative, while the other partner wants to continue the relation. The first partner is confronted with a gain frame, the second with a loss frame. This may cause the second partner to engage in more aggressive, risky behaviour, to maintain the relation, than the first partner, who may be more willing to forgo his profit and run less risk of a harmful separation procedure. One wonders what the adaptive rationale of this difference between a gain frame and a loss frame is, if any. Perhaps it lies precisely in the effect just mentioned: it reduces defection and thereby stabilizes relationships, which may have contributed to survival.[2] This is only a conjecture on my part.

Recall the definition of trust, in Chapter 1, as a four-place predicate: one trusts someone in some respect under certain conditions. It is part of trust, then, to understand another's cognition and motivation, as a function of conditions. This is clearly related to the availability heuristic: 'availability' increases to the extent that one can understand behaviour and empathize or identify with it, or, on the contrary, abhor it. This affects both one's own trustworthiness, in the willingness to make sacrifices for others and one's trust, in the tolerance of behaviour that deviates from expectations. One will more easily help someone when one can identify with his need. One can more easily forgive someone's breach of trust or reliance when one can sympathize or identify with the lack of competence or the motive that caused it. One can more easily accept the blame for oneself. One may sympathize with his action, seeing perhaps that his action was in fact a just response to one's own previous actions. Empathy and identification are both forms of affect-based trust, but in the latter affect is the stronger.

Another reason to attribute blame to oneself when someone else is in fact to blame is to reduce uncertainty or establish a sense of control. This works as follows. If it is perceived to be impossible or very difficult to influence someone's behaviour in order to prevent or redress damage from broken expectations, one may attribute blame to oneself. By doing that, one relieves the stress of feeling subjected to the power of others. For people with little self-confidence or a low self-image, this is a move of desperation and self-blame fits the preconception one had of oneself. For people with self-confidence, self-blame may yield a sense of control: if the cause lies with oneself, one can more easily deal with it. Of course, that may be an illusion, due to overconfidence in oneself.

Another mechanism is that of a belief in a just world, which gives reassurance. By enacting justice, even anonymously, one confirms its existence by contributing to it and thereby maintains a sense of security. However, when the sacrifice for another would be too high to accept, in the view of self-interest, then to avoid a self-perception of callousness one may convince oneself that his hardship is his own fault.

Yet another psychological mechanism is that, in violation of rational behaviour, sunk costs, such as sacrifices made in a relationship, are not seen as bygones that should be ignored in an assessment of future costs and benefits. They are seen as sacrifices that would be seen as in vain if one pulls out after incurring them. This yields what is known as 'non-rational escalation of commitment'. It is associated with cognitive dissonance: cutting one's losses and pulling out would entail an admission of failure, of having made a bad decision in the past. The phenomenon is confirmed in empirical research, which shows that, when the decision to cut one's losses needs to be made by someone not involved in the initial decision, or when the threat of an admission of failure is removed, the rational decision to pull out is made. Again, one cannot say that this mechanism is always bad, because it also demonstrates perseverance in the face of setbacks, which can be a good thing and is in fact a trait of many a successful innovating entrepreneur. This phenomenon can also be connected with the effect of a loss frame versus a gain frame, proposed in prospect theory. The person, or group, that made the initial decision experiences a loss frame, with the inclination to accept further risk in order to prevent acceptance of the loss. The decision maker who enters fresh experiences a gain frame, to make a decision that will offer profit in the future, regardless of past sunk costs and will be less inclined to accept the high risk of continuing losses from sticking to past decisions. The mechanism of non-rational escalation can contribute to the continuation of a relationship where it is not beneficial.

The need arises to go more deeply into the processes underlying 'trust production', including processes of routinization, habituation, perception, absorption, cognitive dissonance, negation, blindness and so on.

## INFERENCE OF RELIABILITY

In Chapter 1, a number of sources of reliability and trustworthiness were identified. Those lie behind behaviour. The question now is to what extent and how one can infer the existence and dependability of those sources from observed behaviour. How does one assess the extent to which different sources of trustworthiness are in operation? What is the basis for inferring the disposition of people to obey social norms and their personal loyalty? We cannot directly observe intentions or capabilities, but only certain personal characteristics and people's actions and we can listen to what they say. An assurance of trustworthiness in mere words is cheap and can be very unreliable. Yet a whole pattern of actions and expressions and 'relational signalling' (Lindenberg, Chapter 3 in this volume) can give us important clues. These include not only actions aimed at ourselves, but also actions aimed at others. Perhaps we can infer something from the way a partner treats a waiter, or his wife and children. The question is, to use the terminology of Zucker (1986), what are the modes of 'trust production'?

The term 'trust production' can raise misunderstanding. It is meant to refer to the way the causes of trust work. Literal production of trustworthiness and trust is problematic. Trust or trustworthiness is not something one can install or inject. The opportunities to 'produce' trust in that sense tend to be overestimated by managers. To impose trust is like imposing spontaneity: if it worked it would not be genuine. We can, however, speak of trust-sensitive management (Sydow, 2000, p. 54). Management can take into account how decisions, forms of contracting, monitoring, communication, events, procedures, forms of punishment and reward can affect the development of trust. This is related to the study of Deanne den Hartog, in Chapter 7, of the effect on trust of different types of leadership. To prevent misunderstanding, it is preferable to speak, not of trust 'production', but of the ways in which one can infer reliability.

Zucker suggested different ways to do this. These are complementary to the sources of reliability and reliance in Tables 1.1 and 1.2 and add to the analysis supplied there. They are given below, in Tables 2.1 and 2.2. Zucker suggested that one may infer reliability from personal characteristics, institutions and the process in which relations develop. Table 2.1 again focuses on intentional trust, in particular benevolence trust (absence or limitation of opportunism) and Zucker's scheme is adapted accordingly. Table 2.2 indicates the result when we focus on competence trust. In that table there is no relation to Table 1.1, since that focuses on intentional, not competence trust.

*Table 2.1   Inference of intentional reliability*

| Basis | Examples | Connection with Table 1.1 |
| --- | --- | --- |
| Characteristics-based trust | membership of family, community, culture, religion | mostly the altruistic sources of social norms and kinship |
| Institutions-based trust | rules, ethics, professional standards | the macro altruistic source of social norms |
| Process-based trust | loyalty, commitment | the micro altruistic sources friendship, habituation |

*Source:*   adapted from Zucker (1986).

Some institutions, such as technical standards or systems of certification, can be developed on the basis of a rational design, although this may take quite some time, since they tend to affect established interests and may entail a political struggle. One can select a partner on the basis of his characteristics, such as being a member of a family or community. However, the association between characteristics and expected trustworthiness is subject to the psychological representativeness heuristic discussed before. It may in fact yield prejudice. One cannot simply buy into characteristics-based trust: one can marry into a family and one can become a member of some communities, but entry selection can be strict and it can take considerable time. Process trust, by definition, has to grow. Such trust can be facilitated by creating favourable conditions. Process trust is as much the outcome of a relation as the basis for it. Sydow (2000) approached this from the perspective of Giddens's structuration theory: to the extent that process trust is already available it provides the basis for a relationship, it is reproduced in the relation, if it goes well and may be further deepened to provide the basis for further extending the relationship.

Zucker (1986) argued that in the United States increasingly, characteristics-based trust related to family and (local, ethnic or religious) community and process-based trust in current relations have eroded. Communitarianism was replaced by individualism and the vacuum had to be filled by

*Table 2.2   Inference of competence*

| Basis | Examples |
|-------|----------|
| Characteristics-based trust | membership of professional associations, educational achievements |
| Institutions-based trust | technical/professional standards, benchmarking |
| Process-based trust | mutual adaptation, learning by doing, routinization |

*Source:*   adapted from Zucker (1986).

means of institution-based trust, which includes the institutional basis for contracts as a source of reliance. This thesis about developments in the USA was later repeated and illustrated by Fukuyama (1995) and documented by Putnam (2000).

The validity of this claim, under current conditions, is doubtful. It is probably accurate for an account of recent history. Currently, however, it seems that there is a re-emergence of the need for characteristics- and process-based trust, for several reasons. One is that governance by contract, based on legal institutions, has its weaknesses, which have become more salient under current economic conditions. Under current uncertainty of technology and markets, it has become more difficult to specify reasonably complete contracts and effectively monitor compliance with them. Another reason for this, next to uncertainty, is that in times of radical innovation knowledge tends to have more tacit elements, which resist the codification needed for legally enforceable contracts (Nooteboom, 2000). For radical innovation one needs flexibility for experimentation and detailed contracts can yield a straitjacket. This suggestion is backed up by the fact that several empirical studies show that contracts have only limited perceived value and effect in the control of relational risk (Macauley, 1963; Berger *et al.*, 1995).

Competence shows itself best when it is stretched. Effort or dedication shows itself best when there is no external pressure for it; that is, when effort cannot well be observed and there are opportunities for slack. Benevolence shows itself best under opportunities for opportunism and temptations or pressures to utilize them. It is especially important to assess whether reliability is intrinsic or extrinsic. In the first case the goal is internal and does not require monitoring. It is based on ethics and conscience, norms and values, affect of empathy, identification, friendship or kinship, or on the enjoyment of trusting relations. In the second case the goal is external and reliability is based on the lack of opportunity for opportunism, dependence or fear of reputational loss. Here monitoring is needed. Routine is an intermediate case, where monitoring is needed only beyond perceived limits of trustworthiness. Connected with this, Deutsch (1973) also recognized the notion of 'focus', with three possibilities: focus on results for the other, on warrantable effort (is one seen to be doing one's reasonable best?) or on doing as one is told. Is one genuinely trying to cooperate or is one intent only on legitimizing one's actions?

So, when a supportive action by X is observed, how does one judge if this is based on benevolence? Table 2.3 gives a sequence of questions that aid such assessment (adapted from Deutsch, 1973). Note that the attribution of trustworthiness requires that all conditions specified in the table be met. Favourable actions have to be intended and go beyond self-interest and entail a risk or sacrifice and the partner must have seen that and he must have had other options of action, before one can attribute trustworthiness, going beyond coercion and self-interest. For complete or incipient mistrust, or doubts about trustworthiness, or at least lack of an increase of trust, only one of these tests has to be failed. The escalation of conflict may be enhanced by the effects of a loss frame identified by prospect theory, as discussed before. The suspicion of loss may trigger an excessive, risky response that calls forth a similar reaction.

*Table 2.3    Attribution of trustworthiness*

| | |
|---|---|
| 1. | Was the outcome intended by X, or was it an unintended result of his action? |
| 2. | Did the action entail significant risk to X? |
| 4. | Was X aware of the risk, and was it not neglected out of impulsiveness? |
| 5. | Did X attach a positive value to this risk, out of masochism, sensation, (self-) image? |
| 6. | Did X have a choice, or was the action dictated by compulsion or conformity? |
| 7. | Was it out of confidence in the system rather than a positive evaluation of the situation? |
| 8. | Was it out of enlightened self-interest? |
| 9. | Was it out of enjoyment of trust relations? |
| 10. | Was it out of ethics, friendship or kinship, habituation? |

*Source:*    adapted from Deutsch (1973).

Deutsch noted that one's power can have an adverse effect not only on the trust of others but also on one's own trust. This can be seen from Table 2.3. If one is very powerful, there is more ground for suspicion that people subjected to one's power are reliable only because they have no choice, not because they are trustworthy in the strong sense. In case of absolute power, the hypothesis that this is the case can never be rejected. Thus power can breed suspicion and absolute power can yield rampant paranoia. Here one recognizes stories about Stalin. The problem here is that mistrust tends to feed upon itself even more than trust does. (Mis)trust by X tends to engender (mis)trust on the part of Y, which justifies and deepens X's (mis)trust. While trust can be falsified because it leads to reliance on others which can be disappointing, mistrust cannot, because it blocks trusting action that might disprove it. This is connected to the issue of trust between leaders and followers, taken up in Chapter 7 by Deanne Den Hartog.

## STAGES OF DEVELOPMENT

The central question now is how process-based trust works. Earlier (Nooteboom, 2002; see also Chapter 1), we proposed that trustworthiness is subject to limits and that trust operates within limits of tolerance. In the process of trust these limits are set and revised in the light of experience and as a result of psychological processes, in interaction with other people. This is subject to psychological heuristics of decision making, as discussed before. The limits of trust and trustworthiness are different with respect to different people; for a given partner, they vary with aspects of behaviour (competence, dedication, benevolence, honesty) and for each aspect they vary with conditions.

How can trust arise when there is no prior basis for it (Sako, 2000, p. 89)? Shapiro (1987, p. 625) proposed: 'Typically . . . social exchange relations evolve in a slow process, starting with minor transactions in which little trust is required because little risk is involved and in which partners can prove their trustworthiness, enabling them to expand their relation and engage in major transactions.' Others later repeated this (for example, Ring and van de Ven, 1992). McAllister (1995) proposed two stages of trust development: 'cognition-based trust' followed by 'affect-based trust'. Lewicki and Bunker (1996) proposed three stages of 'calculus-based', 'knowledge-based' and 'identification-based' trust. This is odd, because calculation and control require monitoring, which requires knowledge, so that calculation can hardly precede the acquisition of knowledge (Nooteboom, 2002).

We may clarify these concepts as follows. First, in the absence of prior trust one may resort to control, which requires monitoring, which requires knowledge of effort, or performance and its conditions. Let us call this 'control-based reliance' (presumably, this is close to Lewicki and Bunker's calculus-based trust). Second, partners begin to know and understand what may lie behind observed behaviour, attributing competence and motives, as a function of conditions. Table 2.3 suggests how this may be done. This enables tolerance levels of real trust, within which one does not exert control. This seems related to what Lewicki and Bunker referred to as 'knowledge-based trust' and what McAllister referred to as 'cognition-based trust'. For this, let us retain McAllister's term. Next, one may develop 'empathy-based trust', where one can imagine oneself in the cognitive frames and the position of the partner. Of course, this does not necessarily support trust. One may learn that the partner is hardly to be trusted, owing to intentions or conditions of survival. Then tolerance levels of trust will be narrow. Here affect begins. This can be positive, where empathy yields sympathy, but also negative, where empathy yields suspicion. When it is positive, one may next develop shared cognitive frameworks, in identification-based trust. As one moves towards identification, on the basis of shared cognitive frameworks, the frame changes from sensitivity to contrasts, to assimilation between self and other. This increasingly adds intrinsic to extrinsic value of the relation. Mutual bonding and friendship may develop. In the identification with a partner's need for help and, within limits, his weaknesses or temptations to break expectations, the tolerance level of trust may widen. As indicated in Chapter 1, this is not necessarily positive in its outcomes. Through identification and 'thick trust', relationships may become too exclusive and may last too long, which may eliminate sources of learning and innovation.

Now, should relations start with control, as Lewicki and Bunker suggest? In the attempt to create conditions for process trust to develop, in trust-sensitive management, control by hierarchical or legal coercion, or incentives and dependence, can be destructive. It can signal mistrust which engenders mistrust, so that mistrust becomes a self-fulfilling prophecy (Macauley, 1963; Zand, 1972). In terms of the psychological anchoring and adjustment heuristic discussed before, mistrust may become the anchor, from which only small adjustments are made even when observed behaviour is manifestly cooperative. This does not imply that contracts always or necessarily destroy the basis for trust in the strong sense. As noted above, particularly in innovation detailed contracts to foreclose opportunism may be infeasible owing to the uncertainty that is part of innovation and they can also constitute a straitjacket that eliminates the scope for unforeseeable activities needed for innovation and learning.

If one engages in a relation which carries great risk, there is no prior basis of trust, it is difficult or undesirable to employ detailed contracts to control risk, for the reasons indicated above, and there are no alternative instruments, one could start small, with low stakes and reduced risk and allow for the emergence of cognition-based, empathy-based and identification-based trust, as the relation unfolds. As partners learn that they can rely on each other, within limits, the stakes may be raised, mutual feelings of appreciation and loyalty may develop and the basis for 'thick trust' may arise. This brings us back to the proposal of Shapiro. Of course, the disadvantage of this may be that the process of small steps takes too long, while speed and reduction of 'time to market' are becoming more important. To speed up the development of trust one may employ go-betweens that facilitate the development of relationships (Nooteboom, 1999). One might create joint experience artificially, to facilitate a speedier development of understanding, empathy and identification. Perhaps a survival course, as practised by some firms, or some other intensive process of socialization, is useful for this.

However, there is no one universally correct or viable way to develop relationships. There are many ways and which is to be chosen depends on a range of contingencies concerning conditions, objectives, preferences and histories. Personal affect may never develop, nor mutual identification, while the relation can still be very fruitful. Conversely, people may start on the basis of affect, as in a family firm or a partnership between friends, and become calculative later. That may destroy trust, but it can also deepen it.

## BREACH AND DEEPENING OF TRUST

As proposed in Chapter 1, trust entails an expectation that things or people will not fail us. However, the disappointment of such an expectation does not necessarily yield a breach of trust. Trust has as many aspects of behaviour as there are causes of things going wrong. One can have trust in a partner's competence, his dedication, his benevolence (absence or limitation of opportunism), his honesty, the availability of means, or external conditions. One may observe that external conditions rather than a partner's behaviour were the cause of disappointing outcomes. It is possible that this cannot be seen, but is claimed by the partner as an explanation. Will the trustor accept the explanation, or will he see it as an excuse for something else: for lack of dedication, competence, or worse, for opportunism? Will he, perhaps, turn a blind eye to the mishap, negate evidence of incompetence or opportunism out of cognitive dissonance, identification or blind trust? Or will he give the partner the benefit of the doubt, but remain alert to future mishaps and their possible causes? Or will he jump to a conclusion of opportunism? Which is the case will depend on a number of conditions: the sources of previous trust or suspicion, the history of the relationship, psychological make-up, personal experience and self-image of the trustor, and external social and economic conditions (for example, intensity of price competition).

People have a natural inclination to judge – to evaluate actions and attribute attitudes or motives to people – and here we often jump to conclusions. Such evaluations are subject to the decision heuristics discussed before. We may be swayed by vivid experiences, in the availability heuristic, by the representative heuristic and by the anchoring and adjustment heuristic. When the expectations of trust are not fulfilled, we need to control this inclination to judge and to grant the benefit of the doubt and assess what has happened as coolly as possible, avoiding the biases that may be involved in the decision heuristics. This is not simple, because heuristics and emotions are not without reason. In Chapter 1, we adopted the notion from Simon that emotions serve to jolt us out of routine behaviour and shift awareness of risk from subsidiary to focal. Without emotions we would be vulnerable to the blindness of routine. So emotions serve to waken us, but we must also control them in order to grant other people the benefit of the doubt.

Note that, in the light of the virtuous role of 'cognitive distance' for the purpose of learning, misunderstanding and conflict of opinion are often creative, in shifting existing views and jointly generating novel insights, in a learning process. This reinforces the idea that the dissatisfaction of expectations does not necessarily break down trust. As Zucker (1986, p. 59) proposed:

> [A violation of expectations] produces a sense of disruption of trust, or profound confusion, but not of distrust. Distrust only emerges when the suspicion arises that the disruption of expectations in one exchange is likely to generalize to other transactions. To distrust, then, implies an attribution of intentionality that continues throughout all interactions or exchanges, at least of a particular type.

The joint solution of conflict can enhance and deepen trust, in several ways. One way is that it yields learning, as just indicated, which confirms the value of the relation and thereby increases mutual commitment. Another way is that a problem is solved by itself, reducing perceived risk in the relation. The conflict yielded a test of the strength of mutual benevolence and the dedication to 'working things out', in a mutual 'give and take'. The fact that the relation survived the test increases trust in the strength and resilience of benevolence and dedication. It increases empathy. This is how the process of continuing and successful relations, with solutions of conflicts, can deepen trust.

The positive effect of the solution of conflicts carries force especially because the reverse is so often observed, that under adverse conditions a relationship breaks down in mutual recrimination and suspicion. This can easily arise, especially when the stakes are high at the beginning of a relationship between strangers. As indicated, when things do not go well, this may be due to accident, lack of dedication, lack of competence, or to opportunism. If in fact the cause is opportunism, this will not be admitted. Knowing this, one may suspect opportunism even when it is denied, or for the suspicious especially when it is strongly denied. In this delicate stage of a beginning relation with high stakes of dependence, a third party may play a useful role in eliminating such incipient misunderstandings and attributions of fault before they become so large and evoke such hostile reactions from the unjustly accused partner, that they escalate beyond repair (Nooteboom, 1999).

Pettit (1995) introduced the notion of 'trust-responsiveness'. It is related to the desire for social recognition and to the notion of social reciprocity, both of which were discussed in Chapter 1. It is also related to the building of empathy. When offered trust, people may reciprocate 'due to the love of regard or standing in one's own eyes and in the eyes of others' (ibid., 1995, p. 203). To the extent that this is true, trust is reciprocated and there is a possibility of an upward spiral of trust. However, the converse may also apply, where mistrust engenders mistrust and then there may be a downward spiral of suspicion.

This is connected with the idea of trust as a default and the notions of a limit of trustworthiness and a tolerance limit of trust. In interaction, one may have developed an explicit or implicit assessment of the partner's trustworthiness and a tolerance limit for deviant behaviour. A positive cycle of reciprocation and increasing empathy can raise the limit of trustworthiness and widen the tolerance limit. Deviant behaviour, on the other hand, triggers awareness and possibly the beginning of suspicion. It may narrow tolerance and reduce the inferred limit of trustworthiness. Events that were previously given the benefit of the doubt, or were not even noticed, may now be scrutinized for evidence of untrustworthiness. As a result, deviant behaviour is sooner perceived and a spiral of suspicion may be set in motion. Again, intermediaries may play an important role here, to provide a more objective, outside test whether suspicion is justified and, if it is not, to stop such a dynamic from getting under way.

## INFORMATION AND COMMUNICATION

In view of this potential self-reinforcing dynamic of trust and suspicion, honesty and trust in honesty are crucial. Honesty here is openness: giving appropriate, truthful and timely information. Dishonesty is the withholding or distortion of appropriate information. Honesty and trust reinforce each other, as suspicion and dishonesty do. Honesty helps to deal with deviant phenomena without narrowing tolerance levels and without reducing perceived limits of trustworthiness. It may even widen both and thereby deepen trust.

When there is no intentional trust (that is, trust in dedication and benevolence), one may be afraid to be honest, lest the partner misuses information for opportunistic purposes or to relax the level of his dedication. If there is lack of trust in dedication, one may think praise will cause slack. If there is lack of trust in benevolence, one may think that information about one's needs, opportunities and their limits, or competencies, will be used opportunistically in power play, cheating, expropriation or treating sensitive information as a hostage (blackmail).

However, when the other party perceives that he is receiving neither trust nor information, he may reciprocate with dishonesty. One elementary lesson is the following. When a disaster is foreseen, one is tempted to keep it secret. This should be resisted. Here is a chance to win trust by announcing the problem before it becomes manifest, asking for help and engaging in a joint effort to redress or mitigate disaster.

However, there is also a subtle reason for dishonesty that is benevolent. One may withhold criticism out of fear of (further) reducing a partner's self-confidence. A special problem here lies in the situation where collaboration has to develop between partners who are unequal in their dependence on each other (Klein Woolthuis, 1999). The most dependent partner may be suspicious because of the one-sided risk he runs, so he starts the relation on the basis of mistrust or apprehension and is on the lookout for signs of opportunistic exploitation of his dependence. His perceived limit of trustworthiness and his tolerance level are narrow. This is a special case of a more general phenomenon that lack of self-confidence engenders mistrust, which breeds mistrust. Here it can be in one's self-interest to soften criticism of the partner, not to make him more apprehensive, defensive and suspicious.

One may go further, not just withholding criticism, but also offering compliments. Compliments, both private and public, especially to new staff, can play a role as an explicit act of policy, in trust-sensitive management. The compliments serve to build trust in two ways. First, they increase self-confidence of new staff and this helps them to grant trust, but not excessive trust, to others. Second, it enhances the trust that others have in the new colleague. It enhances trust-responsiveness between existing and new staff. For this, see the contribution from Frédérique Six in Chapter 10 in this volume. It is crucial that the compliments are not empty and are backed up by perceived quality of performance. Empty compliments have an adverse effect.

Zand (1972) proposed a cycle in which trust engenders openness, yielding information, which provides a basis for the exertion and acceptance of mutual influence, which yields the willingness to demand less and accept more control from the partner, which further engenders trust. In other words, the provision of information based on trust promotes the responsiveness to trust identified by Pettit, which may already be latent but requires a trigger of information that has the dual function of demonstrating trust and reducing the risk of trust reciprocation. This can set a positive dynamic of trust going. Thus Zand (1972, p. 238) included openness in his conceptualization of trust as 'behaviour that conveys appropriate information, permits mutuality of influence, encourages self-control and avoids abuse of the vulnerability of others'. Here we see a positive relation between trust and information: A trusts B and therefore gives information (even if B could use that to the detriment of A), which makes B trust A and give information in return.

Part of the issue concerning the relation between trust and control lies in the ambiguity of the notion of control. When trust is a substitute for control, this refers to formal, contractual control with an imposition of procedures for monitoring. It is a matter of economic reciprocity. The information provided voluntarily in trust may also be called a form of (social) control, but this is in important ways quite different from formal control. It is a form of social reciprocity. First, in trust the information is voluntary. It is not based on demand but on reciprocity. One does not need to demand appropriate information on potential or imminent problems and their true causes because that is already offered. Second, it tends to be less codified and explicit and more tacit and implicit. Third, its conditions for delivery not being specified, it is more flexible, geared to unanticipated contingencies and therefore it is more robust under uncertainty. That is a great advantage, because in formal control such contingencies would generally be impossible to specify completely. Fourth and most importantly, by assumption the information given in trust is truthful, while in formal control truth would have to be tested. In view of the multiple possible causes of disappointing outcomes and the possibility of claiming accidents as an excuse for failure or a mask for opportunism, this is a crucial benefit.

The analysis is reminiscent of what Hirschman (1970) called 'voice', as opposed to 'exit'. In exit, one walks out when dissatisfied, avoiding argument. One quits one's job, fires people, sells shares or part of a firm. In voice, the first response is not to walk out, but to seek amends. One reports one's dissatisfaction, asks for an explanation and asks for and offers help to 'work things out'. The importance of this in inter-firm relations has been indicated and demonstrated in empirical work, in particular by Susan Helper (1990). I propose that the process of voice is as described and analysed above.

# ORGANIZATIONAL PROCESSES

In organizations people have a range of options for including or excluding colleagues to deal with trust and its violation. One can retaliate or voice complaints directly to the antagonist, one can do this privately or in public, one can involve colleagues in gossip or coalitions, or one can go to one's boss and complain or demand action (see Chapters 3, 9 and 10 by Lindenberg, Wittek and Six in this volume). Confrontation in public entails a multiplier effect. Both the loss of prestige, involved in being told off or accepting advice, and the gain of prestige in winning a confrontation or giving advice, are multiplied. Because of such effects, in public confrontation conflict can become more acute than when confrontation is effected in private. However, public confrontation may be needed to muster support and hide behind group interest, masking the personal interest that is at stake. This can be used to reduce the blame that a victim can voice when put under pressure.

Deeper understanding of these phenomena can be achieved by going back to the work of Simmel (1950). He argued that a fundamental shift occurs in going from dyadic to triadic relations (Krackhardt, 1999). In dyadic relations individuality is preserved, in the sense that no coalitions can occur and no majority can outvote an individual. In a triad any member by himself has less bargaining power than in a dyad. The threat of exit carries less weight, since the two remaining partners would still have each other. In a triad, conflict is more readily solved. When any two players enter conflict, the third can act as a moderator, eliminating misunderstandings, proposing a compromise, designing a solution that saves face for the antagonists. This argument can help understanding of processes of trust and trouble within firms. Krackhardt (1999) shows how people who participate in different cliques can become constrained in their public behaviour, because they have to be seen to satisfy the combined norms or rules of all the cliques to which they belong. The paradox is that their multiple membership puts them in a position of potential power, but also constrains them in their use of it.

In groups effects of reputation and prestige arise, which tempt people into 'scoring' behaviour and make them more sensitive to loss of face and hence less inclined to accept compromise. The Simmelian analysis adds two things. One is that, since in dyads stalemates and conflicts are more difficult to resolve, they have to be carried into groups, where solutions are forced through by coalitions. The second is that, while a boundary spanner, involved in multiple cliques, can play a conciliatory role in the privacy of bilateral contacts, he cannot afford to do so in groups that mix the cliques, since he cannot afford to be conciliatory or sympathetic in public to either of the sides. In other words, dyads drive conflicts into groups and there conciliation is more difficult. This leads to confrontation and the need to force issues.

If the above arguments are correct, a dilemma arises concerning group resolution of conflict. On the one hand, a group may be needed to resolve stalemates and conflicts, by the use of coalitions, which cannot be resolved in dyads. On the other hand, in groups the loss of face in losing a conflict is enlarged. Also, in public group meetings, boundary spanners, who are often managers, may not be able to commit themselves to one of a number of interest groups. The solution may be straightforward: resolve conflicts in the minimal group size needed, with as little publicity as possible. However, that leads to backroom deals that have a bad name in a democratic culture.

Speaking more generally, when 'something goes wrong', that is, expectations are not met, the identification and attribution of causes can be enabled, but also blocked and distorted, by organizational conditions and processes. Using third party informants can help, but can also yield destructive gossip that confirms rather than corrects prejudice and misattribution. If Deutsch's 'crude law of social relations', discussed above, is valid, then cooperative or competitive types of relationships can become part of organizational culture, which confirms and propagates such types of relationships. The trust cycle proposed by Zand, discussed above, with its conveyance of appropriate information, mutuality of influence, encouragement of self-control and avoidance of the abuse of the vulnerability of others, can be enabled or obstructed in many ways by organizational structures and processes.

The study of such processes and organizational effects and influences forms an important area for further research. The remainder of this book aims to contribute to that.

## NOTES

1. I thank Gabriele Jacobs for her instruction in elements of social psychology. Any errors of interpretation are of course mine.
2. I do not wish to imply that stability of relations is always a good thing economically, in the sense that it is always conducive to efficiency and welfare. As indicated in Chapter 1, a certain amount of stability may be needed to recoup specific investments, which may in turn be needed to achieve high added value and innovativeness. However, relations can become too stable and exclusive and thereby yield rigidities. The question therefore is how to develop relations that have optimal duration: neither too short nor too long.

## REFERENCES

Bazerman, M. (1998), *Judgement in Managerial Decision Making*, New York: Wiley.
Berger, J., N.G. Noorderhaven and B. Nooteboom (1995), 'The determinants of supplier dependence: an empirical study', in J. Groenewegen, C. Pitelis and S.E. Sjöstrand (eds), *On Economic Institutions; Theory and Applications*, Aldershot, UK and Brookfield, US: Edward Elgar, pp. 195–212.

Cosmides, L. and J. Tooby (1992), 'Cognitive adaptations for social exchange', in H. Barkow, L. Cosmides and J. Tooby, *The Adapted Mind*, Oxford: Oxford University Press, pp. 163–228.

Deutsch, M. (1973), *The Resolution of Conflict: Constructive and Destructive Processes*, New Haven: Yale University Press.

Fukuyama, F. (1995), *Trust, the Social Virtues and the Creation of Prosperity*, New York: Free Press.

Helper, S. (1990), 'Comparative supplier relations in the US and Japanese auto industries: an exit/voice approach', *Business and Economic History*, **19**, 1–10.

Hirschman, A.O. (1970), *Exit, Voice and Loyalty: Responses to Decline in Firms, Organizations and States*, Cambridge, MA: Harvard University Press.

Kahneman, D., P. Slovic and A. Tversky (eds) (1982), *Judgement Under Uncertainty: Heuristics and Biases*, Cambridge: Cambridge University Press.

Klein Woolthuis, R. (1999), '*Sleeping with the enemy: trust, dependence and contracts in inter-organisational relationships*', doctoral dissertation, Twente University, P.O. Box 217, 7500 AE Enschede, the Netherlands.

Krackhardt, D. (1999), 'The ties that torture: Simmelian tie analysis in organizations', *Research in the Sociology of Organizations*, **16**, 183–210.

Lane C. and R. Bachmann (eds) (2000), *Trust Within and Between Organizations*, paperback edn, Oxford: Oxford University Press.

Lewicki, R.J. and B.B. Bunker (1996), 'Developing and maintaining trust in work relationships', in R.M. Kramer and T.R. Tyler (eds), *Trust in Organizations: Frontiers of Theory and Research*, Thousand Oaks: Sage Publications, pp. 114–39.

Lounamaa, P.H. and J.G. March (1987), 'Adaptive coordination of a learning team', *Management Science*, **33**, 107–23.

Luhmann, N. (1979), *Trust and Power*, Chichester: Wiley.

Macauley, S. (1963), 'Non-contractual relations in business: a preliminary study', *American Sociological Review*, **28**, 55–67.

March, J. (1991), 'Exploration and exploitation in organizational learning', *Organization Science*, **2** (1).

McAllister, D.J. (1995), 'Affect- and cognition-based trust as foundations for interpersonal cooperation in organizations', *Academy of Management Journal*, **38** (1), 24–59.

Nooteboom, B. (1999), *Inter-firm Alliances, Analysis and Design*, London: Routledge.

Nooteboom, B. (2000), *Learning and Innovation in Organizations and Economies*, Oxford: Oxford University Press.

Nooteboom, B. (2002), *Trust: Forms, Foundations, Functions, Failures and Figures*, Cheltenham, UK and Northampton, MA, USA: Edward Elgar.

Pettit, Ph. (1995), 'The cunning of trust', *Philosophy and public affairs*, **14** (3), 202–25.

Putnam, R.D. (2000), *Bowling Alone: The Collapse and Revival of American Community*, New York: Simon & Schuster.

Ring, P. and A. van de Ven (1992), 'Structuring cooperative relationships between organizations', *Strategic Management Journal*, **13**, 483–98.

Rosch, E. (1977), 'Human categorization', in N. Warren (ed.), *Advances in Cross-cultural Psychology*, vol.1, New York: Academic Press.

Sako, M. (2000), 'Does trust improve business performance?', in C. Lane and R. Bachmann (eds), *Trust Within and Between Organizations*, Oxford: Oxford University Press, pp. 88–117.

Shapiro, S.P. (1987), 'The social control of impersonal trust', *American Journal of Sociology*, **93**, 623–58.

Simmel, G. (1950), 'Individual and society', in K.H. Wolff (ed.), *The Sociology of George Simmel*, New York: Free Press.

Simmel, G. (1978), *The Philosophy of Money*, London: Rouledge & Kegan Paul.

Simon, H.A. (1983), *Reason in Human Affairs*, Oxford: Basil Blackwell.

Sydow, J. (2000), 'Understanding the constitution of interorganizational trust', in C. Lane and R. Bachmann (eds), *Trust In and Between Organizations*, Oxford University Press, pp. 31–63.

Zand, D.E. (1972), 'Trust and managerial problem solving', *Administrative Science Quarterly*, **17** (2), 229–39.

Zucker, L.G. (1986), 'Production of trust: institutional sources of economic structure 1840–1920', *Research in organizational behaviour*, **8**, 53–111.

# 3.  Governance seen from a framing point of view: the employment relationship and relational signalling

## Siegwart Lindenberg

> We should begin with empirically valid postulates about what motivates real people in real organizations. (Herbert Simon, 1997, p. 223)

## INTRODUCTION

For a long time, it has been accepted that organizations are made up of special relations, most noteworthy the relation between employer and employee. Authority relations and social relations between employer and employee have both been taken very seriously. Simon says that authority is the relation 'that chiefly distinguishes the behaviour of individuals as participants of organizations from their behaviour outside such organizations. It is authority that gives an organization its formal structure' (Simon, 1957, p. 124), building on the work of Barnard (1938). The human relations approach added that there is more than just the authority relation: 'Most of us want the satisfaction that comes from being accepted and recognized as people of worth by our friends and work associates' (Roethlisberger, 1941, p. 24).

Should governance structures concentrate on authority relations, as may be inferred from Simon's observation? If so, why and how? If not, why not? What aspects of relations should be covered by governance structures? Is there a difference for different kinds of organizations? Even though the importance of relations has been recognized for quite some time, there has not been much research on the question of how such relations work and how they are influenced by the governance structures within which they are embedded. As a consequence, authors in the field of organization studies have used the language of relations either to indicate a certain contractual agreement (legal or psychological) or as a synonym for interdependence. It will be argued in this chapter that there is more to relations than agreements and interdependence and that descriptions of governance structures and their workings remain necessarily very incomplete if they do not pay explicit attention to these relational aspects.

## PROTOTYPICAL RELATIONSHIPS

One may define a relationship as a configuration of matching expectations among interacting individuals. Mental models of the essential features of interaction in a variety of situations generate relationships. Thus, in a relationship, interacting individuals define their situation to a certain extent in matching ways.

That interaction takes place mainly within relationships is an assumption common to many classical authors in sociology. The *prototypes of relationships* in these works are based on the distinction between (a) a relationship between equals versus an authority relationship and (b) community (*Gemeinschaft*) versus society (*Gesellschaft*), yielding four basic types. Parsons had elaborated these prototypes in terms of the workings of complementary roles. Anthropologists (such as Polanyi, 1944, and Sahlins, 1972) worked out similar types in terms of the transfer of goods. In more recent times, the social psychologists Clark and Mills (1979) collected experimental evidence for the importance of communal versus exchange relationships. Even more recently, Fiske (1991) has considerably sharpened the delineation of the four types of relationships and has gathered considerable anthropological evidence from his own and other anthropologists' research. Fiske does not speak of roles or exchange of goods but rather of 'generative grammar' or 'script-like schemata' (ibid., p. 21), emphasizing the guide to action implied by the mental model for the relationship. He adds that 'the relational models do not fully specify behaviour in any interaction or situation, but they comprise a set of rules that strongly constrain the possibilities and that organize responses to violations of the rules'.

There is thus much empirical evidence that interaction takes place within the confines of relationships. However, there is also an important missing link: the link to a theory of action. If people use relational models to orient their behaviour, what exactly are they trying to achieve? Why do they use one model rather than another? Under what circumstances is a model particularly vulnerable? How are relationships stabilized over time? What structures are likely to evolve in support of certain relationships? None of these questions can be answered without a theory that links mental models to action and it is here, at present, that the study of relationships has done rather poorly. Even without the rhetoric of roles, the discussion of relationships is still much indebted to the implicit or explicit theory of role-playing behaviour, be that in terms of internalized rules or scripts or 'orientations'. Fiske, for example, moves easily back and forth from the language of 'script-like schemata' to the language of 'constraints' (see above). There is no particular theory of action to which he links the workings of the four prototypes of relationships. Under these circumstances, it is not surprising that relationships seem to take on a rather vague role of being important for simply everything people do. 'Each [relational] model is a standard for reacting to, taking into account, judging and intervening in social relationships and conversely, for accommodating to (and anticipating) others' appropriate judgments of one's own relationships.' Fiske then goes on to summarize: 'The crux of the matter is that each model is simultaneously a goal that people actively seek to realize in their actions toward others, a standard by which they judge their own and their partners' behaviour and a recognized criterion for others' legitimate intervention' (ibid., p. 385). There is no indication of how the relational model that is simultaneously a goal, a standard and a criterion influences behaviour. Maybe the reason Fiske and others have not come up with a suitable theory of action in connection with the workings of relationships is that the task is made difficult by the fact that action seems to be governed by different principles within each relationship and that it is difficult to find a common mechanism that steers these different principles. This chapter aims to address precisely that problem: to find a mechanism that is common to all relationships and that can also inform us about the question of how cooperative relationships within organizations (be they collegial or hierarchical) work, what threatens and what stabilizes them.

## EMBEDDING RELATIONSHIPS WITHIN A THEORY OF ACTION

Where do we begin to find a suitable link of relational analysis to a theory of action that helps us answer the kinds of questions asked above? Assuming that relationships are closely tied to mental models, the choice of possible theories of action is limited. Mental models can only be linked to theories that see the individual as interpreting the world and acting on this interpretation. This leaves either role theory or a theory of goal-directed action. Elsewhere, I have argued in some detail why a role theory is not a good theory of action (Lindenberg, 1989) and I have no room to repeat these arguments here. Suffice it to say that the main criticism of role theory is that it has great difficulty explaining the workings of situational constraints. I thus choose to work with a theory that individuals pursue goals under constraints.

**What is a Mental Model of a Relationship?**

The term 'mental model' is used in many different ways (see Collins and Gentner, 1987) but its basic connotation, quite common to many definitions, is some kind of mental representation that guides reasoning and action. A person is said to create mental models of relevant aspects of his or her physical and social world. One of the major functions of mental models is to allow the individual to *answer questions* about these aspects, be these aspects simple objects, like chairs, or complex processes like the political system of the United States. A subcategory of mental models is prototypes. For example, the prototype of a relationship can be used to answer the question, 'If this is a friendship relationship, what should I do?' Such a model may be taken to consist of five minimal elements. First, there is a set of rules about one's own and the other's behaviour; second, there are expectations about the other's behaviour based on these rules; third, there are the others' surmised expectations; fourth, there are normative expectations about one's own behaviour; and finally, there is coorientation about the expectations (Scheff, 1967), meaning that each partner in a relationship assumes that the other uses the same mental model. For example, the mental model of a friendship relationship could look like this: '*Rules of friendship*: friends are equals; friends don't do anything that would increase the social difference between them; friends don't harm each other; friends help each other in need. *Expectation about other's behaviour*: the other is my friend and thus he will behave according to the rules of friendship. *Expectations from the other*: the other is my friend and he expects me to act according to the rules of friendship. *Normative expectations* about own behaviour: I am his friend and I ought to behave according to the rules of friendship: the other is my friend and therefore uses the same rules and expectations I do.' The mental model of a relationship is thus more than just a social norm about how to behave. It minimally also includes descriptive and normative expectations and coorientation. It is especially this interlocking of expectations that makes mental models so important for interaction.

# MENTAL MODELS, GOALS AND FRAMES

How does a mental model relate to behaviour? As we will see, in order to relate mental models to behaviour, more cognitive aspects have to be considered than are normally considered in the social sciences. The mental model of a friendship relationship clearly contains a prescriptive element: when interacting with a friend, I should behave according to the rules of friendship. Yet, as we have argued above, the simple theory of action that people follow the 'oughts' they glean from a prototype of a relationship will not do. There must be a link to the goal pursuit of the individual. A closer look at mental models of relationships reveals that these models derive their significance from the association with two other elements: a goal and a frame. A *frame* is a process that guides selective attention and it is 'triggered' by a salient goal (see Gollwitzer and Moskowitz, 1996; Kruglanski, 1996). For example, if a person is set on making a profit in a particular interaction (the goal), he or she will 'frame' the situation in such a way that the elements that are relevant for making a profit become salient as well. How does it work?

**Overriding Goal**

When individuals interact with others, their behaviour is affected by an overriding goal. For example, in experiments on negotiation, individuals behave very differently if they are instructed to be cooperative or to be competitive (see Carnevale and Lawler, 1986). What the goal does is activate a certain selective attentional process, called a 'frame'. Because attention is a scarce good, it is selective and what is being attended to is particularly important for determining the kind of action that is taken (see also Fazio, 1990; Higgins and Brendl, 1995). Within a frame, certain bits of knowledge are mobilized and certain categories are activated. The individual is thus more sensitive to one kind of information than to another, relies more or less on certain mental models, remembers certain things better than others, places more value on certain outcomes, and so on.

The importance of this process for the understanding of relationships can hardly be overestimated. What is happening through framing is that some aspects are pushed into the foreground and some aspects are pushed into the background (see Lindenberg, 2001a). Those aspects in the foreground will affect behaviour much more than the ones in the background. We will deal with more details shortly, but let us take an example even before that. If a person meets a friend in a routine social situation (say, with a number of acquaintances during the intermission of a concert), the overriding goal that is likely to come up is 'to act appropriately'. This goal, in turn, will activate a frame with, among others, a mental model that contains more specific aspects of what appropriate behaviour would be in this situation. Note that the mental model of friendship behaviour came up within a frame that steered cognitions to various aspects of appropriate behaviour. Other aspects, such as the goals that relate to guarding against loss or to increasing one's resources are cognitively pushed into the background.

The specific thing about interacting within a friendship relationship is that the mental model of friendship virtually generates the partners' behaviour towards each other. This is possible only thanks to the fact that strongly distracting goals are temporarily out of sight ('framed out'). Conversely, to the partners, the other is only a 'real' friend if he can be assumed to not even think of doing unfriendly things (such as putting him down in public in order to impress one of the bystanders). Friendship, as a relationship, is thus the combination of a cognitive process and behaviour. In that process, mental models are only one, albeit an important, element. In fact, the cognitive processes provide the mechanism by which the same mental models can have quite different behavioural consequences. This is mainly due to the fact that the salience of the frame can vary considerably. Let us have a closer look at this process.

**Salience and Background Goals**

In choice theories that ignore framing effects and salience (such as subjectively expected utility [SEU] theory), the individual's preferences are weakly ordered and he or she will always choose the 'best' alternative of the feasible subset of that ordering. But this is clearly too strong a simplification. For one thing, the choice set is determined not just by feasibility (that is, by the resources) but also by what is selected and ordered by the frame. Second, the assumption that individuals are absolutely sure of their own preference is very unrealistic (see Kahneman, 1999). Individuals may be sure of their own preferences for each aspect, but goods are mostly bundles of aspects. Those aspects that speak for an option will make the individual want to choose it, those that speak against it makes the individual want to choose another option. The actual choice results from the balance of strength between these two tendencies and can best be expressed as a choice probability. When the advantages clearly outweigh the disadvantages, the choice probability for a given option is unity. When it is the reverse, it is zero; otherwise, the probability is in between. Which aspect is most important depends on the framed goal. For example, if my goal is 'to act appropriately' then the 'appropriateness' is the most important aspect for ordering the options.

Other aspects, pertaining to goals in the background, will increase or decrease the salience of the frame and thus the weight of the major aspect vis-à-vis other aspects. The higher the salience of the frame, the more sensitive the individual will be to small differences in the major aspect and thus the more likely that the situationally 'best' alternative will be chosen. In experimental tests of choice behaviour, the fiction of ordered preferences of goods (rather than aspects of goods sensitive to salience effects) can only be sustained by interpreting choice probabilities of, say, 0.51 and 0.96 both as evidence of 'choosing the best', without concern as to where the difference comes from.[1] Once we admit framing and salience effects, we see two important things. First, the 'best' alternative is always relative to the given frame; for another frame, the ordering of alternatives would be different. Second, lower salience of the frame will increase the probability with which second and third best alternatives are being chosen. Take our friendship example. When a person takes out his wallet to help a friend in need, what happens to the goal 'to guard one's resources'? As argued above, the major goal for the person in this situation is to act like a friend and thus the goal concerning his resources is pushed out of sight. What if the friend comes back the next day with another legitimate claim to be helped? What if he returns a third day in a row? We can readily predict what will happen. The degree to which the person will conform to what friendship norms would demand will decline. The contributions will fall increasingly short of the legitimate claim of the needy friend. In fact, the goal in the background 'to guard one's resources' will lower the salience of the goal 'to act as a friend' (the frame), the more so the higher the sacrifice asked of our person. This is so because the two goals are incompatible. From the point of view of the goal 'to act like a friend', lowered salience of the frame will lead to the choice of second and third best alternatives.

The lower the salience the more likely that the frame will switch altogether, so that the background goal becomes the new frame and the old framed goal is pushed into the background. Then the ordering of alternatives changes as well. Now the 'best' alternative is to avoid that person in order to avoid embarrassing social situations of refusal. Note that there is an important difference between a goal within the frame and one in the background. Not only do background goals exert much less influence than goals that are directly in the frame, but by being in the cognitive background they also fail to strike the actor as goals that are being pursued. For this very reason, people are well aware of direct costs (be it money, effort or psychic costs directly expended on the pursuit of the framed goal), whereas they are not well aware of opportunity costs.

In sum, one important point that follows from the consideration of framing and salience is this: a mental model, linked to a frame with a high salience, will lead to different behaviour than the same mental model linked to a frame with low salience will promote. If scripts are part of mental models, they only indicate what the best alternatives are, what would be most appropriate. Even in a normative frame (in which acting appropriately is the overriding goal), the individual does not slavishly follow the script because opportunity costs, even though they are cognitively pushed into the background, still exert influence on behaviour via their influence on the salience of the frame.

**Precariousness of Frames**

Salience effects make frames precarious. As we have seen above, salience of a frame is affected by changing opportunity costs (in the background). They lower the salience and thus the choice probability. Conversely, salience can be increased by background goals that are compatible rather than rival with the goal of the frame. For example, the goal to get social approval is compatible with the goal of a normative frame ('to act appropriately') and will push up the salience of the normative frame. Because frames are subject to varying salience, they are precarious in principle. They can weaken or even switch completely. Frame stability in interaction is vitally important because a certain frame is compatible with a limited range of mental models. For example, if John knows that Jack is in a salient normative frame, he knows that he can rely on Jack's behaviour being strongly influenced by mental models with a prominent normative component. John can safely assume that Jack does not act strategically. For cooperation, that is already a very important message. If John also finds out that Jack's specific mental model in interacting with him is that of friendship, he can relate Jack's behaviour even better to his own frame and mental model and, as a consequence, act in a way that matches Jack's behaviour. However, because of the precariousness of frames, John cannot take Jack's frame stability for granted.

If one just assumes that behaviour is governed by mental models, one is likely to overlook the dependence of behaviour on frames and thus one is likely to overlook the precariousness of frames. For example, in her well-known study of psychological contracts in organizations, Rousseau (1995) also uses mental models to explain how contracts work. According to her, these mental models form and stabilize on the basis of experience of the employee (ibid., p. 31). Keeping to the contractual agreement (as interpreted in the mental model) then becomes a matter of 'scripted behaviour', routine role fulfilment. This view completely misses the precariousness of the frame that is necessary to activate the mental model. In consequence, it also misses the governance structures and patterns of interaction in organizations that deal with this precariousness.[2] For cooperation in organizations, it is vitally important that people be in the right frame, not just for the coordination of their behaviour but also for the interpretation and predictability of their behaviour

In sum, a second and maybe the most important, point that follows from the consideration of framing and salience is this: frame stability is important for coordinated social interaction and yet frames are inherently precarious. Governance structures (aimed at increasing the likelihood of coordinated action) will thus have to address the stability of frames and individuals will be much concerned about the stability of their own frame as well as that of others.

## Differential a Priori Stability of Frames

Frames are the more stable (that is, are the more salient) in a situation the greater the involvement of the individual in the framed goal. For example, when the stakes are high, the framed goal is not likely to be displaced by some other goal. This is common knowledge and people act accordingly. For example, they know that, if they take something away from Jack that is very dear to him, they are likely to trigger Jack's single-minded pursuit in getting it back. In general, one can say that a frame is *a priori* more salient the more the framed goal is (a) tied to (compatible) emotions and (b) tied to direct consequences for self (the more so the less removed in time and the higher the consequences are). There are of course many frames and it would not do to try to list them according to their a priori salience. However, there are three frames that can be considered so general and, given the goals they are attached to, so important for lower-order frames, that it is worth while having a brief look at them (see Lindenberg, 2001a, for more detail). I call them master frames.

A general goal close to emotions and to the self is the wish 'to feel good/better right now'. It is short term and directed at the emotional state of the self in the widest sense of the word. This does not hold only for pos-itive and negative bodily states (such as excitement, hunger, thirst or pain) but also for positive and negative psychic states such as a sense of loss, fear, affection and status. One may call the frame that goes along with this goal the *hedonic frame*. Such a frame has a high a priori salience. A second general goal close to the self is the wish 'to improve one's resources', material or immaterial (such as money and competence). The frame that belongs to this goal can be called the *gain frame*. Such a frame is directly tied to the self, but it is removed emotionally and in time, in the sense that resources must be used before they have any hedonic effect. One can assume that, *a priori* speaking, a gain frame is less salient than a hedonic frame.[3]

A third general goal is the wish 'to act appropriately' belonging to what we have called above a *normative* frame. In such a frame, hedonic and gain-related goals are, if present at all, in the background. The framed goal 'to act appropriately' is directly tied neither to emotions nor to consequences for the self. Side-effects of acting appropriately, such as social approval and avoiding social disapproval, may be important elements in the background, but they do not belong to the framed goal itself. Often, when people do pursue social approval and avoidance of disapproval as the explicit goal (within a hedonic frame), it is noticed socially as a lack of intrinsic interest in moral behaviour and thus will be counterproductive. Having a direct tie neither to emotions nor to the self, a normative frame has an a priori salience lower than that of a gain frame. The consequences of this a priori ordering for questions of governance are very important. The general suspicion of precariousness holds particularly for a normative frame. People who interact are justified in suspecting that a normative frame will give way to a gain or a hedonic frame and, to the degree that their mental models contain important normative elements, in looking for signs in the behaviour of the interaction partners concerning the stability of the normative frame. In order to stabilize a normative frame against the onslaught of a gain or a hedonic frame, special arrangements are necessary. The same holds true for the stabilization of a gain frame against the intrusion of a hedonic frame.

In sum, a third point that follows from the consideration of framing and salience is this: not all frames are equally precarious. When normative and gain frames are deemed desirable for the cooperation of and between employees, individuals will be alert to the possibilities that frames are not stable. They will look for signs in each other's behaviour for frame stability. Management will be likely to establish arrangements that stabilize the weaker frames.

### What is the Right Frame or Combination of Frames?

In organizations, hedonic frames are least likely to be useful for cooperation. They are oriented towards the short term and make people very sensitive to opportunities for fun and against expending effort. A governance structure working with hedonic frames would have to concentrate on creating strong guilt feelings when people do not perform up to a standard. However, such an arrangement requires much monitoring and difficult alignments between guilt feelings and the failure to perform.

If the work requires a considerable degree of routine and if monitoring is costly (so that strictly contingent rewards are out of the question), a strong normative frame is most desirable. The individual's wish 'to act appropriately' is well suited to situations in which appropriate behaviour is well defined. However, because the normative frame is the weakest of the three, it takes the greatest effort to establish. It is especially difficult to keep it from being displaced by a hedonic frame. Bureaucracies usually put in particular effort in fostering normative frames, including the selection of personality types that are by temperament or socialization more sensitive to the lure of appropriateness. Recent moves to make bureaucracies more performance-oriented (that is, fostering a gain frame instead of a normative frame) struggle with the difficulty of redefining a considerable part of routine work as individual achievements. Success is doubtful.

When much individual initiative is needed, a gain frame is more useful than a normative frame because the latter depends on scripted behaviour whereas the former makes full use of the individual's resourcefulness. However, there is a catch. A salient gain frame will make the individual act thoroughly strategically and opportunistically. What does not clearly improve his or her resources will not be done. Conversely, all that clearly does improve his or her resources, no matter what the consequences for the organization, will be done unless it is covered by strong sanctions and a high degree of monitoring. The individual will be a free-rider where they can and a mercenary where they must and an opportunist wherever possible. Thus, for modern organizations, especially knowledge-producing organizations with teamwork, the best solution is what has been called 'weak solidarity' (see Lindenberg, 1998). It consists of two frames that keep each other in check. When the behaviour in a gain frame creates opportunity costs for the goal 'to act appropriately' (in the background), the salience of the gain frame will decline and second and third best options will be chosen. As opportunity costs rise, there will be a frame switch. Gain will vanish into the background and the framed goal will now be 'to act appropriately'. When behaviour in this frame creates opportunity costs in terms of the goal 'to improve one's resources' (in the background), its salience will be lowered until there is a switch back to the gain frame.

In order to make such a balance of frames possible, special arrangements must be in place. These arrangements (a) provide alignment of the individual's gain with organizational goals, (b) guard against the intrusion of a hedonic frame and (c) make relationships important enough for their maintenance alone to boost a wish to act appropriately vis-à-vis the partners in the relationships (see Lindenberg, 2000). We will see later how this is done.

In sum, a fourth point that follows from the consideration of framing and salience is this: for organizations with much routine work and high monitoring costs (such as bureaucracies), fostering normative frames is the best solution. Yet it is not easy to keep a normative frame from being displaced by a hedonic frame and that makes this solution often costly. For organizations that ask for a high degree of individual initiative, such as knowledge-producing organizations with teamwork, a balance of gain and normative frame seems to be the best solution. Such a balance takes sophisticated governance arrangements.

**Frame Interdependence: a Keen Interest in One's Own and Others' Frames**

Master frames are like constraints rather than modes of attending that can be chosen at will. At any given moment, a master frame is given and cannot be willed into otherwise. For example, one cannot will oneself out of a hedonic frame and into a normative frame. The salience of the hedonic frame can thus not be lowered by an act of will, nor can the salience of the normative frame be increased that way. This does mean that frames cannot be influenced. One can choose situations in which it is likely that frames become more or less salient. A good comparison is 'going to sleep'. One cannot choose to sleep but one can choose to lie in bed in the dark and entice sleep to come. In a similar way, one can 'entice' frames by choosing the 'right' environment or avoiding the 'wrong' environment. For example, people may choose to go to church in order to increase the salience of a normative frame, or they may avoid going to certain parties in order not to increase the salience of a hedonic frame. Because frames are so crucial for the mental models used in interaction and for the way they are used, people have a keen interest in managing their own frames. It is generally easier for people to behave in a way they would like to behave when they are in the 'right' frame than when they have to pretend, even though pretending would offer them more flexibility to adjust their behaviour to changing circumstances.

Let us take an example. A businessman, himself in a salient gain frame, would like to enter into a partnership with another businessman. In order to gain the trust of this other businessman he might, in addition to the credible commitments he can give, want to behave in such a way that he does not appear as a pure opportunist. Credible commitments only safeguard against clearly misaligned interests; they do not safeguard against 'myopic opportunism' that exploits golden opportunities that may come along, allows the cutting of corners and generally invites sharp short-term maximization at the margin (see Lindenberg, 2000). Since he is in a salient gain frame, he will not be restrained by a normative frame whenever his own behaviour strongly violates relational norms. To pretend that he is not a pure opportunist means he has to convince the other that his own pursuit of gain is constrained by a normative frame even though it is not. Certainly, there are some con-artists who can do this, but by and large it will be difficult for most people not to give off signs that they are pretending to be in a frame they are not in. The reason that it is so difficult to do this is that most interactions take place within relationships or consist of attempts to build up relationships. The mental models at the basis of the relationships imply complementarity and stability of expectations. Thus, for the kinds of relationships they often enter, people become savvy in reading signals that indicate complementarity and stability or betray the lack of these crucial attributes. Con-artists mostly prey on people who have not much experience with certain relationships, who are not savvy. In short, people are very interested not just in their own behaviour but also in their own frames that are crucial for generating the behaviour. To interact in relationships thus implies regulatory interests in one's own frames.

This regulatory interest points to important links of individuals to governance structures. Such structures should not primarily be seen as control structures by the principal in order to keep the agent in line, but as *joint* production of people who interact in relationships. A governance structure that does not help people to manage their own frames is likely to be highly inefficient. Note that this is compatible with, but different from, the argument by Simon that organizations govern by influencing the employees' premises for making decisions rather than by direct command. Simon does not deal at all with the precariousness of frames or with the frame interdependence between people.

The jointness is reinforced by yet another aspect: *frame resonance*. This phenomenon points to the influence of people's frames on each other. A highly salient frame in one person makes it more likely that the other person will adopt the same frame. For example, it is difficult to maintain a normative frame in a group of people who are in a salient hedonic frame. Similarly, it is much easier to keep a hedonic frame at bay among a group of people who are in a salient normative frame. Thus frame resonance implies that people's regulatory interest in their own frames leads them to be interested in their frame environment, that is, in the frames of others even if they do not interact with these people. At times, this may look like a curious interest in public goods. For example, Mühlau (2000) found that even well-treated employees are slow to commit themselves to the organization if the employer treats other employees badly.

In sum, a fifth point that follows from the consideration of framing and salience is this: master frames cannot be chosen at will even though they are very important for one's own behaviour. They can, however, be influenced by choosing certain environments and avoiding others. Individuals thus have a keen interest in managing their own frames by influencing the environment they are in. This regulatory interest in one's own frame is strengthened by the fact that salient frames of others tend to mobilize similar frames in an individual in their environment (*frame resonance*). Governance structures in organizations are thus, at least to a large extent, to be seen as joint productions for the management of frames rather than control structures to make agents do what principals want.

## RELATIONAL SIGNALS

The precariousness of frames and frame interdependence make people watchful for signals given off by the behaviour of the other. Because interaction takes place mostly within relationships, the most important signals people watch for are relational signals. Such signals indicate the mental model and the frame(s) that sustain it. Watching out for such signals is more efficient than closely monitoring the results of behaviour. There are many results to be monitored, whereas relational signals pertain to relatively few telltale situations in which signals entail sacrifices (such as forgoing part of the control over an extra share for fairness's sake) or cannot be easily suppressed or controlled (such as blushing or forgetting your wife's birthday). The four prototypical relationships (see above) all have their own telltale situations. But what interests us here most are telltale situations that are vital for all kinds of cooperative relationships in organizations, be they authority or collegial relationships: situations that show other regard (or solidarity). Notice that 'other regard' only makes sense if there is something like framing because it means that people who have regard for others do not even think of doing certain negative things. Goals pertaining to these negative aspects are pushed into the cognitive background. People who are in a normative frame with mental models of other regard do not abstain from negative behaviour for strategic reasons (gain frame), or for reasons of favouritism (hedonic frame) but for reasons of the importance of acting appropriately. This is why they can be trusted. People seem to be very quick in assessing general positive or negative clues (see Damasio, 1994) and 'other regard' is always seen as positive by the other because it stands for non-strategic agreement and norm-bound behaviour.

The telltale situations for such a frame are probably only five (Lindenberg, 1998). First, there are *common good situations,* with the signal behaviour of contributing to the common good even if the person could free-ride (the minimal amount of contribution in terms of money, effort, time and so on expected for a signal of 'other regard' varies). Second, there are *sharing situations* (with joint divisible benefits and/or costs), with the signal behaviour of not seeking to maximize what one gets from the benefit and minimize what one gets from the costs but to take one's 'fair share' of both (what the 'fair share' is varies). Third, there are *need situations*, with the signal behaviour of helping others in times of need (what constitutes need and how much help is minimally expected varies). Fourth, there are *breach temptations,* with the signal behaviour of keeping to implicit or explicit agreements, that is, of refraining from hurting others even at a cost to oneself (the minimal amount of cost expected varies). Fifth, there are *mishap situations* in which acts are intended to be solidary but factually turn out to go against the expectation of other regard (in combination with situations one to four). Signal behaviour is showing that one meant to act differently, that one feels sorry that it turned out that way and that one will make amends if the mishap has caused damage to others. Also, if one knows in advance that one will not be able to keep to the agreement, one will warn others in advance, so that they can mitigate the damage.[4]

In game-theoretic experiments, often only the first situation (common good) is being considered. However, because these situations are part of continuing relationships and because the important thing is the stability of the 'right' frame, there is no way one can strategically substitute showing extra 'other regard' behaviour in one of the five kinds of situations and by showing none in any of the others. The signal of signals is consistency across situations. If I make extra contributions to the common good but fail to help others in need, my positive behaviour will be interpreted as strategic rather than generated by other regard.

These relational signals only work under certain conditions and these conditions must be part of the governance structure. For one thing, the group of interacting individuals has to be able to generate or use a language of signals that is specific to the situations in this group. For example, in the apparel industry in New York, things often have to be done so quickly that pricing is done after the deal, creating a typical hold-up situation. Still, it works for stable business relationships (see Uzzi, 1997) because fair pricing after delivery is seen as a relational signal in a sharing situation. This is quite specific to this industry. Other industries will have other signals for fairness in sharing situations. Inside the organization, people must also be able to have joint standards for relational signals. Governance structures can hinder or help the generation of such common signals. Another condition is that signals are not ambiguous. For example, Wittek (1999) describes a situation in a paper factory in which, owing to a change in tasks, helping behaviour could not be well distinguished any more from showing one's superiority. The result was a breakdown of relational signalling and, as a consequence, of efficient cooperation. Mühlau (2000) shows that relational signalling is pervasive in Japanese and American organizations. He also showed that, if an employer was not able or willing to keep his promises (breach temptation), he would have done better with his employees (in terms of their commitment to the organization) if he had not generated any relational expectations in the first place. Lazega's (2001, pp. 201ff) studies show that informal control in an organization only works if the act of control does not simultaneously signal possible strategic behaviour in the guise of relational interest. There is another control aspect connected to selective (performance-contingent) rewards (such as bonuses or promotions). Such reward systems will not work if they interfere with relational signalling. For example, if performance cannot be measured well, then performance-contingent rewards signal, not other regard, but favouritism or strategic behaviour, neither belonging to a normative frame and both eliciting strategic or hedonic responses.

Research on intrinsic motivation has also shown that controlling feedback (for example, 'I would like to see you do so well more often . . .') lowers intrinsic motivation whereas positive informational feedback (for example 'you have done well . . .') heightens it (see Deci and Ryan, 1985). The maintenance of intrinsic motivation is very important where employees are expected to show intelligent effort and where tacit knowledge (that is, knowledge that cannot be referred to in contracts) plays an important role (see Osterloh and Frey, 2000). There is a close relationship between relational signalling and maintaining intrinsic motivation both in the sense of obligation and in the sense of enjoyment (see Lindenberg, 2001b). Thus, in order to keep intrinsic motivation sustainable, one also needs to keep relational signals working well. Governance structures based on principal–agent theory with the basic assumption that the agent tries to do as little as possible for as high a compensation as possible will work against relational signalling and thus also against intrinsic motivation. Similarly, many standard tools for motivating employees make use of individual long-term rewards, such as are offered by internal labour markets. They do offer some perspective but they are largely ineffective if the tournaments that accompany them interfere with effective relational signalling.

### What Kind of Governance Structures?

In sum, what do governance structures have to look like in organizations that are highly dependent on intelligent effort? The short answer to this question is: they have to support mental models of 'weak solidarity'; that is, they have to maintain a balance of gain and normative frames (preferably with frame-compatible hedonic goals in the background, that is, with enjoyment as a side product of gain and normative behaviour). The longer answer begins with the fact that management cannot fake it for long. Frame resonance will create hedonic or pure gain frames in employees if management just pretends to have other regard. Not faking it means that other regard must be part of the *professionalism* of managers rather than a ruse. The second point is that there must be opportunities for improving one's resources (gain). Competition and contingent rewards work positively for a gain frame that is compatible with intrinsic motivation, if jobs allow not just monetary compensation but also improvement in competence, and if there are clear performance standards and even the slightest suggestion of favouritism (as a sign of hedonic frames of the management) is avoided.

Third, there are jointly worked out (or at least consensual) standards of relationally appropriate behaviour throughout all areas of interaction, from keeping promises, to the rule of law, to dealing with control. Without them, normative frames are too weak to curb the gain frame when gain becomes very costly in terms of violation of relational norms. Fourth, the organization of work must be attuned to the five telltale situations in which other regard can be signalled. This means that people who are strongly interdependent in their task performance and joint rewards must be able to exchange informal relational signals, free of ambiguity (for example, without the offer to help being interpreted as an attempt to prove one's superiority). For this, people must be able to meet easily informally (phys-ical proximity and same cafeteria) and they must not be in competition for rewards. For this very reason, interdependence in rewards without task interdependence should be avoided because it creates ambiguity in rela-tional signals (see Van der Vegt *et al.*, 1998). If I help you to work harder, is it that I am interested in you or would I like to be able to get away with doing less? Fifth, there must be much attention paid to relationally positive performance feedback. Normative frames are the weakest of the master frames and need extra support from the realization of compatible goals in the background. The major stabilizer of a normative frame is social approval for having done the right thing and disapproval for having vio-lated relational norms without credible indication that it is a mishap. The people whose approval and disapproval is most effective are those who can shield the employee from negative influence of higher-ups. Ideally, this is a person one rung higher than oneself: they are close enough to notice and not high enough to be dangerous if things have not gone right. Such infor-mal feedback systems take a considerable amount of effort because they require keeping abreast of what others are doing, to do so in terms of per-formance standards and to be willing to engage in potentially embarrass-ing situations of showing disapproval. For this reason alone, governance structures often fall short of stabilizing relational frames through relation-ally positive feedback.

Sixth, there must be a hierarchy for the distribution of responsibility and for coordination of efforts, but there should not be pure chains of command. The solution is a functional hierarchy in which people in a higher position are supposedly better equipped to know what needs to be done. In order to make a functional hierarchy work, it is essential that indi-viduals be well informed about the entire operation and that procedures, interactions and the accompanying rules be transparent. In order to achieve this, employees have to be kept well informed or rotate in their jobs through the organization at least periodically (see Lindenberg, 1993).

It is interesting to note that some recent textbooks often come much closer to these points about governance structures than the older books that rely heavily on transaction cost economics and principal–agent theory. For example Baron and Kreps (1999) mention a number of points for what they call 'high commitment human resource management'. Seemingly, there are some insights in the air. However, without a theory from which these points follow, it remains a matter of luck whether a point strikes home or follows the latest fashion in management talk. For example, Baron and Kreps mention as a prime condition for high commitment human resource management 'egalitarianism in word and deed', so that 'distinctions among workers at different levels of the hierarchy are aggressively de-emphasized' (ibid. p. 190). Here Baron and Kreps mix up egalitarianism with relational signals. Egalitarianism is only a positive relational signal for non-functional distinctions. For example, having separate toilets for supervisors and workers introduces non-functional distinctions that convey little concern for relationships across this divide. By contrast, functional distinctions remain important and do not convey negative relational concern. A similar point can be made about 'employment guarantees', also mentioned by Baron and Kreps. Whether or not giving employment guarantees is interpreted as a negative relational signal depends on culture and context. In Japan, it used to be the super relational signal but, even there, things are changing. Project-related employment is also becoming relationally acceptable in a context in which the distinction between employment and the purchase of services is not always clear. Concrete relational signals may differ by industry and even by organization. The claim here is that they all have one thing in common: they are a common part of many different relationships and their mental models and they all relate to the five telltale situations of other regard. Governance structures for organizations that are highly dependent on the intelligent effort of their employees are likely to focus heavily on the proper workings of these signals.

## CONCLUSION

The current theories of governance in organizations are either still based on transaction costs economics and the principal–agent theory or they are based on the idea that human resources require being treated nicely. The important insight behind the latter idea is that human beings mostly interact in terms of relationships and that in some way positive relationships are best maintained if one is nice to people. A slightly more sophisticated approach to this idea is that people act on the basis of mental models that help them arrive at the behaviour that is adequate for the relationship. So far, the theoretical development in this direction has been hampered by the fact that mental models of relationships are in the literature mostly linked to role-playing behaviour (with scripts and schemas). This does not explain why people use one model rather than another, or under what circumstances a model is particularly vulnerable, or how relationships are stabilized over time and what structures are likely to evolve in support of certain relationships. The situation changed when the relationship between motivation and cognition began to be considered, most importantly framing and salience effects. People attend selectively to aspects of a situation. Certain aspects are at the centre of attention and others are pushed into the background so that the importance given to certain aspects depends on the frame. Frames steer mental models and only if they are relatively stable will relationships work well. Yet the frames that are important for cooperative behaviour are very precarious. Because frame stability is important for coordinated social interaction, governance structures (aimed at increasing the likelihood of coordinated action) have to address the stability of frames. Individuals will be much concerned about the stability of their own frame as well as that of others, which creates a very different point of departure for governance than the principal–agent theory in which individuals are interested in shirking as much as possible. Individuals will look for signs in each other's behaviour for the stability of the other's frame and they have a regulatory interest in structures which help them stabilize their own frames. Management will be likely to establish arrangements that stabilize important but *a priori* weak frames. Such arrangements are quite different from the aspects of governance stressed by transaction cost theory and principal–agent theory and different from more recent relational hype in providing a theory on how relationships work and what aspects help create favourable conditions for effective relational signalling.

## NOTES

1. This is a widespread custom in experimental research on choice behaviour. Even Kahneman and Tversky (1984) do it, although they consider framing effects.
2. On purely empirical grounds, she has to deal with the phenomenon that contracts change 'without any formal effort to alter their terms' (Rousseau, 1995, p. 143). In order to make sense of this 'contract drift', despite the assumption of stable mental models, she introduces a number of unsettling cognitive effects.
3. One can interpret Max Weber's contribution to the explanation of the rise of capitalism as a demonstration of the way, through legal and religious institutions, gain frames became stronger than hedonic frames for many economic agents. The 'normal' microeconomic assumption that a gain orientation is the 'natural' state of human beings is wrong in the light of framing considerations and empirical evidence, especially in developing countries.
4. Note that reciprocity is not one of the five telltale situations. Rather, the given telltale situations cover what would be called reciprocity in a particular kind of relationship. For example, in an exchange relationship failure to reciprocate directly is tantamount to taking more than one's fair share of benefits or less of one's fair share of the burdens. In public good situations, free-riding can be interpreted as violating expectations of generalized reciprocity. It seems preferable to express important aspects that mental models for very different kinds of relationships have in common, rather than to deal with the specific forms of these aspects in the various relationships themselves.

# REFERENCES

Barnard, C. (1938), *The Functions of an Executive*, Cambridge, MA: Harvard University Press..

Baron, J. and D.M. Kreps (1999), *Strategic Human Resources*, New York: Wiley.

Carnevale, P.J.D. and E.J. Lawler (1986), 'Time pressure and the development of integrative agreements in bilateral negotiations', *Journal of Conflict Resolution*, **30**, 636–59.

Clark, M.S. and J. Mills (1979), 'Interpersonal attraction in exchange and communal relationships', *Journal of Personality and Social Psychology*, **37**, 12–24.

Collins, A. and D. Gentner (1987), 'How people construct mental models', in D. Holland and N. Quinn (eds), *Cultural Models in Thought and Language*, Cambridge: Cambridge University Press.

Damasio, Antonio, R. (1994), *Decartes' Error: Emotion, Reason and the Human Brain*, New York: Putnam's Sons.

Deci, Edward L. and Richard M. Ryan (1985), *Intrinsic Motivation and Self-Determination in Human Behavior*, New York: Plenum Press.

Fazio, R.H. (1990), 'Multiple processes by which attitudes guide behavior: the mode model as an integrative framework', *Advances in Experimental Social Psychology*, **23**, 75–109.

Fiske, A.P. (1991), *Structures of Social Life*, New York: Free Press.

Gollwitzer, P.M. and G.B. Moskowitz (1996), 'Goal effects on action and cognition', in E.T. Higgins and A.W. Kruglanski (eds), *Social Psychology. Handbook of Basic Principles,* London: The Guilford Press, pp. 361–99.

Higgins, E.T. and M. Brendl (1995), 'Accessibility and applicability: some activation rules influencing judgment', *Journal of Experimental Social Psychology*, **31**, 218–43.

Kahneman, D. (1999), 'Objective happiness', in D. Kahneman, E. Diener and N. Schwarz (eds), *Well-Being: The Foundations of Hedonic Psychology*, New York: Russell Sage, pp. 3–25.

Kruglanksi, A.W. (1996), 'Motivated social cognition: principles of the interface', in E.T. Higgins and A.W. Kruglanski (eds), *Social Psychology: Handbook of Basic Principles*, London: The Guilford Press, pp. 493–520.

Lazega, M. (2001), *The Collegial Phenomenon: The Social Mechanisms of Cooperation Among Peers in a Corporate Law Partnership*, Oxford: Oxford University Press.

Lindenberg, S. (1989), 'Choice and culture: the behavioral basis of cultural impact on transactions', in H. Haferkamp (ed.), *Social Structure and Culture*, Berlin: de Gruyter.

Lindenberg, S. (1993), 'Club hierarchy, social metering and context instruction: governance structures in response to varying self-command capital', in S. Lindenberg and H. Schreuder (eds), *Interdisciplinary Perspectives on Organization Studies*, Oxford: Pergamon Press, pp. 195–220.

Lindenberg, S. (1998), 'Solidarity: its microfoundations and macro-dependence. a framing approach', in P. Doreian and T.J. Fararo (eds), *The Problem of Solidarity: Theories and Models*, Amsterdam: Gordon and Breach, pp. 61–112.

Lindenberg, S. (2000), 'It takes both trust and lack of mistrust: the workings of cooperation and relational signaling in contractual relationships', *Journal of Management and Governance*, **4**, 11–33.

Lindenberg, S. (2001a), 'Social rationality versus rational egoism', in J. Turner (ed.), *Handbook of Sociological Theory*, New York: Plenum.
Lindenberg, S. (2001b), 'Intrinsic motivation in a new light', *Kyklos*, **54**, 317–42.
Mühlau, P. (2000), *The Governance of the Employment Relation: A Relational Signaling Perspective*, Amsterdam: Thela Thesis.
Osterloh, M. and B. Frey (2000), 'Motivation, knowledge transfer and organizational forms', *Organization Science*, **11**, 538–50.
Polanyi, K (1944), *The Great Transformation*, New York: Rinehart and Co.
Roethlisberger, F.J. (1941), *Management and Morale*, Cambridge, MA: Harvard University Press.
Rousseau, D.M. (1995), *Psychological Contracts in Organizations: Understanding Written and Unwritten Agreements*, New York: Sage Publications.
Sahlins, M. (1972), *Stone Age Economics*, New York: Aldine.
Scheff, T.J. (1967), 'Towards a sociological model of consensus', *American Sociological Review*, **32**, 32–46.
Simon, H. (1957), *Administrative Behavior: A Study of Decision-making Process in Administrative Organizations*, 2nd edn, New York: The Free Press.
Simon, H. (1997), *Rationality in Psychology and Economics, Models of Bounded Rationality. Vol III: Empirically Grounded Economic Reason*, Cambridge, MA: MIT Press, pp. 367–85.
Uzzi, B. (1997), 'Social structure and competition in interfirm networks: the paradox of embeddedness', *Administrative Science Quarterly*, **42** (1), 35–67.
Van der Vegt, G.S., B.J.M. Emans and E. Van de Vliert (1998), 'Motivating effects of task and outcome interdependence in work teams', *Group and Organization Management*, **23**, 124–43.
Wittek, R. (1999), *Interdependence and Informal Control in Organizations*, Amsterdam: Thela Thesis.

# 4. Trust and power as means of coordinating the internal relations of the organization: a conceptual framework

**Reinhard Bachmann**

## INTRODUCTION

The problem of coordinating individual actors' activities within the boundaries of the organization is certainly one of the key issues of organizational theory. Irrespective of whether the nature of the organization is seen as primarily based on contractual arrangements, shared social norms, constellations of economic interests or common cultural orientations, the question of how to integrate different actors' expectations and interaction lies at the heart of any organization's identity. If this function is not fulfilled satisfactorily, organizations will be confronted with serious problems which make it unlikely that they will survive over a longer period of time. However, the simple fact that stable organizations *do* exist and, even more so, that many of them are quite successful in their activities, can be taken as a strong indication that this coordination problem can be tackled and in fact *is* effectively solved every day all around the globe. Undoubtedly, organizations can also look chaotic and indeed may collapse where too many divergent interests render these uncontrollable. But it is an indisputable and – in a theoretical perspective – more remarkable observation that in countless cases complex organizations exist in a stable manner, operate profitably, develop their businesses and even survive when their strategies need to be radically redefined where far-reaching changes in the business environment force them to do so (Luhmann, 1984).

In this chapter, it will be argued that a fruitful approach to understanding the coordination of expectations and interaction within organizations builds on the insight that there must be certain social mechanisms at work, which allow for a swift and relatively frictionless alignment of individual members' behaviour. It will be suggested that trust and power are efficient means to do this job. This chapter will show how these mechanisms function, what the preconditions and consequences of employing them are and how they can be interlinked and thus provide specific regimes of organizational control. The next section of this contribution will deal with the nature and various forms of trust, as well as with the role of power in organizational relations. The third section will discuss two different types of organizational regulation, building on the specific sort and combination of trust and power that occurs in organizational relationships. The conclusion will be a short summing-up of the argument presented in this chapter.

# TRUST

### The Nature of Organizational Trust

As a theoretical starting point, the social mechanism of trust may be conceptualized as being based on a decision by which one social actor selects a *specific positive* assumption among a large number of other – in principle equally *possible* – assumptions about the future behaviour of another social actor (Luhmann, 1979). The proactive party, that is the trustor, makes this selection, communicates it to the trustee and builds his own behaviour onto this assumption. He signals that he is prepared to make decisions generous and favourable to a trustee under the condition of limited knowledge of the *alter ego*'s motives and abilities as well as the impersonal circumstances in which this individual will behave in the future (Nooteboom, 2002). In doing so, he makes a pre-commitment assuming that the other party will not behave opportunistically. Although far from having any guarantees, a trustor chooses to assume that the trustee will simply not take advantage of his vulnerability resulting from his one-sided pre-commitment and ignores all the other possibilities.

Such a pre-commitment need not necessarily be solely interpreted with regard to its normative implications. Often such a behaviour is eminently important to simply provide a first step to initiate any form of social interaction between two actors (Bachmann, 2001). Where neither of the parties finds himself able to offer a one-sided commitment in advance, it may well be that no social communication at all will arise between them. Where one actor, however, makes this first step, the second actor will also be able to select specific assumptions with regard to the first actor's future behaviour and discard all the other possibilities. Thus specific expectations can be selected on a *mutual* basis, a large number of theoretically equally expectable possibilities of *each* actor's future behaviour are rejected and long chains of coordinated social interaction, that is complex social systems, can emerge. Trust, in other words, facilitates the coordination of expectations and allows

for meaningful complex interaction between individuals who might otherwise have little chance to engage in any kind of social relationship.

Unlike other mechanisms of coordinating expectations and interaction
between two social actors, trust unavoidably requires an extrapolation from
the available information on the part of the initiating individual, that is the
trustor. As he has no guarantees as regards the future behaviour of the
trustee he will necessarily have to bear a certain amount of risk as soon as
he decides to invest trust in a social relationship. On the one hand, an
actor's decision to offer trust as the prime coordination mechanism within
a relationship diffuses uncertainty that would otherwise characterize the
situation and paralyse the two potential interactors. But, on the other hand,
it also produces a *binarily* coded risk: the trust investment will *either* pay off
*or* the trustee will misuse the trustor's pre-commitment and not reciprocate
any favours.

Given this inherent characteristic of trust, it seems evident that social
actors who consider this mechanism as a possible basis for their interaction
with another actor usually seek reasons as to why the risk of trust will at
least not exceed certain – more or less acceptable – limits. Although trust
can never be built on complete information, since it would make itself
superfluous in this case, sensible trustors are, by the same token, not keen
to invest 'blind trust'. The latter is not likely to win any social admiration
(especially not if it fails). Potential trustors usually try to assess roughly the
risk that they would buy into with their decision to invest trust in a relationship and then decide whether or not they are prepared to bear this risk.
Social actors, thus, tend to make limited investments of trust. They may, in
their everyday routines, be far from basing their decisions always on explicit
and quantifiable calculation but, at the same time, it would be unrealistic to
assume that there are many cases where they have no consciousness of the
consequences of their behaviour at all.

If this is so, one of the most crucial subsequent questions is: what can
provide *good reasons* (Bachmann, 2001) for a (potential) trustor to believe
that the risk he needs to accept when making a trust investment in the form
of a pre-commitment will not exceed a certain limit of acceptability?
Following Luhmann's argument (1979), the existence or absence of legal
norms may be seen as playing a central role in many situations where trust
is considered as the dominant coordination mechanism in a social relationship. In an environment where clear and reliable legal norms exist, a potential trustor has *good reasons* to assume that the potential trustee, who also
knows these norms, will generally be discouraged from cheating. It is pre-
supposed, however, that the sanctions connected with these legal norms
remain latent. In other words, trust requires that these sanctions are not
considered explicitly by the trustee and that the potential trustor does not

refer to them with the intention of threatening the potential trustee. The mobilization of sanctions is seen as playing a role only in exceptional cases which neither the trustor nor the trustee expects to become reality. Normally, it seems sufficient if social actors orient their behaviour *along the lines of* the existing legal arrangements. If social actors simply accept these without too much critical reflection on worst case scenarios, legal norms do a perfect job. Under these (and only under these!) conditions, legal norms can be seen as an important prerequisite to foster the production of trust in social relationships.

Applying this conceptualization of the trust mechanism to the world of social relations within organizations sheds light on the function of *social* rules that are incorporated in the structure of the organization rather than on *legal* norms that may exist in the institutional environment of the organization. These intraorganizational social rules are represented, for example, in the patterns of division of work and the distribution of responsibilities, the agreements on work duties of each individual member of the organization and so on. Also they include forms of conflict resolution (see Wittek in the present volume) and various other arrangements and practices that may evolve within the boundaries of the organization. All of these are elements of what could be called the *structural inventory* of the organization. Similar to the way in which extraorganizational legal norms do their job with regard to individuals' behaviour, these intraorganizational social rules constitute the internal structural framework of the organization which channels each individual's behaviour according to the identity and dynamics of the organization as a whole. In that these rules have a normative dimension, they imply the *potential* for sanctions which may be used against individual actors who do not comply. Under usual circumstances, however, these sanctions, similar to legal norms existing in the external environment of the organization, are not activated. Their *potential* to sanction individuals' (mis-)behaviour is strong enough to direct individuals' decisions effectively towards certain channels of acceptable behaviour. Explicit threats with sanctions usually seem unnecessary. Where they occur, they constitute an exceptional situation; if they occur repeatedly, they may eventually result in a severe crisis, making a fundamental restructuring of the organization's institutional inventory likely and sometimes unavoidable.

The central function of the rules implied in the structural inventory of the organization is to provide *shared* social and cultural meaning as well as a common set of interpretation categories as regards economic and technical knowledge. This produces a *world-in-common* which, with regard to building trust, plays an eminently important role in organizations. Where the structural inventory of an organization is stable and reliable, its individual members are more likely to find *good reasons* to believe that the risk of investing trust in their relationships with other actors of the same organization is relatively low. The way a potential trustee will behave in the future is simply easier to predict under these circumstances than it is where such a 'world-in-common' is not in place. A strong internal regulation of the organization, in other words, will reduce the inherent risk of trust considerably. Where the structural inventory of the organization is fuzzy and unreliable, it is likely that individual actors will be less inclined to invest trust in their relationships to each other. It simply seems hazardous to invest trust where no or few shared orientations exist and the future behaviour of a colleague, a supervisor or a subordinate worker is difficult to foresee.

This theoretical approach to understanding trust in intraorganizational relations, which has been developed in the present contribution so far, draws substantively on Luhmann's systems theoretical reflections (1979). It also is inspired by conceptual notions developed within the framework of New Institutionalism (Powell and DiMaggio, 1991; Scott, 1995). At least the following three basic features of the phenomenon of trust are agreed by both of these theoretical traditions:

- Trust deals with the problem of predicting another social actor's future behaviour. It is – to use Simmel's words – a state of mind, somewhere between knowing and not knowing (Simmel, 1950) what a potential trustee will do in the future. It is a specific characteristic of trust that it provides a way of bridging this gap by accepting risk.
- It is legitimate and most likely that a potential trustor will seek possibilities to reduce the risk he needs to bear when investing trust. The risk cannot be calculated in exact terms but there must exist *good reasons* to assume that the inherent risk of trust will not exceed certain limits. Otherwise, trust is not justified and will usually not occur.
- Apart from the potential trustees' goodwill and abilities to perform according to the potential trustor's expectations, the institutional framework in which the possible relationship between the two parties will be embedded (Granovetter, 1985) is very important with regard to whether the trustor will decide to invest trust or to refrain from doing so.

**Different Forms of Trust**

The *theoretical* literature on trust makes an important distinction between two fundamental forms of trust: personal trust and impersonal trust. While an everyday understanding of trust tends to see it as a phenomenon that

emerges in an intimate relationship between two individuals, many scholars emphasize the role of impersonal trust, particularly in the field of
organizational relations. One of the central problems with the latter form
of trust, however, seems to be that there exist divergent notions as to
whether this concept should refer to the *object* of trust or to the *environment* in which individuals' social relationships are embedded. In the first
case, the understanding is that individuals trust *in* systems of cultural or
institutional rules. In the latter case, individuals are assumed to trust each
other *in the face of* the structural arrangements surrounding them. Clearly,
these two concepts differ significantly and, thus, at least *three* forms of trust
might be worth discerning:

- personal trust (based on experiences individuals make with each
  other in the course of frequent interaction over a longer period of
  time),
- system trust (trust an individual has *in* the functioning and in the reliability of impersonal social structures),
- institutional trust (trust between individuals vis-à-vis existing impersonal social rules).

The concept of *personal trust* comes closest to the ordinary language con-
notations of trust. It can be fostered by frequently using opportunities to
have face-to-face contacts between individual actors. The usual proximity
of workplaces within organizations can be seen as a seedbed for developing this form of trust. It is often much more difficult to establish it in the
organization's external relationships where personal contacts are often
much rarer. But even within organizations the problem with this form of
trust is that it takes a lot of time to grow. Also, in many cases, it is as such
not sufficient to coordinate effectively expectations and interaction between
individuals, especially not in large and complex organizations. Nonetheless,
it is a form of trust which is and remains important in social relationships.
There seems to be a strong indication that this form of trust, with the
decline of the bureaucratic organization model, has gained renewed importance in many social relationships within organizational contexts (Ebers,
1997; Lane and Bachmann, 1998).

*System trust* is a phenomenon that is deeply rooted in anthropological
conditions of human behaviour. While individuals unavoidably must have
*confidence* – as Luhmann (1988) proposes to say here – in certain rules (for
example, natural laws) and authorities (for example, parents, from a child's
perspective), this form of trust has also become increasingly important
today for a number of man-made, that is *technical* and *social*, artifacts
which in modern times take on a character quite similar to those which can

be viewed as the really unalterable *conditiones humanae*. With reference to this observation, Giddens (1990) argues that modern societies constitutively depend on lay individuals' preparedness to have trust in 'abstract systems' operated by highly specialized experts. Trust in the safety technology and procedures in the commercial aviation industry – to mention an example used by Giddens (ibid., p. 85) himself – is simply a precondition for many people's need to swiftly travel long distances today. Although very few passengers have any idea *why* flying on aeroplanes can be considered one of the safest ways to travel, they – even after seeing the horror scenes of hijacked planes crashing into New York's World Trade Center – do trust in the aviation safety systems and the experts who develop and operate them, just as they trust religious leaders and the law of gravity, or as little children unquestioningly trust their parents.

In a similar vein, system trust that exists within organizations builds on the authority attributed to formal social positions as well as on the reliability of technical systems, standards and procedures. For example, employees of an organization that operates within a strongly hierarchy-based business environment may have the strongest belief that their employer will always make decisions that are to their benefit. Similarly, the workers at an atomic plant may have the infallible belief that the technology they are dealing with simply cannot fail because generations of experts have made the greatest efforts to prevent any possibility of failure. The latter example illustrates particularly well that the object of system trust is usually a large abstract system which primarily exists at the societal level, reaching into the organizational world from its *external* environment (Bachmann, 2000).

One of the most interesting phenomena associated with this form of trust is that, once in a while, some representatives of the systemic abstract authorities whose activities are, in normal circumstances, largely withdrawn from their clients', customers' or workforce's awareness become touchable. The purpose of this is to reassure these individuals that their trust is placed in responsible social actors who are actually in control of the systems they stand for. This is why pilots occasionally speak to their passengers, eloquent nuclear scientists appear in TV talk shows and powerful entrepreneurs as well as high-ranking managers of large corporations suddenly become equal to the lowest-paid cleaner in their organization when sitting next to him on the occasion of a Christmas party. In all these situations individuals lend a personal flavour to the unknown abstract worlds of superior knowledge and power, confirming that these deserve to be trusted. Without these boundary-spanning roles being competently performed on suitable occasions, it would be doubtful that these abstract authoritative and technical systems could – at least in the longer run – be a powerful source of trust.

*Institutional trust* is rooted in a transfer of an organization's control capacity from the level of individual to the level of collective decision. This form of trust emerges where one social actor offers a pre-commitment to another actor vis-à-vis specific institutional arrangements that constitute a world of shared meaning and normative rules of behaviour within organizations. This form of trust, as described in the previous section of this chapter, draws on the institutionalized patterns of the division of work duties and responsibilities as well as other elements of the structural inventory of the organization to which individual actors inevitably have to orient their expectations when interacting with one another. Although the rules that are incorporated in the structural arrangements of the organization may privilege some individuals while restricting others in their chances of influencing collectively binding decisions, they appear as a depersonalized and legitimized institutional order. Thus they have normative power over expectations and interaction between the individual members of the organization, largely irrespective of their situational interests and the resources they might be able to mobilize in order to promote their particularistic interests. Because institutions are blind to individuals' opportunistic interests and the temporary availability of individually attributable resources of power, they can provide an important basis for the constitution of trust within organizations.

The structural inventory of the organization seems to be particularly relevant with regard to the amount of trust that it can swiftly produce among its members. If there exist powerful institutional rules to control the behaviour of individuals within organizations, these can absorb risk and increase the chances of trust becoming a preferred mechanism to coordinate social actors' expectations and interaction. Trust based on organizational institutions is in principle a home-bred phenomenon, constitutively produced *within* the boundaries of the organization. It can thus vary greatly from organization to organization. In contrast, *system trust* is mostly a phenomenon which originates in the *external* environment from where it reaches into the internal world of the organization.

As mentioned above, the characteristics of the national or regional business system in which an organization operates have a strong impact on the quality of intraorganizational relations (Sorge, 1996; Streeck, 1997; Whitley, 1999). Thus they can significantly foster the development of system trust relevant for the organization's internal activities (Bachmann, 2002). At the same time, it can be assumed that this external environment also has a strong impact on the conditions under which *institutional trust* is generated within the organization. In highly regulated territorial business systems, organizations are likely to adapt their internal structures to the business environment in so far as they place specific emphasis on generalized rules and standardized procedures to attain their organizational goals and to realize their strategies. Conversely, situational decision making in which the idiosyncrasies of individuals become influential is generally more likely to occur in organizations which operate in national and regional business systems that are characterized by a weak form of structural regulation and a low level of trust (Fox, 1974; Bachmann, 2001).

**Power in Organizations**

Without doubt, trust is part of *social capital* (Bourdieu, 1979; Coleman, 1990) which can become very valuable with regard to an organization's strategic competitiveness. It can contribute considerably to saving on transaction costs, speed up business processes and produce a work atmosphere which can be conducive to the innovativeness and creativeness of the organization's management and workforce. Thus, when compared to other means of fulfilling the same function, for example power or money, trust can be deemed a highly attractive mechanism to coordinate social relationships (Bradach and Eccles, 1989). However, it cannot be ignored that there are also disadvantages to overreliance on this coordination mechanism. *Personal trust*, in particular, is fragile and can break down without any chance of being quickly restored. In similar vein, it cannot be excluded that, under certain conditions, *institutional trust* may fade away where organizations go through periods of severe crisis (Kern, 1998). Even *system trust* may turn out not to be completely safe against erosion, as could be illustrated with reference to large-scale technological disasters such as Chernobyl or the gradual decline of the charismatic leadership model in the past three decades or so.

Looking at these problems that can occur with trust, it is worth considering other mechanisms which might also be utilized for the coordination of internal activities of the organization. For example, power can be assumed to be a mechanism which, as counterintuitive as it may seem, works on the basis of principles quite similar to those involved when trust is present. At the heart of both of these mechanisms lies a process in which one social actor *selects* specific assumptions about the future behaviour of another actor. In this respect, there is no difference between a trusting actor and a powerful actor. Each of them makes such a selection knowing that other choices are equally possible. Similar to a trustee, a (potentially) power-accepting actor is – at least in principle – free to choose whether or not he will behave according to what the powerful party sees as a preferable way of their dealing with each other in the future. However, the powerful actor does not select a positive assumption about the other party's future behaviour, as a trustor does. Rather, he selects a negative possibility of how the (potentially) power-accepting actor could behave and presents it to him as a choice that would not be in either party's interest and hence as a possibility that should be avoided. From an analytical point of view, the result is not altogether different from what trust can achieve in a social relationship. Each of the two mechanisms can provide an effective solution to the problem of coordinating social actors' activities.

Also, as in the case of a trust-based relationship, any calculation that the (potentially) power-exerting and accepting actors may be inclined to make must necessarily remain incomplete and imprecise. If the sanctions connected to the negative hypothetical assumption that the powerful actor has selected with regard to the power-accepting actor's behaviour need to be mobilized, he has already lost his power and the quality of the relationship – if it does not simply end at this stage – takes on the form of coercion or violence (Clegg, 1989). In the case of this event, power collapses in a way similar to the breakdown of trust when legal and/or explicit sanctions are activated against cheaters. The similarities between the two mechanisms of coordinating expectations and interaction of organizational actors are thus quite striking. This, however, is not to say that there are no differences at all (Luhmann, 1979).

The decision to use power as the preferred means of coordinating expectations and interaction between social actors in an organizational context buys into risk just as the decision to trust would do. But power does not – at least in normal circumstances – have the same *moral* weight that trust has. Power is, in this respect, generally more robust and one can expect that, if power breaks down, this usually does not imply the same disastrous effects on interpersonal relationships and/or the organizational climate, as the disappointment of trust is likely to produce. This can be seen as an important advantage of power and one may conclude that power thus suggests itself as the preferable option for coordinating social actors' expectations and interaction in many situations, particularly where trust, from a potential trustor's point of view, appears too risky. In this case, a potential trustor might well prefer using his resources of power, presupposing – of course – that he has (a sufficient quantity of) these available. They can have the form of social reputation, privileged access to specific knowledge, superior communication skills and so on. Whenever a (potential) trustor finds that he might foster his interests with less effort, faster and/or with less risk if he decides to draw on his resources of power, one should assume that he will in fact take this option, disregarding the positive effects that a trust-based relationship might yield. The question of whether trust or power appears as the preferable option to the proactive party of the relationship might also depend on the psychological disposition of the individual actors and the existing and/or expected dynamics in a current relationship (see

Nooteboom in the present volume). By and large, however, this prediction should hold true if there are no exceptional extra- or intraorganizational factors which might additionally influence social actors' decisions.

To conclude, on the one hand, trust can be betrayed and – if this happens – the relationship between two individuals is likely to be destroyed for a long period of time. On the other hand, power can also be challenged. If this occurs it is likely that open conflict will be the result, which may do considerable harm not only to the specific relationship between two individual actors but also to the organization as a whole. In usual circumstances, the advantages of a relationship that is predominantly based on trust are likely to supersede the possible advantages of a power-based relationship. Trust is a highly effective lubricant in many relationships which may increase with using it (Hirschman, 1984). Power, by way of contrast, has generally a lower value as social capital and can hardly produce any self-controlled dynamics. There are, however, numerous cases where a powerful (potential) trustor has *good reasons* to consider power as his first choice. It may minimize risk more effectively and facilitate the alignment of other views with his own ideas in a more efficient manner.

## TWO DIFFERENT TRUST/POWER CONTROL PATTERNS

In practice, the distinction between trust and power is a lot less sharp than it may seem at the analytical level. In fact, social relationships within (and between) organizations are normally based on a combination of both of these mechanisms. The empirically interesting question is often simply whether trust or power is dominant over the other mechanism in a specific relationship. In this (and only this) sense, one can speak of *alternative options* between which an individual actor can choose, provided that both mechanisms are available to him at all. The latter, of course, is not always the case. Where, for example, a subordinate actor has no or few resources of power to draw on, the choice between trust and power is virtually non-existent for him. In such a situation this actor may hope that the powerful party will offer trust to be used as the central coordination mechanism in the relationship. But, evidently, it will be the powerful actor who will have the choice between running the risk that his pre-commitment may be misused by the potential trustee and relying on the assumption that the potentially power-accepting party will actually take the fact that he has significant resources of power available as a *good reason* to acknowledge his claim. Thus it largely depends on social status and situational circumstances whether or not a social actor will have a serious choice. Of course, theoretically one can assume that a powerless actor is always free to refuse acceptance of the powerful actor's selection of negative possibilities as regards his future behaviour and to favour instead an option which has been presented to him as one which should be avoided. But this has little relevance for the empirical world. Both parties are simply not equal in their chances of deciding which coordination mechanism should be dominant in the relationship. Rather, it seems that it is invariably the powerful party that ultimately determines which specific mixture of trust and power will dominate the relationship. There are, of course, cases where both of the parties can draw on significant resources of power which they may use against each other. But then, this mechanism dramatically decreases its effectiveness as a means of coordinating expectations and interaction within the organization. The possibilities of developing trust in relationships increase accordingly under these circumstances.

Where trust and power appear as more or less distinct options, it is likely that *personal trust* is the form of trust that is in debate. By contrast, in cases of *system trust* and *institutional trust*, it is hardly a question of individual choice whether trust or power should have more weight in a relationship. The latter observation, of course, then raises the question, what other kind of interrelationship between these two mechanisms could also be considered as possible? The answer is simple: impersonal trust – in the form of *system trust* or *institutional trust* – and impersonal power can each appear as a precondition of the impact of the other mechanism on individual actors' behaviour. The underlying assumptions and the theoretical consequences of this notion, however, are a little more challenging to unravel.

As has been explained above, internal institutions and structural arrangements in the environment of the organization can be deemed a prime source of trust at the level of interpersonal relationships. Largely irrespective of the situational circumstances, potential trustors will often find enough *good reasons* to assume that the risk of misplaced trust is low where the *structural inventory* and the *systemic elements of the external world* of the organization are stable and reliable. Under these conditions, trust is predominantly produced in a depersonalized manner and will thus mostly appear in the form of impersonal trust, that is as *institutional trust* and/or *system trust*. If this is the case, it can be assumed that the level of trust will generally be high within the organization. For a potential trustor, it would simply seem not sensible to believe that a potential trustee is very likely to behave in an unforeseen manner unless there are exceptional circumstances to be considered, which recommend special precaution. A potential trustee can simply be trusted with less risk when he acts within 'social structures in which it is in . . . [his] interest to behave trustworthily' (Coleman, 1990, p. 111).

Such structures which bundle social actors' interaction along the lines of generally accepted behaviour can be interpreted as *powerful* with regard to relationships within organizations. Power in this sense is of course different from the form of power that is based on the resources an actor can individually draw on. This form of power is incorporated in the institutional inventory of the organization and/or the structures of the authoritative and expert discourses that reach into the organization from its external environment. This impersonal form of power can be seen as a *precondition* of the existence and development of *institutional trust* and *system trust* within the organization. In the face of *institutional power* and/or *system power* – to use a terminology that closely connects with the distinctions made above with regard to trust (second section) – individual actors tend to recognize *good reasons* to assume that the risk of misplaced trust is low and that investing trust in their relationships with each other is preferable to relying on individual resources of power (always provided that this is a realistic option for one of them at all).

The latter marks a fundamental difference between strongly and weakly regulated organizations. Where *institutional power* and/or *system power* foster the development of impersonal trust between members of an organization, a generally high level of trust is likely to prevail in their relationships. If, in contrast, a low level of organizational regulation exists, individual actors have a choice between either putting more effort into developing trust at the interpersonal level or – which indeed is more likely to happen then – falling back on their individual resources of power. The development of *personal trust* – although often considered as in principle preferable – would often simply seem too costly in terms of time and effort to be made (Zucker, 1986).

Within organizational contexts where highly generalized and powerful rules exist, individuals may find it relatively easy to develop trust (system trust and institutional trust) in their relationships while, paradoxically, the need for trust seems relatively low. Where a high level of impersonal trust is present, social actors have fewer incentives to develop *personal trust* in their relationships. At the same time, they are also systematically discouraged from utilizing their individually available resources of power. Attempts to draw extensively on the latter would at best be ignored within an organization built on strong institutional and/or systemic regulation. More realistically, an individual frequently questioning the structural order of the organization and insisting on using his individual resources of power to coordinate expectations and interaction with other individuals would be seen as a person who is useless or even dangerous with regard to the organization's identity and stability. In contrast, under conditions of a low level of impersonal regulation, the same behaviour may well appear as an acceptable – if not essential – means of coordinating activities within the organization. Where few generalized norms and standards of behaviour exist, individuals almost inevitably have to draw on individually attributable resources of power where – which is a likely case – personal trust cannot be produced swiftly and in sufficient quantity. If they refused to do so, a serious lack of coordination of individuals' behaviour would be the unavoidable consequence and the organization as such would sooner or later cease to exist.

Against the background of this argument, two ideal-types of organizational regimes emerge. First, there are strongly regulated organizations where power primarily exists in the form of abstract rules and procedures. This form of power (that is impersonal power) is highly conducive to the production of institutional trust and system trust within the organization. Individual social actors trust each other because the institutional inventory of the organization as well as the external environment in which it is embedded provide a reliable framework for individuals' expectations and interaction. In these organizations, a latent threat of collectively legitimized sanctions is always present but is rarely made explicit or even mobilized.

Secondly, there are more flexible organizations where much depends on individuals' idiosyncratic interests and the situational circumstances in which they make their decisions. In these organizations, individuals develop trust in their relationships primarily on the basis of interpersonal contacts. These play a vital role in coordinating expectations and interaction between the members of the organization. But as developing trust in the form of personal trust requires considerable efforts on the part of the individual actors and may, even when these efforts are made, still seem quite risky, organizational actors will often find it preferable or even unavoidable to draw on their resources of *personal power* to achieve a sufficient level of coordination of activities within the organization.

These ideal-typical reconstructions of organizational regimes mark the two ends of the scale, whereas empirical cases can be expected to be located more at medium positions. System trust, in particular, is a form of trust which is rooted in anthropological conditions of human behaviour and/or the cultural basis of the business system in which the organization's identity is embedded. Irrespective of whether a highly or a weakly institutionally regulated organization is concerned, none of these is likely to exist without any system trust. At the same time, impersonal forms of power and trust have lost part of their impact on individuals' behaviour in the past three decades or so. Modern organizations, in other words, tend to move away from the traditional model of strong and bureaucratic regulation and foster flexibility as well as more decentralized processes of decision making. These developments are directly connected to the rediscovery of *personal* relationships and, in particular, personal trust in the post-bureaucratic organization (Grey and Garsten, 2001). Thus it can be concluded that system trust plays a stabilizing role in weakly regulated organizations, while even in strongly regulated organizations it has a decreasing potential to absorb completely individual actors' agency.

## CONCLUSIONS

The analysis of trust and power as two central mechanisms of coordinating relationships between individual social actors within an organizational context leads to the conclusion that, depending on the forms of trust and power and their specific combination, two distinct patterns of organizational control can be reconstructed. In strongly regulated organizations, impersonal forms of trust and power tend to link into each other in such a way that powerful intraorganizational and environmental structures breed trust between individual actors in a highly efficient manner. In a weakly regulated organization, by contrast, individual efforts to establish cooperation between relevant actors in the organization become more important. In this case, individuals often see trust and power as two different mechanisms to draw on when interacting with one another. Often power is then preferred, since trust may well promise many advantages for a relationship but is also quite awkward to build without strong impersonal safeguards.

The central aim of this chapter was to present a conceptual approach to analysing different regimes of organizational control. The argument presented above is thus based on analytical conceptualizations rather than empirically existing cases. The latter, of course, vary greatly over history and different cultural backgrounds. Nonetheless, in order to gain a deeper understanding of how organizations function and what strategies might be useful when strategic interventions are considered, the conceptual differentiation of the two suggested modes of organizational governance may be helpful as an analytical framework. In a neorealistic view (Layder, 1997; Reed, 2001), these ideal-typical patterns of control might be understood as 'generative mechanisms' which do not determine the ways of (re-)producing and transforming social relationships within organizations. But they certainly do provide indispensable channels and viable configurations of coordinated interaction between individuals pursuing their interests in the context of organizational arrangements.

## ACKNOWLEDGMENTS

I am particularly thankful to Bart Nooteboom, Gerry Redmond, Frédérique Six and Arjen van Witteloostuijn for their stimulating comments on earlier versions of this chapter.

## REFERENCES

Bachmann, R. (2000), 'Die Koordination und Steuerung interorganisationaler Netzwerkbeziehungen über Vertrauen und Macht', in Jörg Sydow and Arnold Windeler (eds), *Steuerung von Netzwerken. Konzepte und Praktiken*, Opladen: Westdeutscher Verlag, pp. 107–25.

Bachmann, R. (2001), 'Trust, power and control in trans-organizational relations', *Organization Studies*, **22** (2), 337–65.

Bachmann, R. (2002), 'The role of trust and power in the institutional regulation of territorial business systems', in Thomas Brenner and Dirk Fornahl (eds), *The Influence of Co-operations, Networks and Institutions on Regional Innovation Systems,* Cheltenham, UK and Northampton, MA, USA: Edward Elgar.

Bourdieu, P. (1979), *La Distinction: Critique sociale du jugement,* Paris: Les Éditions de Minuit.

Bradach, J.L. and R.G. Eccles (1989), 'Price, authority and trust: from ideal type to plural forms', *Annual Review of Sociology*, **15**, 97–118.

Clegg, S. (1989), *Frameworks of Power*, London: Sage.

Coleman, J. (1990), *Foundations of Social Theory*, Cambridge, MA: Belkamp Press.

Ebers, M. (ed.) (1997), *The Formation of Inter-organizational Networks*, Oxford: Oxford University Press.

Fox, A. (1974), *Beyond Contract: Work Power and Trust Relations*, London: Faber.

Giddens, A. (1990), *The Consequences of Modernity*, Stanford: Stanford University Press.

Granovetter, M. (1985), 'Economic action and social structure: the problem of embeddedness', *American Journal of Sociology*, **91**, 481–510.

Grey, C. and C. Garsten (2001), 'Trust, control and post-bureaucracy', *Organization Studies*, **22** (2), 229–50.

Hirschman, A.O. (1984), 'Against parsimony: three easy ways of complicating some categories of economic discourse', *American Economic Review*, **74**, 88–96.

Kern, H. (1998), 'Lack of trust, surfeit of trust: some causes of the innovation crisis in German industry', in Christel Lane and Reinhard Bachmann (eds), *Trust Within and Between Organizations: Conceptual Issues and Empirical Applications*, Oxford: Oxford University Press, pp. 203–13.

Lane, C. and R. Bachmann (eds) (1998), *Trust Within and Between Organizations: Conceptual Issues and Empirical Applications*, Oxford: Oxford University Press.

Layder, D. (1997), *Modern Social Theory*, London: University College London Press.

Luhmann, N. (1979), *Trust and Power*, Chichester: Wiley.

Luhmann, N. (1984), *Soziale Systeme: Grundriß einer allgemeinen Theorie*, Frankfurt/Main: Suhrkamp.

Luhmann, N. (1988), 'Familiarity, confidence, trust: problems and alternatives', in

Diego Gambetta (ed.), *Trust, Making and Breaking Cooperative Relations*, Oxford: Blackwell, pp. 94–108.

Nooteboom, B. (2002), *Trust: Forms, Foundations, Functions, Failures and Figures*, Cheltenham, UK and Northampton, MA, USA: Edward Elgar.

Powell, W.W. and P.J. DiMaggio (eds) (1991), *New Institutionalism in Organizational Analysis*, Chicago: University of Chicago Press.

Reed, M. (2001), 'Organization, trust and control: a realist analysis', *Organizational Studies*, **22** (2), 201–28.

Scott, W.R. (1995), *Institutions and Organizations*, Thousand Oaks: Sage.

Simmel, G. (1950), *The Sociology of Georg Simmel*, K.H. Wolff (ed.), New York: Free Press.

Sorge, Arndt (1996), 'Societal effects in cross-national organization studies: conceptualizing diversity in actors and systems', in Richard Whitley and Peer Hull Kristensen (eds), *The Changing European Firm: Limits to Convergence*, London: Routledge, pp. 67–86.

Streeck, Wolfgang (1997), 'German capitalism: does it exist? can it survive?', in Colin Crouch and Wolfgang Streeck (eds), *Political Economy of Modern Capitalism*, London: Sage, pp. 33–55.

Sydow, J. (1998), 'Understanding the constitution of interorganizational trust', in Christel Lane and Reinhard Bachmann (eds), *Trust Within and Between Organizations: Conceptual Issues and Empirical Applications*, Oxford: Oxford University Press, pp. 31–63.

Whitley, Richard (1999), *Divergent Capitalisms: The Social Structuring and Change of Business Systems*, Oxford: Oxford University Press.

Zucker, L. (1986), 'Production of trust: institutional sources of economic structure 1840–1920', *Research in Organizational Behavior*, **8**, 53–111.

# 5. Calculativeness, trust and the reciprocity complex: is the market the domain of cynicism?

## Henk de Vos and Rudi Wielers

### THE MARKET SOCIETY AND THE PROBLEM OF TRUST

In almost all modern societies market exchange is a taken-for-granted part of daily life and participation in market transactions is an essential precondition for making one's livelihood. Market societies emerged in a long process of commercialization and commodification. During this process money became established as the medium of exchange and labour got commodified, just as a wide array of human artifacts and services, and mass production and mass consumption emerged. A relatively recent phase in this complex historical process, absolutely impossible to take in at a glance, is the global spread of the net of market relations.

Attending to this process reminds us of the fact that market societies simply did not exist for by far the largest part of the history of humankind. In this long period people made a livelihood by way of an array of activities such as gathering, plant protection and propagation, some horticulture, some hunting, some game management and some domestication of animals. There was of course no money. There was exchange, but almost totally within the sphere of personal and durable relations, and in forms such as delayed exchange, mutual aid and sharing of food and useful information (in one word: reciprocity). People were strongly interdependent, not by way of a far-flung division of labour and the impersonal price mechanism, but by way of reciprocity in long-lasting personal relationships. For these kinds of societies, Redfield (1963) coined the term 'folk society'.

It is easy to observe that in our times the growth of the market has not yet come to an end. In the very recent past, we had some real-life experiments with central planning as an alternative to the market (but not less impersonal), but these attempts failed dramatically, with a large waste of resources and a lot of human misery. It seems that due note has been taken of these failures. Worldwide, the advantages of the market, as the impersonal coordination mechanism that promotes wealth and freedom, are fully emphasized. And in their daily living people experience the effects of continuing market penetration in social life. On the one hand, governments facilitate and create markets by way of deregulation and privatization, thereby reducing the working of governments to what are considered their essential tasks. On the other hand, services that were formerly provided within the sphere of personal relations, nowadays are more and more taken over by the market (are commercialized and commodified). The proportion of convenience food in daily intake is increasing. An increasing array of household chores is entrusted to commercial household service providers. Leisure time is increasingly filled with commercially provided recreation and amusement (instead of socializing with family, friends and neighbours). Familial, friendly and neighbourly help in times of inconvenience or need is increasingly replaced by easy access to a wide range of shops with ample business hours, and by a diversity of professional support providers, such as psychotherapists, consultants, lawyers, mediators and insurance companies. The process is too complex to be easily summarized in a few sentences, but it seems to us that there exists a widespread expectation that the market will further penetrate our way of living in the near and distant future.

The transformation of folk societies into market societies of course took many generations and the changes were sweeping. This means that the way members of one generation, in a certain phase of the historical process, experience their daily living and their life course is probably forgotten within the next few generations. Being members of the present generation, we can only vaguely and superficially experience how it must have felt to live as a hunter–gatherer in the Pleistocene, or as a peasant, a few thousands or even a few hundred years ago. And at the same time it inevitably takes considerable effort to realize fully that the way we live now is very peculiar relative to the way our ancestors lived.

In modern societies people are born and raised in families that are socially isolated to a high degree in comparison with the strongly socially embedded families in the past. Also nowadays, several times during their life course, people experience radical changes in their social networks. Ties with friends are severed, or are maintained less easily and probably with less satisfaction and by making use of modern means of transport and communication, or they simply fade away, and new friends enter the scene. While in the past people were naturally embedded within a community of long-term relationships, nowadays relationships are much more precarious and can much less be taken for granted. And of course nowadays people have a lot of interactions with others with whom they simply have no or a very restricted common personal history. This is in complete accordance with the image we have of a market society, and of the process of its emergence. The transfor-mation of folk society into market society was vividly described, by Karl Polanyi, as a process of delocalization and social disembedding, of the li-quidation of organic society (Polanyi, 1957). It is also in accordance with the conditions for the proper working of the market, as formulated by the economic discipline: 'The price system is the mechanism that performs this task . . . without requiring people to speak to one another or to like one another' (Friedman and Friedman, 1980). The market destroys traditional communal networks of mutual obligation and reciprocal support. And the resulting social atomization should not be deplored, because allegedly it is precisely what the market needs for its (further) development.

Different interpretations and evaluations of this large-scale historical trend exist in the social scientific literature. Hirschman (1986) ordered them in two main contradictory propositions: the 'doux-commerce' thesis, and the self-destruction thesis.

The first one stressed the so-called 'uncivilized' aspects of pre-market society: enmity, violence and turmoil. The market was seen as the new and to be welcomed civilizing agent, as the system that made individuals useful to each other, and because of this induced them to be deliberate, honest, reliable, orderly, disciplined, prudent and more friendly and helpful.

Contrary to this optimistic interpretation, the self-destruction thesis stated that the market destroys the moral values (inherited from pre-market society) that are its own essential underpinnings. A 20th-century sophisti-cated formulation of this pessimistic thesis was given by Fred Hirsch in his *Social Limits to Growth* (Hirsch, 1978). According to Hirsch, the greater anonymity and greater mobility of the market society directed individual behaviour increasingly to individual advantage, to calculativeness and opportunism, thereby destroying the social virtues based on communal attitudes and adherence to communal objectives, such as truthfulness, trustfulness, restraint and obligation. And precisely these virtues are needed for the functioning of an individualistic, contractual economy.

So, on the one hand, we have an optimistic view: the market creates the social virtues, and the concomitant behaviour that it needs for its proper functioning. On the other hand, the opposite view also has its adherents: the market destroys those virtues without which its further development is seriously thwarted.

This is without any doubt a serious issue, for its intellectual as well as its societal implications. Therefore it is no surprise that it is widely discussed, roughly within the fields of economic sociology, law and society, law and economics, and transaction cost theory (TCT). Forerunners of the more recent discussions are Macaulay (1963), Dore (1992), MacNeil (1980) and of course Durkheim (1964). That the societal implications are indeed far-reaching can be understood from two popular books by Fukuyama (1995; 1999), from their content as well as from their circulations. But we think that it is a fair statement to say that the issue is still unresolved. As we see it, the problems that still have to be solved are partly conceptual and partly empirical.

First, there is a conceptual problem: what precisely are those social virtues, mostly referred to with that simple term 'trust'? In the next section we consider Williamson's (1993) proposal to make a strict distinction between (personal) trust and risk as an important contribution to an eventual solution, but we think it is only partly satisfactory. This is so because he exclusively assigns trust to the very special relations with family, friends and lovers, and denies any role for trust in market transactions because it would immediately be exploited by essentially cynical transaction partners. We think this gives a very implausible and unrealistic view of real-life market behaviour, and of modern market society. This view not only clearly contradicts our personal experiences as market participants but also contradicts results of several empirical studies of market behaviour.

Therefore, in the third section we attempt to improve and to proceed further, by way of turning to several sociological, social–psychological, anthropological and evolutionary–theoretical sources. These sources seem to us of the utmost pertinence to the problem, because they allow for embedding the concept of trust in a more general, empirically plausible, if not supported, theory of human social needs and motives. According to this theory, human social behaviour is strongly moulded by a set of emotions and expectations that we shall call the 'reciprocity complex'. It will then become clear that we should not consider the 'proper functioning' of the market as the only relevant value in the discussion. Often the existence or non-existence of trust is considered only important in so far as trust is potentially a factor that promotes market functioning (and human welfare as promoted by market functioning). Many (including the present writers) think that this is a deeply wrong way to approach the problem. We think that 'the existence of trust' is a thing that is (also) valued by humans in itself. This refers to the positive feelings that are connected with being involved in reciprocal relationships; that is, relations in which partners are concerned for each other's welfare (feelings of commitment and belongingness). In such relationships people trust each other, not as a result of a deliberate and calculated decision, but just because the possibility of distrust does not easily enter the mind.

Human welfare is a wider concept than is covered by the concept of 'economic welfare', that is, the set of all benefits that are provided by way of market transactions. The things that are not covered can be called social–emotional gratifications, or 'social welfare' in short, not in the sense of established welfare economics (as in the work of Arrow), but in the sense of welfare that is provided by the sheer existence of reciprocal relationships with other human beings. Social welfare simply is the welfare that is derived from having (reciprocal) relationships, and can be distinguished from the welfare that is generated by market transactions in which relationships are instrumental to the output of these transactions.

The full realization of this essentially social component of human welfare gives us a different perspective on the real-life functioning of the market than the well-established and often taken-for-granted economic view. If people have indeed specifically social motives, next to economic motives, for which relationships are instrumental, the issue arises of when, in which situations, the one or the other motive is, so to speak, at the wheel. As we will show, in the final section, it cannot simply be assumed (as Williamson does) that in the case of real market transactions only the economic motive is driving.

## WILLIAMSON ON TRUST AND RISK

Williamson's (1993) article is an attempt to make sense of the growing literature on trust in economic relationships. Most of this literature is, he argues, about calculated risk. That is, with contracts being incomplete, there is a chance of the agent not fulfilling the contract, thus causing damage to the principal. In this literature mechanisms are sought or developed to make the agent act up to the contract. A main mechanism is to incorporate incentives in the contract, such that the agent's utility increases if the contract is fulfilled. Williamson argues that it is superfluous and confusing to interpret such contracts in terms of trust. It is superfluous since such transactions can be analysed in terms of calculated risk, and it is confusing since it implies a deeper relationship than an economic relationship in which gains are maximized.

Trust, on the other hand, should be considered as disinterested and uncalculative. It implies that people are prepared to incur costs, without a compensating gain. Williamson defines trust relationships as relationships characterized by (1) the absence of monitoring, (2) favourable or forgiving predilections, and (3) discreteness, that is to say that the relationship is not subject to market incentives. He also uses 'personal trust', for distinguishing this concept from trust as calculated risk. We think this usage should be avoided, because calculated risk should simply not be called trust. And then the adjective 'personal' is superfluous (and confusing).

Williamson argues that trust no doubt exists, but that it is irrelevant for market relationships. Placing personal trust in an economic partner is asking to be exploited, since the world of commerce is organized in favour of the cynics, and against the innocent (Williamson, 1993). The relevance of personal trust is therefore limited to the world of family, friends and lovers; commercial relations do not qualify. We return to this issue in later sections.

As for the conceptual problem, Williamson clearly struggled with the problem of how precisely to distinguish calculativeness and trust. On the one hand, he argues that people are not calculative if acting in a trust relationship. Calculativeness would devalue the relation, making it instrumental instead of a goal in itself. On the other hand, he is not fully satisfied with this firm statement:

> It is mind-boggling to contemplate the absence of calculativeness. That is not to say that calculativeness cannot be suppressed or to deny that some actions are more spontaneous than others. Indeed, I shall argue that it is sometimes desirable to suppress calculativeness. If, however, the decision to suppress calculativeness is itself purposive and calculative, then the true absence of calculativeness is rare if not nonexistent. (Ibid.)

So, on the one hand he embraces the idea that people sometimes are not calculative, but on the other hand he shies away from the idea that calculativeness could be fully absent. Now we think he deserves to be admired for finding his way out of this struggle to a considerable degree: let us say halfway. First we summarize how he covers the first half of the route, and then we describe how we think the argument should be completed. It will turn out that contemplating the absence of trust might be just as mind-boggling as contemplating the absence of calculativeness.

Williamson's way out of the struggle boils down to stating that trust is nearly non-calculative. Thereby he is inspired by the so-called 'economics of atmosphere' on the one hand, and the idea of trust as a human passion (for which he uses this 'personal trust') on the other. From the economics of atmosphere he takes up the lesson that calculativeness can be taken to dysfunctional extremes. We dwell for a moment with his example of the matter of externalities between employees. Would it be wise for a company to try to meter all externalities with net gains? The answer is a clear no, because this policy would transform 'harmless by-products of *normal social intercourse*' (Williamson, 1993, emphasis added) into compensable injuries. Suddenly, all kinds of grievances would be 'felt' and demands for compensation would be made accordingly. Now it is very interesting to observe the two reasons Williamson gives for his negative verdict on the metering of externalities. One reason is that the overall impact of metering and compensation could easily be negative in terms of efficiency. This reason falls within the normal neoclassical economic discourse. But the other reason does not. It introduces a new kind of satisfaction: individuals 'find the exchange of reciprocal favors among parties with whom uncompensated spillovers exist to be satisfying' (ibid.). This refers to a special kind (special, seen from an economic perspective) of satisfactions. They are characterized not only by their non-pecuniary nature, but also by their special relationship to interpersonal relations. Normally (again, seen from an economic viewpoint) satisfactions are derived from the outputs of transactions, which may be embedded in relationships between transaction partners. But this reason refers to a relationship in which reciprocal favours are exchanged, and that is therefore valued in itself, and not (only) for its outputs. Williamson mentions Nozick's description of Love's Bond as an instance of such a relationship, and as an explanation of the existence of this special kind of satisfaction. The idea is that partners in a loving relationship have the intention to form a 'we' and to identify with it as an extended self. Of course, if your self is extended, so as to include another person, then the impacts your actions have on that person acquire a completely different meaning than in a relationship in which your self is not extended.

Williamson's second source of inspiration is Dunn's concept of trust as a human passion. According to Dunn, trust as a passion is the confident expectation of benign intentions by another person. In a relation of mutual trust, each partner is predisposed to ascribe good intentions to the other. As a consequence, they consciously refuse to monitor each other's behaviour, and they tend to view the other's behaviour in a favourable way, insisting on reform rather than doing better if things go wrong.

What are basically the results of this short review that Williamson gives of the theoretical background of the idea of trust? The first insight is that people are able to value relationships in themselves, and that this will happen if they identify with the partner as part of their extended self. And the second insight is that people are able to ascribe benign intentions to another person. These two insights can easily be combined (in a way that is not discussed by Williamson). If person A extends his self to include person B, and confidently assumes that person B extends his self to include person A, then this naturally causes person A to ascribe good intentions to person B (and of course person B to ascribe good intentions to person A).

## GOING FURTHER: TRUST AS PART OF THE RECIPROCITY COMPLEX

In this section we attempt to complete Williamson's analysis by embedding it in the wider social scientific literature on the concept of reciprocity.

Williamson's arguments clearly refer to this concept, as it was developed within sociology, social psychology, anthropology and evolutionary theory. By tapping these sources we are able to develop a deeper and more systematic view on the concept of trust, which also allows us to discover how trust relates to relevant other concepts, such as reciprocity, fairness and commitment. And, above all, we will have a perspective for assessing Williamson's assertion that trust is confined to the very limited field of very special relations, those between family, friends and lovers. We start by discussing Gouldner's (1960) article on reciprocity, because we think it deserves to be rescued from oblivion. We will see that it gives us a completely different, and roughly to be preferred, view on the problem of trust from Williamson's. Thereafter we attempt to summarize the empirical work on reciprocity and related issues since Gouldner's seminal article, in order to have a more complete picture of the feelings, the beliefs and the ways of behaving that the concept refers to: in short, the reciprocity complex (see later). We conclude this section with a discussion of the wider question of how our findings fit in an evolutionary perspective on human social motives and emotions.

**Gouldner on Reciprocity**

In the previous section we mentioned Williamson's introduction of this 'new' kind of satisfaction: the satisfaction of being involved in the exchange of reciprocal favours. This is accompanied by a reference to the well-known in-depth study by Alvin Gouldner of an industrial corporation in the 1950s (Gouldner, 1954). Gouldner observed a kind of employee behaviour that prompted him to give thought to this special kind of satisfaction. This resulted in an article that was published six years later (Gouldner, 1960) on the norm of reciprocity.

Following older authors such as Hobhouse, Thurnwald, Westermarck and Malinowski, and contrary to the then popular cultural relativism, Gouldner asserted that the principle of reciprocity should be seen as a set of sentiments and beliefs about social interaction that is universal to human societies. He formulates the principle as an internalized norm that makes two interrelated minimal demands: (1) *people should help those who have helped them,* and (2) *people should not injure those who have helped them.* That a special kind of satisfaction is connected with the principle should be derived from the norm having been internalized: *internalization implies that the act of following the norm generates positive feelings.* (By the way, we do not need to accept the social determinism that is in the background of the then popular concept of internalization. The issue is simply that it feels good to be involved in a reciprocal relationship.)

It is worth while to dwell for a moment with what Gouldner thought about the issue of whether reciprocity will always be present in social life and the issue of how reciprocity is related to the purely economic model of exchange.

He deals with two aspects of the first issue: does the norm function in different cultures in different degrees, and is the norm operative in every instance of an interaction? His answer to the first question is straightforward: in some countries (he mentions the Philippines as an example) the norm governs almost all relations, but it is also endemic in more bureaucratized countries (nowadays we would say 'market societies') such as the United States. In such countries it may not be imposed by the dominant culture, except for friendships, kinship and neighbourly relations, nonetheless it is commonly found in all institutionalized sectors, even the most rationalized. On the other hand, as an answer to the second question, it will not be operative in every case: a lack of reciprocity is not socially impossible. For example, a relation may be coercive, and as such stable, with little or no reciprocity. Nevertheless, some general notions that apply to these cases may be seen as compensatory mechanisms, such as the notions of 'noblesse oblige' and clemency. It should be explicitly noted that Gouldner does not mention market behaviour as an instance of lack of reciprocity. This is explained in his dealing with the second issue.

This issue is about how reciprocity is related to the economic model. About this there is a very interesting passage in the Gouldner article. He points to the difficulty a purely economic or utilitarian model has in accounting for the manner in which transactions begin. Say that Ego and Alter could both profit from an exchange of valuables, and suppose that each feels that the only motive the other has is the anticipated gratification of the net return that the transaction will bring.

> Each may then feel that it would be advantageous to lay hold of the other's valuables without relinquishing his own. . . . under such circumstances, each is likely to regard the impending exchange as dangerous and to view the other with some suspicion. . . . Thus the exchange may be delayed or altogether flounder and the relationship may be prevented from developing. (Gouldner, 1960)

Things would be totally different if Ego and Alter were steered by reciprocity. This would be the case for two reasons, of which Gouldner mentions only the first. It holds that both Ego and Alter feel an obligation to repay a received benefit and know that the other feels it. This provides grounds for confidence that the one who first parts with his valuables will be repaid. So there will be less hesitancy in being the first. But there is also a second reason that could even have been mentioned by Gouldner: if being involved in a reciprocal exchange relationship generates a special kind of satisfaction, this gives an extra motive for beginning a relationship. This will make the beginning more probable, especially if we also assume that Ego and Alter both know this of each other. In other words (and this certainly is surprising after just having digested the Williamson article), the reciprocity principle may be necessary for the creation of the trust that is needed for market transactions taking place. Divided by a third of a century, these two authors contemplated roughly the same issue.[1] The more recent one came to a conclusion (trust is not relevant for market transactions; it applies exclusively to interactions between family, friends and lovers) that is diametrically opposed to what the earlier one concluded (trust is necessary for market transactions; and trust is provided by the reciprocity principle that is common to a wide array of interactions in virtually all human societies).

In the next subsection we further investigate the concept of reciprocity. Now we conclude with bringing out the difference between the economic quid pro quo and the reciprocity principle that we encountered by contrasting the views of Williamson and Gouldner. According to Williamson the market is organized in favour of the cynics: market participants do not trust each other, they only calculate the risks of the transactions that they face. According to Gouldner, market transactions would be impossible if the parties were exclusively interested in the anticipated gratification of the net return that the transaction would bring. In real transactions, people trust each other because, first, they feel obliged and because they derive satisfactions from being involved in relationships in which partners trust each other, and second, because they know this of each other.

## The Nature of Reciprocity

As said above, we think that the problem of what it means to trust and the problem of the kinds of interactions to which trust applies should be seen from the wider perspective of reciprocity. Now we should take a moment to draw up an inventory of the feelings, beliefs and ways of behaving that, taken together, form the meaning of this concept. We will refer to this inventory as the 'reciprocity complex'. Although we give references to the literature, these may be far from exhaustive.

### Non-calculativeness
People who are involved in a reciprocal relationship have a non-calculative attitude towards the outcomes of the relationships. An implication of this is that benefits that are exchanged need not be comparable, and that the non-comparability of benefits is interpreted as typical of a reciprocity relationship. A returned benefit that is incompatible with a received benefit (for example, a ride home is 'returned' for being treated to a lunch, instead of

also treating to a lunch) is perceived as an attempt to fulfil a need or to please the other, both intentions that are typical of a reciprocal relationship (see below) (Clark, 1981). Another implication is that the members of the relationship do not keep track of each other's inputs in joint tasks, because such record keeping is not required in order to distribute rewards according to needs or because of the wish to demonstrate concern for the other (Clark, 1984). Because of this non-comparability of benefits and the non-record keeping, parties in a reciprocal relationship do not like the use of money as a repayment for help received. The relationship is seen as too special to be conducted with general-purpose money (Webley and Lea, 1993; Zelizer, 1989; Foa and Foa, 1980).

### Diffuse temporal expectations

Members of reciprocal relationships have diffuse expectations of the moment of return of benefits, that is, they are willing to accept imbalances for a non-determined period. This attitude can be interpreted in two different, but not necessarily mutually exclusive, ways. In the first place it can be seen as evidence for the existence of an assumption of eventual balance, but more in the sense of a confidence that 'It will all work out', than in the sense of a calculated risk (O'Connell, 1984). The other interpretation is that donor and receiver perceive the giving as a response to a need and as a sign of concern for the receiver (see below). If the receiver insisted on repaying immediately or too soon, it would cause embarrassment on the part of the donor and would disturb the relationship (Clark and Mills, 1979; Schwartz, 1967).

### Responding to each other's needs

Instead of expecting that benefits be immediately returned, partners in a reciprocal relationship expect from each other that they respond to the other's needs. And a willingness to respond to the needs of the other can easily be perceived as a concern for the other's welfare, that could be a result of extending the self so as to include the other (Cialdini *et al.*, 1997). An implication of this is, for example, that members of a reciprocal relationship respond positively to the sadness of the other person (instead of avoiding a sad person) (Clark *et al.*, 1987; Clark and Mills, 1979; Uehara, 1995; Deutsch, 1975). Mutual awareness of the responsiveness to each other's needs produces a basic feeling of safety, an affect state identified by Chance as the hedonic mode (Chance, 1988).

### Feelings of obligation and guilt

Although partners in a reciprocal relationship accept imbalances to a considerable degree, this does not mean that persons who overbenefited do not feel obliged to return benefits. They do feel so, but this is caused by feelings of uneasiness or even guilt, and not by their wish to avoid giving the donor power to impose certain demands as the price for assistance. In short, people in a reciprocal relationship in general would prefer a state of balance over a state of imbalance, but if balance is not possible, they avoid overbenefiting more than underbenefiting (Uehara, 1995; Van Tilburg, 1992). We may say in passing that this eventual preference for underbenefiting is probably one factor in producing the phenomenon of the 'potlatch', the contest of presenting each other with larger and larger gifts.

### Diffuse expectations regarding identities of donors and receivers in densely-knit networks of reciprocal relationships

If persons are embedded in a densely knit social network of reciprocal relationships, they feel that they are relieved of the burden of keeping track of who helped whom. A pairwise momentary imbalance is not perceived as such, because the overbenefitor has provided help for others in need in the past, and is fully intending to provide for others in the future, should needs arise (Uehara, 1995). In these circumstances the self is extended to include more than one other person, either specific others or even impersonal collectives or categories (Brewer and Gardner, 1996). In both cases the person feels that he belongs to a reciprocity group, either a real one or a more or less mentally constructed one.

### Non-instrumental concern

The concern members of a reciprocal relationship have for each other's welfare inevitably gives the relationship a value in itself. Being a member provides a feeling of safety, of always being able to call in a person's aid in times of need. This positive feeling is of course also present in times without need, so indeed 'having the relationship' is a value in itself. This implies that members are willing to benefit the other, or to exert themselves in order to maintain the relationship, even in cases in which the other is not informed about the identity of the sender of the benefit or about the offers the other made (Halpern, 2001). Not only do people have this non-instrumental attitude towards the relationship; they also expect this from each other (O'Connell, 1984). Non-instrumental concern also seems to imply that costs are accorded a different meaning than in a contingent exchange relationship. In a longitudinal study of friendship, Hays asked his respondents to list the 'costs' and 'benefits' of their friendships. He found that friendship intensity was more highly correlated with the benefits-plus-costs score than with the benefits-minus-costs score (Hays, 1985). If people are embedded in a close-knit network of reciprocal relationships, this same non-instrumental concern leads to positive feelings towards the group ('we' feelings, belongingness, connectedness) (Lee and Robbins, 1995; Bollen and Hoyle, 1990).

We think that this list of feelings, beliefs and ways of behaving gives a reasonably complete description of what is generally understood by the concept of reciprocity. But we have to admit that in the second half of the 20th century the concept gained an enormous popularity and that the term is used so frequently that it is a sheer impossibility to keep track of all the different definitions that have been proposed. One well-known way in which the concept is used, that we clearly did not follow, is the meaning of a simple preference for equity or tit-for-tat. Reciprocity in the sense of tit-for-tat came into vogue after Axelrod used it as a synonym for the tit-for-tat strategy in his computer tournaments. Our list implies that we use the 'reciprocity complex' with a meaning that explicitly excludes the calculativeness and contingency of exchange that is implied by concepts such as equity and tit-for-tat. We also see that the 'reciprocity complex' is much more encompassing than Gouldner's two interrelated minimal demands: (1) people should help those who have helped them, and (2) people should not injure those who have helped them.

It is quite clear that reciprocity implies trust. People in a reciprocity relationship are responsive to each other's needs and know that they are. Therefore each one feels confident that he can count on the other in case of need. Probably the soothing thought behind this confidence is the feeling that there exists another one who shares your concerns, who extends his self to include yours. This is indeed trust in the deep sense that Williamson refers to. The idea that trust is implied by reciprocity can also be found in many definitions of trust. A review of these definitions concluded that trust involves not only the appraisal of partners as reliable and predictable, but also (1) the belief that partners are concerned with one's needs and can be counted on in times of need, and (2) feelings of confidence in the strength of the relationship (Rempel *et al.*, 1985).We think that other concepts that are discussed a lot by social scientists, such as justice (or fairness), morality and altruism, are also implied by the 'reciprocity complex'.

Another issue that deserves to be pointed out is that emotions, such as sympathy, obligation, guilt, feelings of safety, connectedness and belongingness, are part and parcel of reciprocity. Now everyone knows that emotions may affect our behaviour without (fully) entering our consciousness. From an evolutionary standpoint (see the next subsection) emotions are ancient steering mechanisms of behaviour. The emergence of (self-)conscious deliberations is a very recent phenomenon in evolutionary history and it is restricted to humans and perhaps one or two other primates. This explains the quite common (human) experience that our behaviour often is 'driven' by unconscious emotional states that can only be raised to full awareness by way of more or less effort. Readers will have recognized the list of feelings and beliefs we gave, but will also be prepared to admit that a lot of their daily behaviour is steered by these feelings and beliefs without their being (fully) aware of this. Apparently, we do not need to know that a relationship is based on reciprocity in order to act according to it.

We conclude this subsection by returning to the issue that was raised in the first section: to what domain of social life does trust apply? This question should now be viewed from the perspective of trust being a part of the wider emotional, cognitive and behavioural 'reciprocity complex'. According to Williamson, trust only applies to the domain of family, friends and lovers. In the social domain of market relationships trust cannot (stably) exist, because it would be immediately exploited by the opportunism and calculativeness of competitors. This brings us to the question of how limited or extended the social domain is to which the 'reciprocity complex' applies. Does the complex only describe our behaviour when we interact with our family, our friends and our lovers? Given that we have only a limited conscious access to the steering principles of our behaviour, this is by no way a trivial question. To find an answer we think that it is absolutely necessary to turn to the evolutionary perspective. This we now do.

### An Evolutionary Perspective on the Reciprocity Complex

In the first section of this chapter we referred to an insight that seems to us of great importance, namely that human beings lived by far the largest part of the existence of humankind in pre-market societies; that is, in societies in which the reciprocity complex dominated social life. According to Rodseth, Wrangham, Harrigan and Smuts, our ancestors lived in a social order of communities, of closed or semi-closed social networks, larger than conjugal families, with fission–fusion subgroups (Rodseth *et al.*, 1991). Within these communities the interactions were reigned by reciprocity, in contrast to the relations between communities that were more competitive. This way of living was an adaptation to a risky and heterogeneous environment; that is to say (1) resources were spatially and only partly predictably spread, had to be found on a daily basis and did not lend themselves to storage, and (2) if they were found, they were often so abundant that they could be shared with others. In such an environment a social arrangement is adaptive in which individuals spread out, and return at the end of the day to the base camp, where those who found food share it with those who did not. This is especially so if the identities of the finders and the not-finders change over time on a more or less random basis (Winterhalder, 1986). Apparently, our ancestors were selected for this way of living, probably in contradistinction to several other hominoids that did not succeed and became extinct. The selection process must have involved a whole spectrum of features, morphological as well as cognitive and emotional. It is commonly thought that the reciprocity feelings and beliefs find their origin in this long period when human pre-market societies existed (Cosmides and Tooby, 1992; Tooby and Cosmides, 1998; Deacon, 1997; Ridley, 1997; Sober and Wilson, 1998; Wright, 1995). An implication of this is that the 'reciprocity complex' would also be pervasive in foraging societies that were still extant when observed by social scientists, which is indeed the case (Kent, 1993; Cashdan, 1985; Boehm, 1999; Kelly 1995).

Since we cannot go back to the time when this selection process is supposed to have happened, another important kind of evidence that results from computer simulations and tournaments should also be taken into account. By far the majority of these simulation studies made use of the iterated Prisoner's Dilemma game paradigm, inspired by the work of Maynard Smith, one of the founders of evolutionary game theory, and of Axelrod (1984). By and large, these studies showed that tit-for-tat-like strategies can successfully compete with cheating strategies. The original tit-for-tat strategy (designed by Rapoport) starts a game with a cooperative move and mirrors the opponent's move thereafter. This kind of strategy is very similar to the calculative behaviour that Williamson thinks is typical of market behaviour (although Axelrod, very confusingly, referred to tit-for-tat as reciprocity). These results suggest that it is calculativeness, and not reciprocity, that was selected in evolutionary history. However, this would be a serious misinterpretation. An important disadvantage of iterated Prisoner's Dilemma evolutionary studies is that players do not have the chance to select partners. They are simply forced to interact with whatever other player is assigned to them. It has been pointed out that the results of these studies, because of this element of forced play, overemphasize the importance of the ability of strategies to detect cheaters and to retaliate; that is, of calculativeness (De Vos and Zeggelink 1997; De Vos *et al.*, 2001). Simulations with a model in which partner selection is part of the problems that the strategies have to solve showed very different results. Because of the relevance of these results for our present argument, we give a short summary of this study (De Vos *et al.*, 2001).

The simulation environment was one in which the willingness to help another who is in need is potentially conducive to survival, but at the same time this willingness can be exploited by cheaters. The simulations served to find out the conditions under which the positive effects of willingness to

help outweigh the negative effects of being exploitable. Individuals enacting a strategy had a probability of getting in need, and the only way to
survive a period of need was to find another individual willing to provide
help. Providing help incurred costs, in the form of an increase in the probability of getting in need in the next round of the simulation. The success
of two different non-cheating strategies was investigated, both having to
compete with one and the same cheating strategy. One of these two strategies was called 'Keeping Books Balanced', because individuals enacting
this strategy are always willing to help if asked for the first time, but thereafter persistently try to be even with those they have helped. This aspect of
calculativeness shows that this strategy was inspired by the principle of tit-
for-tat. The other strategy, called 'Commitment', was much less calculative:
individuals enacting this strategy also always help if asked for the first time,
but thereafter they are more benevolent towards the ones that had helped
them. For example, they are willing to help the same person repeatedly,
without having received help in between from that person. We consider
'Commitment' a rather unambiguous expression of the 'reciprocity complex'. Finally, individuals who enacted the exploiting strategy are indeed
cheaters, in the sense that they always ask for help when in need, but never
provide help when asked. (Actually, the strategies are more complex than
can be described here.)

It turned out that in all the conditions that were studied the non-cheating
strategies were able to resist an invasion by the cheaters if the latter entered
the population one at a time. When the simulation started with populations
of cheaters, the non-cheaters were only able to enter the population if they
entered with at least a few at the same time and exclusively in the harshest
conditions, that is, with the highest probabilities of getting in need.
However, and this is the point we want to stress, 'Commitment' did better
than 'Keeping Books Balanced'. In the harsh conditions, it only needed an
initial threshold of two individuals, a lower threshold than 'Keeping Books
Balanced' needed. In general, it was concluded that 'Commitment' was
more successful because (1) it is better at profiting from the presence of
other non-cheaters in the population, and (2) it is better at contributing to
the survival of the other non-cheaters as soon as they have found each
other, so that they continue to be present as providers of help in the future
(De Vos *et al.*, 2001). The results show that the kind of behaviour that is
induced by the 'reciprocity complex' is more successful in competition with
cheaters than a much more calculative kind of behaviour. This indicates
that the 'reciprocity complex' could have been selected, given of course that
conditions were present in which individuals needed each other's help for
survival and in which they had to select partners.

That reciprocity emotions and beliefs are selected does not necessarily imply that they are completely hard-wired. Let us dwell for a moment on the definition Nesse gives of emotions: 'The emotions are specialized modes of operation shaped by natural selection to adjust the physiological, psychological, and behavioural parameters of the organism in ways that increase its capacity and tendency to respond adaptively to the threats and opportunities characteristic of specific kinds of situations' (Nesse, 1990). For the reciprocity emotions, the threats and opportunities characteristic of specific kinds of situations refer to the risky and heterogeneous environment that our ancestors found themselves in. These emotions 'told' them to attend to the presence of others as possible partners to share with, to stay close to these others, to return to them, or, more abstractly, to stay in relationship with them even without continuous face-to-face contact, to suppress their inclinations for competition and dominance with regard to them, to sanction those that attempt to dominate and so on. (See Boehm, 1999, for a description of the egalitarian ethos that is closely connected with the 'reciprocity complex'.) Now of course there is some hard-wiredness in the ability to be steered by emotions, as is suggested by the finding that specific emotions can be elicited by stimulating specific brain loci. But on the whole we know that being steered by emotions is not the same as being totally subjected to a fixed pattern of responses. We know that we are able to decide in another way than we are told by our emotions, but we also know that this can demand a lot of effort and may involve so-called emotional costs (stress).

The issue of the degree of flexibility of these specialized modes of operation is of particular importance if the environmental threats and opportunities change. A specific emotion is by definition adaptive in the environment in which it was selected (although not necessarily in an ideal sense), but it can be neutral or maladaptive if the threats that existed in that environment disappeared or changed so fast that the process of natural selection did not have time to do its work. (This seems to explain why the number of species that became extinct exceeds by far the number of still existing species.) For example, we have an innate fear of snakes that is not completely hard-wired, as is shown by those people that have fought down the fear and keep snakes as pets. This fear was very adaptive for some long period in our ancestral past. In our present environment it is probably neutral or perhaps even maladaptive. An innate fear of cars would suit us much better, given the high number of yearly fatal accidents in which cars are involved.

Because of the transformation of the communal societies of the past into modern market societies this issue of flexibility is of course of the utmost pertinence to the 'reciprocity complex'. In communal societies, people were born into an existing dense network of reciprocal relationships of which they remained a member for the rest of their lives, experiencing of course the turnover of membership by way of mortality and increase. (Probably, this was somewhat different for women, who were often married off into another group, but with continuing contact with, and control by, their original community.) This means that the special satisfactions of having reciprocal relationships (social welfare) were received almost for nothing. They could be taken for granted, as a natural concomitant of the normal life course. This gradually changed with the transition to a sedentary way of living, with higher population densities, and with domestication of plants and animals. It went along with a development of the emergence of gradually more and more individualized, property rights in land, livestock, storaged food, edifices and implements. This historical development is described as a sequence of shifts from the Paleolithic foragers to hunting nomads, to acephalous tribes, to big man societies, to sedentary foragers, to chiefdoms and finally to primitive kingdoms (Boehm, 1999) or as a gradual shift from egalitarian to non-egalitarian hunter–gatherers (Kelly, 1995). In short, step by step, all elements of the market society as we know it entered the scene. What was the role of the 'reciprocity complex' in this large-scale historical process? Was human nature so flexible that the complex simply gave way to the supposedly advancing cold-blooded market mentality with its calculativeness and instrumentality? Was it so flexible that the applicability of the complex was neatly restricted to the shrinking domain of relations with family, friends and lovers, thereby making room for the entirely new abilities (that lay dormant?) that served market participation? Or was the process seriously delayed and hampered by the 'old-fashioned' and 'conservative' 'reciprocity complex', and were perhaps its outcomes deeply influenced by the complex; and can this influence still be observed in modern market behaviour?

These questions are of course far too big to be satisfactorily answered in this chapter. But what we can do is to give a short review of some pieces of evidence that in our opinion should in any case be considered. This we do in the closing section.

## THE RECIPROCITY COMPLEX IN MARKET SOCIETY

The emergence and spread of market societies caused increasing permeability and fragmentation of the close-knit communities of the past. This meant that people were confronted by an entirely new phenomenon: meeting strangers much more than incidentally. So a new challenge had to be faced: how to behave to strangers? Or, more precisely, how to behave to this stranger in this particular circumstance, and how to behave to that stranger in other particular circumstances and so on. For successfully meeting these challenges, two more or less automatic modes of behaving, with their concomitant emotions and cognitions, lay ready to use: the hedonic mode, allowing for a reciprocity relationship if operative on both sides, and the agonic mode, leading to hostile competition and eventually to a stable status relationship if operative on both sides (Chance, 1988).

First, an encounter with a stranger could be the beginning of a new recip-rocal relationship. Given that existing networks of reciprocal relationships had fragmented and diminished, it may be assumed that a need for new rela-tionships existed to a certain degree. So if this need happened to exist on both sides, and if the parties were able to discover this to be the case, the behaviour of both could successfully be steered by the 'reciprocity complex'. The operation of the hedonic mode would result in the development of a new reciprocity relationship that would in the language of market societies be called a friendship. A new friendship would add to the community domain. So community does not only exist as a matter of course, as in folk society, but also emerges as a thing that is more or less consciously made. It seems to us that the practice of gift giving is a phenomenon that at least partly arose as a social invention to deal with the uncertainties that come along with the existence of relationships that are not yet well defined as rec-iprocity relationships. That this practice is so common in modern society, as well as in agrarian societies and in complex extant hunter–gatherer societies, is in agreement with the fact that indeed many relationships in these kinds of societies cannot be taken for granted as reciprocity relationships.

Second, a meeting with a stranger could be the beginning of a conflict. A stranger could be and could begin to act as a competitor in the struggle for scarce resources, including mating opportunities (sexual competition). If a meeting is seen as a potentially competitive one, an evolutionary much older mode of behaving (and feeling and perceiving) lies ready to become effective: the agonic mode. In such a case both parties are eager to estimate their differential capabilities to mobilize relevant resources. At the same time they will try to face the other down. Depending on the outcome of the estimations and the bluffing on both sides, or on the outcome of a real fight, a stable status relationship will eventually be established. The party that sees himself and is seen as the winner is going to act dominantly. The party that sees himself and is seen as the loser is going to act submissively, so as to show that he admits his loss and to avoid (further) damage. Then the interaction is finished if the loser runs for safety. But also a relationship may emerge if the loser estimates that staying with the winner is more profitable provided that he acts submissively, and becomes a follower. In this way the agonic mode is a basis for a kind of group formation that is characterized by a stable status hierarchy. This is in contradistinction to the hedonic mode of group formation, which is characterized by reciprocity, an egalitarian ethos and the presence of the hedonic mode (Chance, 1988).

So if we witnessed the very first beginnings of market societies, we would probably observe a shrinking of the domain of reciprocity relationships, some new additions to this domain by way of establishing friendships, and the emergence of stable status hierarchies in the form of big man societies, chiefdoms and primitive kingdoms. The status hierarchies that we observed would probably be a mixed expression of status competition and reciprocity, in the sense that followers more easily accept leadership if the leaders act generously and that leaders are in general willing to do so (conferring the notions of 'noblesse oblige' and clemency that were referred to by Gouldner).

Now the interesting problem is: was this a situation in which cold-blooded, calculative and instrumental market relationships, according to Williamson part and parcel of our modern market, could easily emerge? At first sight one would say not. On the basis of the hedonic mode you would tend to characterize humankind as Homo Reciprocans. And on the basis of the agonic mode you would think of Homo Hierarchicus. But on what basis would you arrive at the idea of Homo Economicus?

But now of course the issue of human flexibility enters. At some phase in the evolutionary history of early humans, probably in connection with the selection for the cognitive, emotional and morphological characteristics of the 'reciprocity complex', our ancestors became equipped with (self-)representational and language skills. This allowed for mental time travel and empathy. The combination of these two made it possible to represent and attend to one's own and others' history and future in connection to each other. This involved the possibility of (self-)conscious and deliberate, planned action on the individual level, and coordination of plans with others on the collective level. We do not know to what degree these newly acquired abilities were immediately adaptive (by way of increasing survival and procreation through sharing in reciprocal relationships) or to what degree they were simply neutral side-effects. It may be that the ability to empathize, that allowed for being involved in reciprocity relationships, laid the basis for deliberate and abstract thinking as an adaptively neutral side-effect that only became adaptive in later stages of human history. However this may be, as is always the case in evolution, these new capabilities that were selected did not replace the older ones. The agonic and hedonic modes are still present in the human emotional (physiological and neurological) systems. If we act deliberately we may succeed to a certain degree in suppressing these modes and finding a new way of action. But the general idea is that this takes trouble.

The least that we can say is that humans were able to imagine the 'cold-blooded market mentality' and to devise the economic model of action as a scientific theory to match. The neoclassical economic model is the most elaborated and refined version of this. It was constructed at the end of the 19th century, with Alfred Marshall as one of the main figures and the author of what became the most influential economic handbook. It is interesting to note that even then objections were raised that pointed to the problem that social–emotional motives such as the need for status were totally ignored in the economic model. And although some renowned economists (Jevons, Edgeworth) recognized the problem, Marshall decided that the model would be made too complex by taking these social motives into account (Mason, 1998). This decision was probably of greater significance than is often understood, because the neoclassical model started to lead its own and independent life. Apparently human beings are so flexible that their ideas and behaviour can be influenced by simply getting to know the economic model: students who followed a course on economics acted more calculatively in a Prisoner's Dilemma experiment after that course than before (Frank *et al.*, 1993).

What do these considerations tell us about the significance of the 'reciprocity complex' for the behaviour of market participants? First, we should face the fact that humans are able to act calculatively and cold-bloodedly (let us say, rationally), but with the provision that this takes more or less effort.[2] Second, this is so because the 'reciprocity complex', with its hedonic mode, on the one hand, and the, let us say, 'status competition complex' with its agonic mode on the other hand, always lie ready as kinds of default options, telling a person what to do without much deliberation necessary. Third, this suggests that the two complexes are sort of slots in which it is easy to land, and that it is always precarious to remain in the small interjacent field of deliberate rationality. In terms of economic theory (and somewhat ironically), rationality is possible, but it is not an equilibrium. And fourth, it suggests that we should not place calculative behaviour as an intermediate form on the same level as the reciprocity behaviour and the status competition behaviour.[3]

Now that we have made up our mind, it remains to be investigated whether our conclusions are proof against the available evidence. We think that at least the following two pieces of evidence should be considered when contemplating the issue of the actual and potential role of the 'reciprocity complex' in modern market societies. First, it should be considered that much of the resistance that existed and still exists to the expansion of the market could be interpreted as being caused by the continuing attractiveness of the 'reciprocity complex'. Second, those findings should be taken into account that show that the 'reciprocity complex' heavily influences the behaviour of participants in experimental and real-life markets. As part of this last piece of evidence we especially pay attention to what is known about within-firm relationships and behaviour.

## The Reciprocity Complex as a Source of Resistance to the Penetration of the Market

The historical process of the spread of the market and of its continuing penetration of daily life has always been attended with concerns and debates about the valuation of its social consequences. Clues for this are of course restricted to the rather recent period of literacy, and depend on whether documents are preserved. But, from what we know, it can be derived that, although the increasing wealth was of course welcomed, the penetration of the market in daily social life was received with mixed feelings. The spread of the market went along with the emergence of trade, and therefore of a new category of people: those who specialized in trade. In a society with a still strong communal basis, traders, who apparently were less integrated within a community, were treated with suspicion, had low standing and were kept at a distance (Fisher, 1976). Even more despised were those who traded in money, the usurers (Nelson, 1969). All four great world religions had, and some of them still have, a ban on interest, which is easily understood if seen from the perspective of societies that were still dominated by the 'reciprocity complex'.

More recently, in the centuries of the Industrial Revolution, the resistance to the market found its expression in the wealth of deliberate attempts to construct communities, intended as a kind of shield against the intruding market. Often these attempts were spiritually inspired. They existed in the Old World, but the opening up of the American continent offered an opportunity to move together to the New World, often in response to being persecuted, and to start an economic and social way of life totally of one's own making. The greatest wave of community building in America occurred in the middle of the 19th century. Well-known examples are the Shakers, the Oneida Community, the Amana and the Hutterites. Their strivings for building a communal life have been concisely described as attempts 'to repersonalize a society that they regard as depersonalizing and impersonal, making person-to-person relations the core of their existence' (Kanter, 1972, p. 213). A second wave of community building in the United States occurred in the 1960s and 1970s. A more recent, less radical, expression is the rise of the so-called 'Local Exchange Trading Systems', that are intended to revitalize local economic and social life and that use their own monetary units without interest (Pacione, 1998). Of course other more widely known phenomena, such as the endurance and probable increase of formal and informal voluntary work in market societies, and the resistance to bringing human blood and organs under market rules, are easily interpreted as a result of attempts inspired by the feelings of the 'reciprocity complex'.

Often this resistance to the market is quickly condemned as nostalgia. But the evidence is accumulating that the satisfactions that are generated by being involved in a network of reciprocity relationships contribute significantly to people's health and well-being. Excellent reviews of findings are Schwarzer and Leppin (1991) and Uchino *et al.* (1996). This strongly suggests that the 'reciprocity complex' is much more than a relic of the past. Although being involved in a network of reciprocity relationships is not as easily realized in present-day market society as it was in the past, it represents a way of living that contributes significantly to people's well-being and health. Although material wealth is of course also an important factor for well-being and health, it appears that, above a certain level of wealth, more wealth is no longer associated with more subjective well-being or happiness (Diener and Suh, 1999; Veenhoven and Timmermans 2000). This indicates that material wealth is a poor substitute for social welfare. It also seriously qualifies the optimistic ideas about the flexibility of human nature.

### The Influence of the 'Reciprocity Complex' on the Behaviour of Participants in Experimental and Real Markets and in Organizations

Do people who act in the context of a market, be it a market as simulated in the laboratory or a real-life market, behave as calculatively and cynically as the standard economic model predicts? No doubt they often do. But there is also a considerable amount of evidence that often their behaviour is more or less strongly influenced by the 'reciprocity complex'. As for simulated markets, we may refer briefly to studies by Kollock, Lawler and Yoon, and Fehr *et al.*[4]

Kollock found that his subjects had a tendency to remain with an exchange partner despite better offers from other potential partners. Although this tendency was highest in conditions in which change of partners could involve risking future benefits, it was also present in conditions in which no risk was involved. Kollock therefore suggests that 'commitment will be present to some degree in any exchange system' (Kollock, 1994). Similar results are reported by Lawler and Yoon, who formulated and tested a theory of relational cohesion, that asserts that frequent exchanges between two actors in a network make their relation an expressive object, valuable in its own right, because positive emotions are produced by successful exchanges (Lawler and Yoon, 1996). And Fehr *et al.* showed that, in an experimentally simulated labour market in which excess supply of labour created enormous competition among the subjects acting as workers, the subjects acting as firms did not take advantage of this fact. Instead of this, their wage offers were solely governed by reciprocity considerations (Fehr *et al.*, 1998).

As for real-life markets, an important line of research is formed by the empirical sociological studies of social embeddedness of market transactions, often inspired by Macaulay's (1963) study of non-contractual relations in business. For example, Uzzi studied how social embeddedness affected the acquisition of financial capital in middle-market banking. He concluded that the market participants he observed, bank personnel who made lending decisions and who interacted with clients, built networks with their clients with the expressed motive to gain access to private information. But it appeared that enacting these relationships attenuated 'the narrow aims that may have motivated it originally, because such ties tend to create expectations that normally accompany noneconomic attachments. [Apparently] even in a business culture that uses the yardstick of money to gauge value, bankers and clients develop expressive bonds that affect their economic decisions' (Uzzi, 1999).

Finally, at least some economists believe that the behaviour of participants on the labour market is strongly influenced by the 'reciprocity complex'. An example is Akerlof's analysis in which labour contracts are seen as partial gift exchanges. As a result of this behaviour the labour market does not clear, which at least partially explains the existence of involuntary unemployment (Akerlof, 1982, 1990). This points to the literature on organization studies and on the employer–employee relationship. Within the economic framework the existence of firms is explained by way of the principle of efficient boundaries. Williamson (at the end of this chapter we meet him again) used this principle to explain the decision a firm makes on whether to make a component itself or to buy it from an autonomous supplier; that is, to explain where the market ends and the firm begins. According to him, given recurrent transactions, market contracting will be efficacious whenever assets are non-specific to the trading parties, and internal organization will displace markets as assets take on a highly specific character (Williamson, 1981). Asset specificity exists when investments are specialized for a particular transaction, thereby transforming a market relation into a bilateral exchange relation. In the words of Williamson himself:

> Inasmuch as the value of specific capital in other uses is, by definition, much smaller than the specialized use for which it has been intended, the supplier is effectively 'locked into' the transaction to a significant degree. This is symmetrical, moreover, in that the buyer cannot turn to alternative sources of supply and

obtain the item on favorable terms, since the cost of supply from unspecialized capital is presumably great. Accordingly, where asset specificity is great, buyer and seller will make special efforts to design an exchange that has good continuity properties. (Ibid., p. 555)

Now it is interesting to notice what Williamson mentions as the advantages of an exchange that has good continuity properties, that is of a firm. First, common ownership reduces the incentives to suboptimize. Second, internal organization is able to invoke fiat to resolve differences, instead of costly adjudication. And third, internal organization has easier and more complete access to the relevant information when dispute settling is needed (ibid., p. 559). It seems to us that the first two of these advantages are easily interpretable if we assume that the prospective of an enduring relationship and the awareness of common fate may release within the members of the firm the emotions, cognitions and perceptions of the 'reciprocity complex'.

More generally, *much of the organization literature shows that a significant part of organizational behaviour is difficult to interpret in any other way than as stemming from the 'reciprocity complex'*. We illustrate this by giving three examples. First, it was found that employers perform better and are more helpful towards the organization and towards their colleagues if they believe the organization values their contributions and cares about their well-being. Significantly, and completely in line with the 'reciprocity complex', this association was mediated by feelings of obligation and positive mood (Eisenberger *et al.*, 2001). A second line of research is about so-called '*organizational citizenship behaviour*'. This concept refers to helpful activities of employees over and above their formal job duties that contribute to the organization's success. It was argued that organizational citizenship behaviour is promoted by the degree to which a so-called '*psychological contract*' exists between employer and employee and the degree of *perceived procedural justice* within the organization (Cropanzano and Byrne, 2000). The idea of a psychological contract is that each party feels obligations towards the other and that the relationship is characterized by high levels of trust and mutual support. Third, several studies of organizational behaviour showed that the affective commitment of members to their organization, that is the extent to which they experience *a sense of identification and involvement with the organization*, furthers various aspects of their work performance (Mathieu and Zajac, 1990).

By and large, all these studies show that, under various conditions, organizational behaviour easily lands within the slot of the 'reciprocity complex'. We should add, however, that there are two important limitations to the degree of reciprocity behaviour that can exist in organizations. The first is that there is always competition between organizations, especially between firms operating on the market. Although this may promote the experience of common fate within the organization (a signal for evoking the 'reciprocity complex'), it also creates an ever-present prospect of lay-offs and reorganizations. This prospect sets upper limits to the degree that employees feel that they have a common future, a condition for the 'reciprocity complex' being in full swing. The second limitation is that an organization always by definition is a hierarchy. This hierarchical feature may evoke the 'status competition complex' in the members of the organization, leading to dominant behaviour of the leaders and submissive behaviour of the subordinates – and, of course, to all kinds of unproductive investments in the struggle for defending and attaining leadership positions. Actually, this is the big problem of organization in our present society: how to profit from the 'reciprocity complex', given that organizations have to compete and need some hierarchy.

## NOTES

1. The time period considered is actually much longer if we realize that Gouldner was strongly influenced by Durkheim's *Division of Labor*, that first appeared in 1893 (Durkheim, 1964).
2. We do not go into the issue of interindividual differences in the amount of effort this would take (Mealy, 1995).
3. This happens in those attempts to categorize behaviour that are not informed by evolutionary considerations, such as Fiske (1992) and Lindenberg (1988).
4. If we are right in suggesting that the 'reciprocity complex' and the 'status competition complex' are slots in which it is easy to land, than it should also be possible to show that the behaviour of market participants is influenced by the latter complex. That this is so for consumers was already observed by Veblen, and later by Hirsch and Frank (Frank, 1999; Hirsch, 1978). That businessmen and managers are driven by the 'status competition complex' is often described in popular novels, recently, for example, in Tom Wolfe's *A Man in Full*. It seems that the energy that many firms invest in becoming one of the two or three biggest companies of their trade often cannot be justified by sound economic considerations.

## REFERENCES

Akerlof, G. (1982), 'Labor contracts as partial gift exchange', *Quarterly Journal of Economics,* **97**, 543–69.
Akerlof, G. (1990), 'The fair wage-effort hypothesis and unemployment,' *Quarterly Journal of Economics,* **105**, 255–83.
Axelrod, R. (1984), *The Evolution of Cooperation*, New York: Basic Books.
Boehm, C. (1999), *Hierarchy in the Forest: The Evolution of Egalitarian Behavior*, Cambridge, MA: Harvard University Press.
Bollen, K.A. and R.H. Hoyle (1990), 'Perceived cohesion: a conceptual and empirical examination', *Social Forces,* **69** (2), 479–504.

Brewer, M.B. and W. Gardner (1996), 'Who is this "we"? Levels of collective identity and self representations', *Journal of Personality and Social Psychology,* **71** (1), 83–93.

Cashdan, E.A. (1985), 'Coping with risk: reciprocity among the Basarwa of Northern Botswana', *Man (N.S.)*, **20**, 454–74.

Chance, M.R.A. (1988), 'Introduction', in M.R.A. Chance (ed.), *Social Fabrics of the Mind*, London: Erlbaum, pp. 1–35.

Cialdini, R.B., S.L. Brown, B.P. Lewis, C. Luce and S.L. Neuberg (1997), 'Reinterpreting the empathy–altruism relationship: when one into one equals oneness', *Journal of Personality and Social Psychology*, **73** (3), 481–94.

Clark, M.S. (1981), 'Noncomparability of benefits given and received: a cue to the existence of friendship', *Social Psychology Quarterly*, **44** (4), 375–81.

Clark, M.S. (1984), 'Record keeping in two types of relationship', *Journal of Personality and Social Psychology,* **47** (3), 549–57.

Clark, M.S. and J. Mills (1979), 'Interpersonal attraction in exchange and communal relationships', *Journal of Personality and Social Psychology*, **37** (1), 12–24.

Clark, M.S., R. Oulette, M.C. Powell and S. Milberg (1987), 'Recipient's mood, relationship type, and helping', *Journal of Personality and Social Psychology*, **53** (1), 94–103.

Cosmides, L. and J. Tooby (1992), 'Cognitive adaptations for social exchange', in J.H. Barkow, L. Cosmides and J. Tooby (eds), *The Adapted Mind. Evolutionary Psychology and the Generation of Culture*, Oxford: Oxford University Press, pp. 163–228.

Cropanzano, R. and Z.S. Byrne (2000), 'Workplace justice and the dilemma of organizational citizenship', in M. van Vugt, M. Snyder, T.R. Tyler and A. Biel (eds), *Cooperation in Modern Society*, London: Routledge, pp. 142–61.

Deacon, T. (1997), *The Symbolic Species. The Co-evolution of Language and the Human Brain*, Harmondsworth: Penguin Books.

Deutsch, M. (1975), 'Equity, equality, and need: what determines which value will be used as the basis of distributive justice?', *Journal of Social Issues*, **31**, 137–49.

De Vos, H. and E. Zeggelink (1997), 'Reciprocal altruism in human social evolution: the viability of reciprocal altruism with a preference for "old-helping-partners"', *Evolution and Human Behavior*, **18**, 261–78.

De Vos, H., R. Smaniotto and D.E. Elsas (2001), 'Reciprocal altruism under conditions of partner selection', *Rationality and Society*, **13** (2), 139–83.

Diener, E. and E.M. Suh (1999), 'National differences in well-being', in D. Kahneman, E. Diener and N. Schwartz (eds), *Well-Being. The Foundations of Hedonic Psychology*, New York: Russell Sage, pp. 434–50.

Dore, R. (1992), 'Goodwill and the spirit of market capitalism', in M. Granovetter and R. Swedberg (eds), *The Sociology of Economic Life*, Boulder: Westview Press, pp. 159–80.

Durkheim, E. (1964), *The Division of Labor in Society*, New York: Free Press.

Eisenberger, R., S. Armeli, B. Rexwinkel, P.D. Lynch and L. Rhoades (2001), 'Reciprocation of perceived organizational support', *Journal of Applied Psychology*, **86** (1), 42–51.

Fehr, E., E. Kirchler, A. Weichbold and S. Gächter (1998), 'When social norms overpower competition: gift exchange in experimental labor markets', *Journal of Labor Economics,* **16** (2), 324–51.

Fisher, N.R.E. (1976), *Social Values in Classical Athens*, London: Dent.

Fiske, A.P. (1992), 'The four elementary forms of sociality: framework for a unified theory of social relations', *Psychological Review,* **99** (4), 689–723.

Foa, E.B. and U.G. Foa (1980), 'Resource theory: interpersonal behavior as exchange', in K.J. Gergen, M.S. Greenberg, and R.H. Willis (eds), *Social Exchange: Advances in Theory and Research*, New York: Plenum.

Frank, R.H. (1999), *Luxury Fever. Why Money Fails to Satisfy in an Era of Excess*, New York: Free Press.

Frank, R.H., Gilovich, T. and D.T. Regan (1993), 'Does studying economics inhibit cooperation?', *Journal of Economic Perspectives*, **7**(2), 159–72.

Friedman, M. and R. Friedman (1980), *Free to Choose. A Personal Statement*, London: Secker & Warburg.

Fukuyama, F. (1995), *Trust. The Social Virtues and the Creation of Prosperity*, New York: Free Press.

Fukuyama, F. (1999), *The Great Disruption. Human Nature and the Reconstruction of Social Order*, New York: Free Press.

Gouldner, A.W. (1954), *Industrial Bureaucracy*, New York: Free Press.

Gouldner, A.W. (1960), 'The norm of reciprocity: a preliminary statement', *American Sociological Review,* **25** (2), 161–78.

Halpern, J.J. (2001), 'Elements of a script for friendship in transactions', *Journal of Conflict Resolution,* **41** (6), 835–68.

Hays, R.B. (1985), 'A longitudinal study of friendship development', *Journal of Personality and Social Psychology*, **48** (4), 909–24.

Hirsch, F. (1978), *Social Limits to Growth*, London: Routledge & Kegan Paul.

Hirschman, A.O. (1986), 'Against parsimony: three easy ways of complicating some categories of economic discourse', in A.O. Hirschman (ed.), *Rival Views of Market Society and Other Recent Essays*, New York: Viking Penguin, pp. 105–41.

Kanter, R.M. (1972), *Commitment and Community. Communes and Utopias in Sociological Perspectives*, Cambridge, MA: Harvard University Press.

Kelly, R.L. (1995), *The Foraging Spectrum. Diversity in Hunter–Gatherer Lifeways*, Washington: Smithsonian Institution Press.

Kent, S. (1993), 'Sharing in an egalitarian Kalahari community', *Man (N.S.),* **28**, 479–514.

Kollock, P. (1994), 'The emergence of exchange structures: an experimental test of uncertainty, commitment and trust', *American Journal of Sociology*, **100**, 313–45.

Lawler, E.J. and J. Yoon (1996), 'Commitment in exchange relations: test of a theory of relational cohesion', *American Sociological Review*, **61**, 89–108.

Lee, R.M. and S.B. Robbins (1995), 'Measuring belongingness: the social connectedness and the social assurance scales', *Journal of Counseling Psychology*, **42** (2), 232–41.

Lindenberg, S.M. (1988), 'Contractual relations and weak solidarity: the behavioral restraints on gain maximization', *Journal of Institutional and Theoretical Economics,* **144**, 39–58.

Macaulay, S. (1992), 'Non-contractual relations in business: a preliminary study', in M. Granovetter and R. Swedberg (eds), *The Sociology of Economic Life*, Boulder: Westview Press, pp. 265–83.

MacNeil, I. (1980), *The New Social Contract: An Inquiry into Modern Contractual Relations*, New Haven: Yale University Press.

Mason, R. (1998), *The Economics of Conspicuous Consumption. Theory and Thought Since 1700*, Cheltenham, UK and Lyme, US: Edward Elgar.

Mathieu, J.E. and D.M. Zajac (1990), 'A review and meta-analysis of the antecedents, correlates, and consequences of organizational commitment', *Psychological Bulletin*, **108**, 171–94.

Mealy, L. (1995), 'The sociobiology of sociopathy: an integrated evolutionary model', *Behavioral and Brain Sciences*, **18**, 523–99.

Nelson, B.N. (1969), *The Idea of Usury. From Tribal Brotherhood to Universal Otherhood*, Chicago: University of Chicago Press.

Nesse, R.M. (1990), 'Evolutionary explanations of emotions', *Human Nature*, **1** (3), 261–89.

O'Connell, L. (1984), 'An exploration of exchange in three social relationships: kinship, friendship and the marketplace', *Journal of Social and Personal Relationships*, **1**, 333–45.

Pacione, M. (1998), 'Toward a community economy – an examination of local exchange trading systems in West Glasgow', *Urban Geography*, **19** (3), 211–31.

Polanyi, K. (1957), *The Great Transformation. The Political and Economic Origins of Our Time*, Boston: Beacon Press.

Redfield, R. (1963), *The Primitive World and Its Transformations*, Ithaca, NY: Great Seal Books.

Rempel, J.K., J.G. Holmes, and M.P. Zanna (1985), 'Trust in close relationships', *Journal of Personality and Social Psychology*, **49**, 95–112.

Ridley, M. (1997), *The Origins of Virtue*, Harmondsworth: Penguin Books.

Rodseth, L., R.W. Wrangham, A.M. Harrigan and B.B. Smuts (1991), 'The human community as a primate society,' *Current Anthropology*, **32** (3), 221–41.

Schwartz, B. (1967), 'The social psychology of the gift,' *American Journal of Sociology*, **73**, 1–11.

Schwarzer, R. and A. Leppin (1991), 'Social support and health: a theoretical and empirical overview', *Journal of Social and Personal Relationships*, **8**, 99–127.

Sober, E. and D.S. Wilson (1998), *Unto Others. The Evolution and Psychology of Unselfish Behavior*, Cambridge, MA: Harvard University Press.

Tooby, J. and L. Cosmides (1998), 'Friendship and the banker's paradox: other pathways to the evolution of adaptations for altruism', *Proceedings of the British Academy*, **88**, 119–43.

Uchino, B.N., J.T. Cacioppo and J.K. Kiecolt-Glaser (1996), 'The relationship between social support and physiological processes: a review with emphasis on underlying mechanisms and implications for health', *Psychological Bulletin*, 119, 488–531.

Uehara, E.S. (1995), 'Reciprocity reconsidered: Gouldner's 'moral norm of reciprocity' and social support', *Journal of Social and Personal Relationships* **12** (4), 483–502.

Uzzi, B. (1999), 'Embeddedness in the making of financial capital: how social relations and networks benefit firms seeking financing', *American Sociological Review*, **64**, 481–505.

Van Tilburg, T. (1992), 'Support networks before and after retirement', *Journal of Social and Personal Relationships*, **9**, 433–45.

Webley, P. and S.E.G. Lea (1993), 'The partial unacceptability of money in repayment for neighborly help', *Human Relations*, **46** (1), 65–76.

Williamson, O.E. (1981), 'The economics of organization: the transaction cost approach', *American Journal of Sociology*, **87** (3), 548–77.

Williamson, O.E. (1993), 'Calculativeness, trust, and economic organization', *Journal of Law and Economics*, **36**, 453–86.

Winterhalder, B. (1986), 'Diet choice, risk, and food sharing in a Stochastic environment', *Journal of Anthropological Archaeology*, **5**, 369–92.

Wright, R. (1995), *The Moral Animal: Why We Are the Way We Are?*, London: Little, Brown and Company.

Zelizer, V. (1989), 'The social meanings of money: "special moneys"', *American Journal of Sociology*, **95**, 342–77.

# 6. Understanding the nature and the antecedents of trust within work teams

**Ana Cristina Costa**

## INTRODUCTION

Trust has been one of the most controversial research topics during the last decade of the past millennium. Because trust is so central in human relationships several conceptualizations have been proposed from a variety of perspectives. Until recently these perspectives have appeared largely disconnected, rather ignoring one another or criticizing each other's research methods and accomplishments. Acknowledging that trust reflects a multitude of roles, functions and levels of analysis, and that it is applicable to different contexts, has been a recent turning point for theory and research. Instead of focusing on the differences between conceptualizations, scholars are starting to concentrate on the common elements across perspectives in order to develop coherent knowledge with regard to trust (for example, Hosmer, 1995; Rousseau *et al.*, 1998; Kramer, 1999). One of these elements concerns the importance of trust for the functioning and well-being of organizations.

Recent research shows that trust can be associated with a number of favourable outcomes for teams and organizations. Zand (1972) found that high-trust groups performed better on eight specific criteria than did low-trust groups. Morgan and Hunt (1994) showed that work relationships characterized by trust engender cooperation, reduce conflicts, increase the commitment to the organization and diminished the tendency to leave. Costa (2000) demonstrated that trust within teams relates not only to specific team outcomes, such as high task and role performance, low stress, team satisfaction and relationship commitment, but also to more general and organizational-related outcomes such as low continuance commitment, high satisfaction and affective commitment to the organization. While trust should not be seen as the ultimate solution for all organizational problems, teams where individuals feel tense, unsatisfied and less emotionally committed may become extremely unproductive (Costa *et al.*,

2001). In the long run, these conditions can lead to a higher rate of absenteeism (Katz and Kahn, 1978), which may be detrimental to the organization. In order to remain effective organizations will need to invest in conditions that facilitate trust among members.

Trust becomes a vital concept when there are significant risks involved (that is, vulnerability) and when there is objective uncertainty about future consequences of trusting (Morris and Moberg, 1994). Within teams in organizations, uncertainty and vulnerability can arise for different reasons. Contingency theories advocate that team processes be dependent on three major factors, that is, the composition of teams, work characteristics and organizational context (for example, Gladstein, 1984; Hackman, 1987). Each factor contains specific variables that may influence trust within teams in different ways. The purpose of this chapter is to understand the nature of trust and explore the relevancy of each of these factors as a condition to trust in teams.

## TRUST WITHIN TEAMS

One problem of studying trust is the vast applicability of the concept 'trust' to different contexts and levels of analysis. Within the organizational literature trust has been studied with regard to interpersonal work relationships, teams, organizations, governance structures or even societies as a whole. A delimitation of the domain of research is, therefore, necessary in order to understand what is meant by trust and how to define it.

Trust within teams refers to the extent to which team members trust each other as a team. The interpersonal literature on trust has emphasized several important characteristics of this concept. One of these concerns the specificity of trust with regard to person(s) and situations. People trust others on the assumption that these others will behave in a certain way (Mayer *et al.*, 1995) and that this will provide them with an expected desirable outcome (Deutsch, 1962). Consequently, people choose whom to trust in a given circumstance, or at least they will not confer the same trust to different people across the same range of actions. Several researchers have defended the importance of situational trust in specific others as opposed to propensity (general willingness) to trust in generalized others (for example, Butler, 1991; Butler and Cantrell, 1984). However, it is important to mention that the general propensity to trust might help to explain variations in trust levels between individuals. In particular, as situations become increasingly unfamiliar, the influence of a propensity to trust on behaviour grows (Rotter, 1980). Yet propensity to trust should be viewed as a more situation-specific trait affected by both personality and situational factors (Mayer *et al.*, 1995). Since trust involves granting latitude to others over actions that will have an impact on ourselves, decisions to confer trust do probably involve assessments of the accompanying risks and alternatives available to avoid such risks (Morris and Moberg, 1994).

Another characteristic relates to the dynamic character of trust. Scholars agree that trust changes and develops over time as relationships go through various phases such as building, declining or renewal (for example, Lewicki and Bunker, 1996). Shapiro *et al.* (1992) argue that trust may take on a different character in the early, developing and 'mature' stages of a business relationship: starting from developing trust based on deterrence, business relationships may develop towards trust based on knowledge, and finally identification. However, not all business relationships develop fully and trust may not develop past the first or second stage. Moreover, 'trust is typically created rather slowly, but it can be destroyed in an instant by a single mishap or mistake' (Slovic, 1993, p. 677). Also dynamics within work relationships may bring trust to a lower level than the one achieved before (Lewicki and Bunker, 1996). This not only reflects the dynamic character of trust but emphasizes the importance of its maintenance for the development of a healthy team climate (see King and Anderson, 1995).

An equally important characteristic of trust relates to its multi-component nature. Sociologists were the first to propose that an adequate analysis of trust begins by recognizing its 'multifaceted' character. To Lewis and Weigert (1985) trust is a highly complex phenomenon with distinct cognitive, emotional and behavioural dimensions. People trust on the basis of cognitive processes that discriminates others as being trustworthy, untrustworthy or unknown as well as on emotional bonds. The behaviour reflects the significance of the earlier dimensions, which enables the individuals to act upon their judgments (ibid.). This multidimensional structure is present in many other conceptualizations of trust. Within economics, Cummings and Bromiley (1996) use the same dimensions to define trust between individuals or groups in more work-related contexts. Focusing more on dyadic work relationships, psychologists such as McAllister (1995) distinguish between contents of cognition-based and affect-based trust and the specific factors that influence the development of each form. Mayer *et al.* (1995) propose further that cognitive and affective dimensions of trust influence and are influenced by a general propensity to trust others, which develops from general beliefs about the treatment individuals expect to receive from others. In turn, these expectations are closely linked to the engagement of, or the willingness to engage, behaviours of trust when interacting with others (Deutsch, 1962; Kramer *et al.*, 1996).

On the basis of these considerations, trust can be defined as 'a psychological state that manifests itself in the behaviours towards others, is based

on the expectations made upon behaviours of these others and on the perceived motives and intentions in situations entailing risk for the relationship with those others' (Costa, 2000, p. 52). In this definition trust is viewed
as an attitude held by an individual in relation to another individual or
group of individuals and it is applicable to work relationships in team contexts. This definition conceptualizes trust as a multi-component construct
composed of the general propensity to trust others, perceived trustworthiness and the trust behaviours. Costa (2000) found that individuals who
trust their teams have a high propensity to trust others, strongly perceive
other team members as being trustworthy, often engage in cooperative
behaviours and do not monitor the work of their colleagues. It is according to this definition that trust is approached in this chapter.

## ANTECEDENTS OF TRUST WITHIN WORK TEAMS

According to Rousseau *et al.* (1998), risk and interdependence are the two
necessary conditions for trust to arise. Within teams there are significant
risks associated with the work process as well as different degrees of vulnerability and uncertainty among members (Morris and Moberg, 1994).
Most teams hold some degree of interdependence among members and
some degree of differentiation in roles and tasks in order to produce some
type of outcome. During the process of accomplishing this outcome, team
members need to interact to a certain extent by way of exchanging information, sharing resources and coordinating with or reacting to one another
(Guzzo, 1995). Furthermore, teams operate in an organizational context
that is able to generate significant risks associated with either the nature of
the employment relationship, rewards system, career development or
norms of conduct. Therefore trusting in such conditions is one means of
dealing with uncertainty and becoming vulnerable.

Contingency models of group behaviour posit that not only the composition of teams, but also the characteristics of tasks performed by the team and
other organizational variables are relevant inputs in team processes. We will
describe next the variables included in these factors that are expected to relate
to trust. The conceptual model used in this study is described in Figure 6.1.

### Team Composition

Work teams vary in many respects and can be defined according to several
characteristics (Hackman, 1987). Although there is no unified view about
which personal factors should be considered as determinants of team
process, there is a shared view that certain combinations of people in a

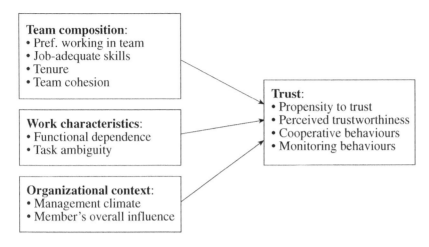

*Figure 6.1    Hypothesized model*

team are more likely to result in greater performance effectiveness than others. In most studies team composition refers to the individual differences among members that can be described in terms of personal characteristics, tenure in the job and the organization, adequate job skills and so on (for example, Gladstein, 1984). Having the adequate skills to perform the job deals with trust based on expectations of competent performance. Competence-based trust is of particular importance in work relationships and may involve expert knowledge, technical facility or everyday routine performance (for example, Barber 1983). Variables such as team cohesiveness can also be related to trust within teams. For instance, Cartwright and Zander (1968) speak of coexistence in teams of 'person-oriented motives' and 'group-oriented motives'. It is the interdependence or the compatibility of these motives that leads team members to engage in cooperative or competitive interactions. In Chapter 1 of the present volume Bart Nooteboom and Frédérique Six provide a similar distinction by referring to self-interest and altruism as two sources of intentional reliability. The presence of strong or weak altruism motives may also be related to the individual preference for working on a team and to tenure. By preferring to work in team contexts, individuals are more likely to feel committed to it and to generate a coherent identity (Anderson and Birch, 2001). Tenure often reflects knowledge of either the team or the organization and can be seen as a mechanism that induces predictability, in terms of what to expect of team members when acting in good faith. Trust presupposes prediction based on former knowledge and is only possible with a reliable background (Luhmann, 1979).

Although team composition research is rarely associated with trust, we suggest that preference for working in teams, adequacy of job skills, tenure and cohesion will be related to trust within teams.

*Proposition 1a:* high preference for working in team contexts will be associated with high levels of trust within teams.
*Proposition 1b:* having the adequate skills to perform the job will be associated with high levels of trust within teams.
*Proposition 1c:* tenure will be positively related to trust between team members.
*Proposition 1d:* teams with high cohesion among members will display higher levels of trust than teams with low cohesion.

## Work Characteristics

The nature of tasks can be classified according to complexity, interdependence and environmental uncertainty (Lawrence and Lorsch, 1967). These dimensions determine the information requirements of the task. In order to be effective, teams must have information-processing capacity that matches the requirements of their tasks (Gladstein, 1984). For instance, when tasks are complex there is a need to discuss alternative performance strategies in order to achieve high levels of performance effectiveness (Hackman *et al.*, 1976), whereas, if tasks are simple, team members can use standard operating procedures, and discussion of alternative methods is not necessary (Gladstein, 1984). Morris and Moberg (1994) suggest that functional dependence and task ambiguity are two relevant working conditions that increase uncertainty and vulnerability between members.

Functional dependence refers to the extent to which the successful job performance of a given worker directly or indirectly depends on the contributions of another worker (Morris and Steers, 1980). Functional dependence may be considered a facilitator of trust because it encourages information exchange, discussion of possible strategies and open communication, which gives room for acceptance and personal involvement. Functional dependence is also believed to increase proximity and personal involvement within groups (Zand, 1972), which at the same time are considered to be important prerequisites for trust (Lewicki and Bunker, 1996). In this way, it is expected that teams where members are highly functionally dependent will show higher levels of trust:

*Proposition 2a:* teams where members are highly functionally dependent will display higher levels of trust than teams where members are less functionally dependent.

Task ambiguity refers to the lack of work specifications, or standard operating procedures provided by the organization or colleagues, that can define expectations about what resources and actions will be required for successful task accomplishment (Morris and Moberg, 1994). In such situations, the worker's vulnerability towards others increases and trust becomes very important, especially in relation to 'technical competence' and 'fiduciary responsibility' of the trustee (Barber, 1983). According to a human sciences point of view, ambiguity might lead to trust because it increases the need for open discussion of possible alternatives (ibid.). In opposition, the transaction costs point of view of Williamson (1975) suggests that in ambiguous situations the risk of opportunism is high, which might increase protective or defensive behaviours. With regard to this variable we adopt the economic point of view and hypothesize that teams with high ambiguity of task will show lower levels of trust.

*Proposition 2b:* high levels of task ambiguity will lead to low trust within teams.

### Organizational Variables

The organizational variables that systematically appear as inputs in models of team performance effectiveness are normally related to supervision, degree of influence, reward systems, training opportunities and technical consultation (for example, Gladstein, 1984; Hackman, 1987). In the present study we focus on these same issues using two slightly different variables, management climate and members' overall influence.

Management climate is related to the perceptions of supervision as being classic and bureaucratic versus work-centred and personal, and it is conceptualized in terms of the distinction between theory X and Y of McGregor (Ten Horn and Roe, 1988). In this perspective, management climate is assessed from the point of view of the subordinates. Workers evaluate behaviours of supervision in terms of information sharing, degree of participation, and decision making, and determine how they experience these behaviours as being helpful, friendly, tense and so on. The work of Creed and Miles (1996) and of Cangemie *et al.* (1989) suggests that behaviours and philosophies of leadership play a central role in developing and sustaining trust among workers. They serve to focus expectations and attributions as well as to shape the nature of interactions and statements of reciprocity (Creed and Miles, 1996). Although no consistent body of research exists on the effect of leadership on trust, the literature suggests that trust within teams is mostly reflected through climates that emphasize sharing of information, participation in decision making and personal involvement.

*Proposition 3a:* management climates more in line with work-centred and personal leadership styles will be associated with higher levels of trust within teams than management climates that are characterized by classic and bureaucratic leadership styles.

Members' overall influence relates to the influence of team members in the distribution of their work, budgets, evaluation and rewards. Recent research shows the importance of empowerment of individuals and teams as well as the provision of tools and skills to enable them to become self-managing (De Vries, 1997). To a certain extent, effective coordination requires employees to make decisions and commit resources, in order to move forward with a particular strategy or course of action. This is only likely to enhance collaboration and performance if trust between members and managers develops. Team members that are interdependent and trust each other operate with more latitude in doing what is required to achieve effectiveness (Shaw, 1997).

*Proposition 3b:* members' overall influence in the organization is positively related to trust between team members.

## METHOD

### Sample

We administrated a questionnaire to 552 employees dispersed over 131 teams in three Social Care institutions in the Netherlands. From these, only 395 (71.5 per cent) provided data via the questionnaire, enabling the identification of 112 teams. The teams fulfilled two criteria: they had a minimum of three members each, and their work activity was related to 'people' and/or 'information'. The teams included management teams, supervision teams, supporting teams, facilitating teams and staff teams; no production teams were involved in this study. The size of the teams ranged from three to six, with an average of 4.25 individuals per team. The age average was 40.5 (sd = 10.3 years), the average tenure was 4.3 years (sd = 3.4). Of these teams, 55 (49 per cent) included only male respondents, eight (7 per cent) included only female respondents and 49 (43.8 per cent) included respondents from both genders.

### Instruments

#### Trust
In accordance with our definition, four scales were used to measure this concept. These scales consisted of self-report items scored on a seven-point

Likert scale (1 = completely disagree, . . . 7 = completely agree). In a previous work we have described the methods and procedures used in the development of these scales and reported the results of internal consistency and validation of the trust measures (see Costa, 2000). The final scales consisted of seven items measuring propensity to trust: for example, 'People usually tell the truth, even when they know they would be better off by lying'; eight items measuring perceived trustworthiness (for example, 'In my team some people have success by stepping on other people' (reversed item); eight items measuring cooperative behaviours (for example, 'In my team we provide each other with timely information'); and three items measuring monitoring behaviours (for example, 'In my team people check whether others keep their promises'). Reliability results showed satisfactory levels of internal consistency for all scales ($\alpha > 0.70$). The alpha coefficient for propensity to trust was 0.84, for perceived trustworthiness 0.87, for cooperative behaviours 0.81 and for monitoring behaviours 0.71.

**Team composition**
The variables were assessed with the measurements of team tenure and the scales team cohesion, job-adequate skills and preference for working in a team. Items were scored on a seven-point Likert scale (1 = completely disagree, . . . 7 = completely agree). The scale measuring team cohesion (five items, $\alpha = 0.84$) was adapted from Podsakoff and Mackenzie (1995) by De Vries (1997). Job-adequate skills (six items, $\alpha = 0.80$) and preference for working in a team (five items, $\alpha = 0.73$) were scales adapted from the Organizational Assessment Inventory – OAI (Van de Ven and Ferry, 1980).

**Work characteristics**
Functional dependence and task ambiguity were adapted from existing measures developed by Roe *et al.* (1997). The items were answered with a seven-point Likert scale (1 = completely incorrect, . . . 7 = completely correct). Functional dependence was measured with six items ($\alpha = 0.76$). An example of a functional dependence item was 'In order to do my work I'm dependent on the work of my team members.' Task ambiguity was measured with five items ($\alpha = 0.72$). An example of task ambiguity item was 'There are no written rules or manuals to conduct my job.'

**Organizational variables**
The management climate scale contained eight items concerning the behaviour of supervisors towards their subordinates (Roe *et al.*, 1997). The items were answered using a four-point Likert scale. The alpha coefficient for management climate was 0.81. The members' overall influence was measured with a four-item scale from Koopman-Iwema (1980). The

answers were scored on a five-point Likert scale (1 = very little influence . . .
5 = very much influence). The alpha coefficient for members' overall
influence was 0.81.


# RESULTS

### Within-team Agreement and Scale Characteristics

The team scores were obtained by aggregating the individual scores on each
item within the teams. This aggregation was obtained by computation of
means to allow comparisons across teams without variances in the sample
size. In order to examine the level of agreement within teams we conducted
an analysis of variance ANOVA ($F$ ratio) and calculated the within-group
inter-rater agreement index – $rwg(j)$ – of James *et al.* (1984, 1993). Values
of $rwg(j)$ equal to 0.70 or above demonstrate high consistency within
groups and justify the aggregation within that team.

In Table 6.1 the results of the one-way analysis of variance ANOVA
show that the between-group variance was significantly greater than the
within-group variance in all scales ($F > 1.96$). This justifies the aggregation
of scores at team level in this study. For the trust scales, the highest
difference was for perceived trustworthiness ($F = 2.34$, $p < 0.01$) and the
lowest for monitoring behaviours ($F = 1.97$, $p < 0.05$). The level of within-
group agreement of these scales was satisfactory ($rwg(j) > 0.70$). The

*Table 6.1   Scale characteristics and within-group agreement*

|     |                            | No. | M | sd | F | rwg(j) |
|-----|----------------------------|-----|------|------|---------|--------|
| 1.  | Propensity to trust        | 6   | 4.22 | 1.02 | 2.13** | 0.85 |
| 2.  | Perceived trustworthiness  | 6   | 5.40 | 0.98 | 2.34** | 0.86 |
| 3.  | Cooperative behaviours     | 6   | 4.86 | 0.85 | 2.10** | 0.89 |
| 4.  | Monitoring behaviours      | 3   | 4.79 | 0.91 | 1.97*  | 0.78 |
| 5.  | Pref. working in a team    | 5   | 5.23 | 0.84 | 2.03** | 0.87 |
| 6.  | Team cohesion              | 5   | 5.45 | 0.72 | 2.40** | 0.89 |
| 7.  | Job-adequate skills        | 4   | 5.43 | 0.67 | 1.90** | 0.89 |
| 8.  | Functional dependence      | 6   | 5.13 | 0.70 | 2.00** | 0.91 |
| 9.  | Task ambiguity             | 5   | 3.17 | 0.90 | 2.76** | 0.86 |
| 10. | Management climate         | 6   | 3.00 | 0.35 | 3.14** | 0.89 |
| 11. | Members' overall influence | 5   | 2.29 | 0.70 | 1.91** | 0.90 |

*Notes:* No. is the reliable number of items in each scale, M is mean scale, sd is standard
deviation, $F$ is ratio ANOVA, $rwg(j)$ is the within-group inter-rater agreement; $*p = <0.05$,
$**p = <0.01$.

highest within-group agreement was for cooperative behaviours ($rwg(j) = 0.89$) and the lowest for the scale monitoring behaviours ($rwg(j) = 0.78$). With regard to the antecedents of trust, organizational climate obtained the highest $F$ ratio ($F = 3.14$, $p < 0.01$) and job-adequate skills the lowest ($F = 1.91$, $p < 0.01$). Also in these scales the level of within-group agreement shows high levels of reliable consensus within the teams. The highest within-group agreement is for functional dependence ($rwg(j) = 0.90$) and the lowest is for task ambiguity ($rwg(j) = 0.86$).

## Model Testing

Structural equation modelling (SEM) was the statistical procedure used to test the model described in Figure 6.1. This procedure tests simultaneously all relationships in the entire model and determines the extent to which the model is consistent with data (Byrne, 1998). Using Lisrel 8.30 (Jöreskog and Sörbom, 1993) the model was tested and fitted to the data with correlation matrices. To evaluate the fit of the model to the data the following indices were inspected: the chi-square ($\chi^2$), the goodness of fit indices (GFI and AGFI), the comparative fit index (CFI) and the residual indices (RAMSEA and RMR). Non-significance of the chi-square reflects a good model fit. Goodness of fit and comparative fit indices above 0.90 indicate an adequate fit. Values of RMSEA $<0.80$ indicate a good fit and $<0.50$ a very good fit (Browne and Cudeck, 1989). For the RMR, in general values $<0.50$ indicate a good fit (Byrne 1998). The results of the structural equations are expressed in standardized scores.

Table 6.2 describes the results concerning the adequacy of fit of our hypothesized model. With 28 degrees of freedom, the $\chi^2$ equals 36.03 ($p = 0.14$), GFI $= 0.95$, AGFI $= 0.87$ and CFI $= 0.95$. This suggests that the model fits the data well. The residual fit indices RMR and RMSEA also suggest a good model fit, 0.05 and 0.04, respectively.

With regard to the multi-component nature of trust, perceived trustworthiness is the strongest component ($\gamma2 = 0.91$) and alone explains 80 per cent of the total variance of trust ($R^2 = 0.80$). Cooperative behaviours explain 57 per cent of the total variance of trust ($R^2 = 0.57$) and obtained the second strongest result ($\gamma3 = 0.75$). Propensity to trust explains 10 per cent of the total variance of trust ($R^2 = 0.10$) having a standardized score equal to $\gamma1 = 0.32$. Monitoring behaviours explain the lowest percentage of trust, only 4 per cent ($R^2 = 0.04$) and their relation with trust is negative ($\gamma4 = -21$). These results show that in this study trust within teams is essentially explained by perceived trustworthiness and cooperative behaviours. Although propensity to trust and monitoring activities seem to be less central to trust, the initial estimates were highly significant (t-values $>1.96$).

*Table 6.2 Fit indices and structural relations*

| | [γ / λ] | Error | R² | [χ²] | [GFI] | [AGFI] | [RMSEA] | [RMR] | [CFI] |
|---|---|---|---|---|---|---|---|---|---|
| Hypothesized model | | | | 34.81 (df = 28; p = 0.17) | 0.95 | 0.87 | 0.04 | 0.05 | 0.98 |
| | | | | | | | | | |
| Trust | | | | | | | | | |
| Propensity to trust | 0.32 | 0.26 | 0.74 | | | | | | |
| Perceived trustworthiness | 0.91 | 0.90 | 0.10 | | | | | | |
| Cooperative behaviours | 0.75 | 0.19 | 0.80 | | | | | | |
| Monitoring behaviours | −0.21 | 0.43 | 0.57 | | | | | | |
| | | 0.95 | 0.05 | | | | | | |
| Antecendents | | | | | | | | | |
| Pref. working in teams → trust | 0.22 | | | | | | | | |
| Team cohesion → trust | 0.36 | | | | | | | | |
| Job-adequate skills → trust | 0.31 | | | | | | | | |
| Tenure → trust | −0.12 | | | | | | | | |
| Functional dependence → trust | 0.15 | | | | | | | | |
| Task ambiguity → trust | 0.10 | | | | | | | | |
| Organizational climate → trust | 0.16 | | | | | | | | |
| Members' influence → trust | 0.10 | | | | | | | | |

*Note:* Independent model χ² = 372.50 (df = 66).

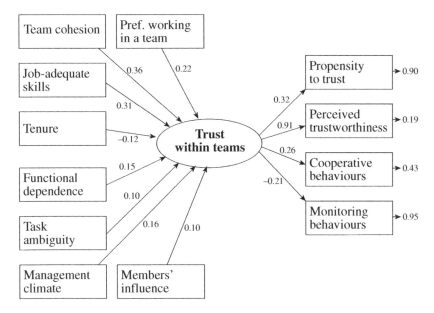

*Figure 6.2    Structural relations*

The strongest relations between the antecedents and trust are for the team composition variables, team cohesion and job-adequate skills, $\lambda 2 = 0.36$ and $\lambda 3 = 0.31$, respectively (see Figure 6.2). Preference for working in a team is also positively related with trust ($\lambda 1 = 0.22$). However, tenure shows a negative relation with trust ($\lambda 4 = -0.12$). The initial estimate for the relation between tenure and trust shows a t-value $<1.96$, indicating that this relation is not statistically significant. Looking at the proposed relationships between variables, it appears that the results support the expected positive effects of preference for working in a team, team cohesion and job-adequate skills on trust. Our results fail to support proposition 1c because the effect of tenure was negative. Observing the correlation matrix between latent variables (see Table 6.3), we noted that tenure is negatively correlated with trust and with preference for working in a team, respectively $r = -0.18$ and $r = -0.12$. These correlations suggest that individuals who work longer for their organization and perform the same function for a long time, not only have less trust in their teams but also prefer to work more on their own. With the other team composition variables tenure obtained almost zero correlations.

Our results also indicate that trust is associated with work characteristics and organizational variables. Management climate, functional dependence and members' overall influence are positively related to trust within teams, $\lambda 7 = 0.16$, $\lambda 5 = 0.15$, $\lambda 8 = 0.10$, respectively. The relation between task

*Table 6.3   Correlations between variables in the model*

|  | | 1 | 2 | 3 | 4 | 5 | 6 | 7 | 8 | 9 |
|---|---|---|---|---|---|---|---|---|---|---|
| 1. | Trust | 1.0 | | | | | | | | |
| 2. | Pref. working in a team | 0.45 | 1.0 | | | | | | | |
| 3. | Team cohesion | 0.62 | 0.17 | 1.0 | | | | | | |
| 4. | Job-adequate skills | 0.60 | 0.17 | 0.45 | 1.0 | | | | | |
| 5. | Tenure | −0.18 | −0.12 | 0.06 | 0.02 | 1.0 | | | | |
| 6. | Functional dependence | 0.38 | 0.20 | 0.27 | 0.16 | 0.09 | 1.0 | | | |
| 7. | Task ambiguity | 0.36 | 0.22 | 0.16 | 0.15 | 0.14 | −0.04 | 1.0 | | |
| 8. | Management climate | 0.48 | 0.22 | 0.19 | 0.30 | 0.19 | 0.35 | −0.06 | 1.0 | |
| 9. | Members' overall influence | 0.32 | 0.18 | 0.03 | 0.01 | 0.12 | 0.30 | 0.35 | −0.54 | 1.0 |

ambiguity and trust is also positive, although significantly weaker than the other antecedent variables ($\lambda6 = 0.10$) with an initial estimate not statistically significant (t-value < 1.96). The results thus confirm propositions 2a, 3a and 3b.

Contrary to proposition 2b, task ambiguity shows a positive relation with trust. In the correlation matrix obtained for the latent variables (see Table 6.3), both task ambiguity and functional dependence correlate positively with trust, $r = 0.38$ and $r = 0.36$, respectively, which is consistent with the direction of the relationships found in the model. This suggests that ambiguity of tasks may be a condition of trust between team members rather than a condition of opportunistic behaviour, as often proposed in the economic literature.

## DISCUSSION

In this study trust seemed based more on perceptions of trustworthiness and cooperative behaviours than on general propensities to trust others or lack of monitoring. Propensity to trust and lack of monitoring behaviours explained, respectively, 10 per cent and 5 per cent of the total variance of trust. However, we consider that both components still should be viewed as important aspects of trust. In the first place, we were dealing with teams where individuals had already known each other for some time (tenure average 4.3 years), therefore it makes sense that trust between members may be based more on attributions of trustworthiness shown to one another than on general expectancies. Different trust components may be more important in some contexts than in others, depending on the degree of familiarity between members (Bigley and Pearce, 1998).

With respect to which antecedents are relevant for trust within teams, team composition factors seemed the most significant. Teams with a high level of cohesion, where members have a preference for teamwork and possess the adequate skills to perform tasks, have the best composition to enhance trust. These conditions reflect a high-level interaction between members, strong identity, and are usually positively associated with social involvement (Cartwright and Zander, 1968). Although trust probably develops and changes over time, as a consequence of members having a history of interaction, in this study tenure did show a negative relation to trust. Even though this relation was not statistically significant, further analyses indicated that tenure was also negatively related to preference for working in a team. Roberts and Hunt (1991) have argued that tenure combined with age can generate a more calculative relation with the organization, which may justify the need to monitor and diminish perceptions of trustworthiness in these teams. This can be related to lack of career perspectives or promotion, as age and the tenure in the organization increase. Another explanation may be related to what Bart Nooteboom and Frédérique Six in Chapter 1 of this volume refer to as 'shadow of the future'. This notion concerns the calculative assessment of future benefits, such as reputation, based on present cooperation. If team members know that they will work together for a long period of time, they may be more calculative, and not want to damage their reputation, than when they know that the team will be dissolved or when they are near retirement.

Work and organizational factors showed less influence on trust than team composition. Yet, from this study, we learned that trust is not context-free and that some conditions are more likely to enhance trust than others. When the contacts with supervisors are experienced as friendly, and there is an emphasis on openness and information sharing, trust between team members is likely to occur. Furthermore, the degree of influence on the organization of tasks, evaluation of budgets and rewards systems presumably enhances trust within teams. The importance of empowerment of individuals and teams in the development of trust at different organizational levels has been emphasized by recent economic theories. Trust based on the assumption that individuals are willing to produce a common good for the organization increases the likelihood that workers will act in a trustworthy manner (Bromiley and Cummings, 1995). Furthermore, the more trust there is, the more it is likely to develop and generalize to different organizational levels (Dasgupta, 1988).

Characteristics of the work such as the degree of functional dependence between team members and the level of ambiguity of tasks were positively related to trust. In teams with high functional dependence, members need to cooperate more, and they must depend on one another to a certain degree (Morris and Moberg, 1994). Although trust does not necessarily lead to cooperation, functional dependence creates conditions for information exchange and proximity, which may give room for acceptance and increase vulnerability. Ambiguity of tasks also creates vulnerability between members and uncertainty about how to perform tasks, as well as how to go about the job (ibid.). The transaction costs point of view posits that ambiguity creates conditions for opportunism, which increases the need for monitoring or defensive behaviour, and therefore will lead to less trust (Williamson, 1975). Our research does not confirm this point of view. When tasks are ambiguous, members do not necessarily take advantage of these conditions and do not act in an opportunistic manner vis-à-vis their teams. On the contrary, ambiguity may reinforce interdependence and the need to collaborate, which in turn promotes trust. This is consistent with the claim that, under uncertain conditions, there is increased need for contribution of others with complementary competence (see Bart Nooteboom in Chapter 2 of this volume), also found by Nathalie Lazaric in Chapter 8.

## CONCLUSIONS

Trust within teams is influenced by the composition of the teams as well as by work and organizational contextual factors. According to the variables considered in this study, we identified three major conditions that influence the level of trust within teams; that is, the quality of interaction among team members, the level of interdependence and the degree of participation and influence in the organization. Trust within teams is essentially created through positive interactions among members. Preference for working in a team can be a major determinant of interpersonal interaction within teams, since it brings people together that favour working in such contexts. Having adequate skills to perform jobs provides a kind of equality in the work process. Members that consider their colleagues to have adequate skills are less afraid of having to cover up for someone that does not perform well, or have fewer tendencies to monitor the work of others. Cohesiveness within a group not only provides interpersonal harmony but creates a common identity and commitment in relation to the tasks performed. Without considering these conditions as static, the quality of interaction within teams may improve social and work-related aspects of the team and enhance trust.

Contextual factors such as the level of interdependence between team members, the degree of participation in decision making, and the degree of influence on the organization also affect trust. Teams with highly interdependent or ambiguous tasks are more likely to enhance trust, since both conditions create the need for collaboration among members. In less interdependent teams, trust might also be achieved though reputations or past experiences (for example, Hill, 1990). However, as members become more familiar with each other they will start comparing reputations with present experiences. Participation in work decisions and having influence on the organization issues such as organization of work, budgets, systems and so on, generates trust by providing a sense of transparency and fairness between individuals and the organization they work for. This research seems to suggest that, in order to enhance trust in teams, managers should look at different factors related either to the composition of teams, work characteristics or organizational context.

Although this study may represent a step forward in establishing the relevant antecedents of trust within teams, several limitations are associated with these results. The foremost limitation relates to the fact that the teams in this study came from organizations within a single sector of activity, which makes it inappropriate to generalize these conclusions to other sectors of activity. Cautions in the interpretation of these results are also associated with using self-ratings scales. Furthermore, although we studied different factors affecting teams in organizations, we probably did not exhaust all possible determinants of trust.

## REFERENCES

Anderson, N.R. and J. Birch (2001), 'Selecting for teamwork: development of the selection team inventory (STI)', paper presented at the Annual Conference of the British Psychological Society, January, Blackpool, UK.

Barber, B. (1983), *The Logic and Limits of Trust*, New Brunswick, NJ: Rutgers University Press.

Bentler, P.M. (1990), 'Comparative fit indexes in structural models', *Psychological Bulletin*, **107**, 238–46.

Bentler, P.M. and D.G. Bonnet (1980), 'Significance tests and goodness of fit in the analysis of covariance structures', *Psychological Bulletin*, **88**, 588–606.

Bigley, G.A. and J.L. Pearce (1998), 'Straining for shared meaning in organization science: problems of trust and distrust', *Academy of Management Review*, **23**, 405–21.

Bromiley, P. and L. Cummings (1995), 'Transaction costs in organizations with trust', *Research on Negotiations in Organizations*, **5**, 219–47.

Browne, M.W. and R. Cudeck (1989), 'Single sample cross-validation indices for covariance structures', *Multivariate Behavioral Research*, **24**, 445–55.

Butler, J.K. (1991), 'Toward understanding and measuring conditions of trust:

evolution of a conditions of trust inventory', *Journal of Management*, **17**, 643–63.

Butler, J.K. and R.S. Cantrell (1984), 'Communication factors and trust: an exploratory study', *Psychological Reports*, **74**, 33–4.

Byrne, B. (1998), *Structural Equation Modelling with LISREL, PRELIS, and SIMPLIS: Basic Concepts, Applications and Programming*, Mahwah, NJ: Erlbaum.

Cangemie, J.P., J. Rice, and C.J. Kowalski (1989), 'The development, decline and renewal of trust in an organization: some observations', *Psychology. A Journal of Human Behavior*, **27**, 46–53.

Cartwright, D. and A.W. Zander (eds) (1968), *Group Dynamics Research and Theory*, 3rd edn, New York: Harper & Row.

Costa, A.C. (2000), 'A matter of trust: effects on the performance and effectiveness of teams in organizations', dissertation, Tilburg, Ridderkerk.

Costa, A.C., R.A. Roe and T. Taillieu (2001), 'Trust within teams: the relation with performance effectiveness', *European Journal of Work and Organizational Psychology*, **10**(3), 225–44.

Creed, W.E.D. and R.E. Miles (1996), 'Trust in organizations: a conceptual framework linking organizational forms, managerial philosophies, and the opportunity costs of controls', in R.M. Kramer and T.R. Tyler (eds), *Trust in Organizations: Frontiers of Theory and Research*, Thousand Oaks, CA: Sage Publications, pp. 16–38.

Cummings, L.L. and P. Bromiley (1996), 'The organizational trust inventory (OTI): development and validation', in Roderick M. Kramer and Tom R. Tyler (eds), *Trust in Organizations: Frontiers of Theory and Research*, Thousand Oaks, CA: Sage Publications, pp. 302–30.

Dasgupta, P. (1988), 'Trust as a commodity', in D. Gambetta (ed.), *Trust Making and Breaking Cooperative Relations*, New York: Basil Blackwell, pp. 49–72.

De Vries, R.E. (1997), *Need for Leadership: A Solution for Empirical Problems in Situational Theories of Leadership*, Tilburg, Enschede: FEBO.

Deutsch, M. (1962), 'Cooperation and trust: some theoretical notes', *Nebraska Symposium on Motivation*, Lincoln: University of Nebraska Press, pp. 275–319.

Giffin, K. and B.R. Patton (1971), 'Personal trust in human interaction', *Basic Readings in Interpersonal Communication*, New York: Harper & Row.

Gladstein, D.L. (1984) 'Groups in context: a model of task group effectiveness', *Administrative Science Quarterly*, **29**, 499–517.

Guzzo, R.A. (1995), 'Introduction: at the intersection of team effectiveness and decision making', in Richard A. Guzzo and Eduardo Salas (eds), *Team Effectiveness and Decision Making in Organizations*, San Francisco: Jossey-Bass Publishers, pp. 1–8.

Hackman, J.R. (1987), ' The design of work teams', in J.W. Lorsch (ed.), *Handbook of Organizational Behavior*, pp. 315–42.

Hackman, J.R., K.H. Brouseau and J.A. Weiss (1976), 'The interaction of task design and group performance strategies in determining group effectiveness', *Organizational Behavior and Human Performance*, **16**, 350–65.

Hardy, K. and A.L. McGrath (1989), 'Dealing with cheating in distribution', *European Journal of Marketing*, **23** (2),123–9.

Hill, C.W.L. (1990), 'Cooperation, opportunism, and the invisible hand: implications for transaction cost theory', *Academy of Management Review*, **15**, 500–513.

Hosmer, L.R.T. (1995), 'Trust: the connecting link between organizational theory and philosophical ethics', *Academy of Management Review*, **20**, 379–403.

James, L.R., R.G. Demaree and G. Wolf (1984), 'Estimating within-group interrater reliability with and without response bias', *Journal of Applied Psychology*, **69**, 85–98.

James, L.R., R.G. Demaree and G. Wolf (1993), 'RWG: an assessment of within-group interrater agreement', *Journal of Applied Psychology*, **78**, 306–9.

Janis, I.L. (1982), *Groupthink: Psychological Studies of Policy Decisions and Fiascos*, Boston: Houghton Mifflin.

Jöreskog, K.G. and D. Sörbom (1993), *LISREL8e*, Mooresville: Scientific Software.

Katz, D. and R.L. Kahn (1978), *The Social Psychology of Organizations*, New York: John Wiley and Sons.

Keen, P. (1990), *Shaping the Future: Business Design Through Information Technology*, Harvard: Harvard Business School.

King, N. and N.R. Anderson (1995), *Innovation and Change in Organizations*, part of the Routledge New Essential Business Psychology series, London: Routledge.

Koopman-Iwema, A.M. (1980), *Macht, motivatie en medezeggenschap: een studie naar de determinanten van participatief gedrag van leden van overlegorganen in industriële bedrijven*, Proefschrift UvA Amsterdam, Assen: Van Gorcum.

Kramer, R.M. (1999), 'Trust and distrust in organizations: emerging perspectives, enduring questions', *Annual Review of Psychology*, **50**, 569–98.

Kramer, R.M., M.B. Brewer and B.A. Hanna (1996), 'Collective trust and collective action: the decision to trust as a social decision', in R.M. Kramer and T.R. Tyler (eds), *Trust in Organizations: Frontiers of Theory and Research*, Thousand Oaks, CA: Sage Publications, pp. 357–89.

Lawrence, P.R. and J.W. Lorsch (1967), *Organization and Environment: Managing Differentiation and Integration*, Boston, MA: Harvard University.

Leifer, R. and P.K. Mills (1996), 'An information processing approach for deciding upon control strategies and reducing control loss in emerging organizations', *Journal of Management*, **22**, 113–37.

Lewicki, R.J. and B.B. Bunker (1995), 'Trust in relationships: a model of development and decline', in Barbara Benedict Bunker and Jeffrey Z. Rubin (eds), *Conflict, Cooperation and Justice: Essays Inspired by the Work of Morton Deutsch. The Jossey-Bass Management Series and The Jossey-Bass Conflict Resolution Series*, San Francisco, CA: Jossey-Bass, pp. 133–73.

Lewicki, R.J. and B.B. Bunker (1996), 'Developing and maintaining trust in work relationships', in Roderick M. Kramer, Tom R. Tyler (eds), *Trust in Organizations: Frontiers of Theory and Research*, Thousand Oaks, CA: Sage Publications, pp. 114–39.

Lewis, J.D. and Weigert, A. (1985), 'Trust as a social reality', *Social Forces*, **63**, 967–85.

Luhmann, N. (1979), *Trust and Power*, New York: John Wiley and Sons.

Mayer, R.C., J.H. Davis and F.D. Schoorman (1995), 'An integrative model of organizational trust', *Academy of Management Review*, **20**, 709–34.

McAllister, D.J. (1995), 'Affect- and cognition-based trust as foundations for interpersonal cooperation in organizations', *Academy of Management Journal*, special issue: Intra-and Interorganizational Cooperation, **38**, 24–59.

Morgan, R.M. and S.D. Hunt (1994), 'The commitment-trust theory of relationship marketing', *Journal of Marketing*, **58**, 20–38.

Morris, J.H. and D.J. Moberg (1994), 'Work organizations as contexts for trust and betrayal', in Theodore R. Sarbin, Ralph M. Carney and Carson Eoyang (eds), *Citizen Espionage: Studies in Trust and Betrayal*, Westport, CT: Praeger Publishers/Greenwood Publishing Group, pp. 163–87.

Morris, J.H. and R.M. Steers (1980), 'Structural influences on organizational commitment', *Journal of Vocational Behavior*, **17**, 50–57.

Nunnally, J.C. (1978), *Psychometric Theory*, New York: McGraw-Hill.

Podsakoff, P.M. and S.B. MacKenzie (1995), 'An examination of the psychometric properties and nomological validity of some revised and reduced substitutes for leadership scales', *Journal of Applied Psychology*, **79**(5), 702–13.

Roberts, K.M. and D.M. Hunt (1991), *Organizational Behavior*, Boston, MA: PWS-Kent.

Roe, R.A., L. Ten Horn, I. Zinovieva and E. Dienes (1997), 'Expanded Delft measurement kit: technical guideline', report on the European research program on work motivation and quality of work life, WORC, Tilburg University.

Rotter, J.B. (1980), 'Interpersonal trust, trustworthiness, and gullibility', *American Psychologist*, **35**, 1–7.

Rousseau, M.T., S.B. Sitkin, S.B. Burt and C. Carmerer (1998), 'Not so different after all: a cross-discipline view of trust', *Academy of Management Review*, **23**, 393–404.

Shapiro, D.L., B.H. Sheppard and L. Cheraskin (1992), 'Business on a handshake', *Negotiation Journal*, **8**, 365–77.

Shaw, R. B. (1997), *Trust in the Balance: Building Successful Organizations on Results, Integrity and Concern*, San Francisco: Jossey-Bass.

Sheppard, B.H. and D.M. Sherman (1998), 'The grammars of trust: a model and general implications', *Academy of Management Review*, **23**, 422–37.

Slovic, P. (1993), 'Perceived risk, trust and democracy', *Risk Analysis*, **13**, 675–82.

Ten Horn, L.A. and R.A. Roe (1988), 'De Delftse Meetdoos voor Kwaliteit van arbeid; oriëntatie voor gebruikers', Faculty of Technical Social Sciences, Delft University of Technology.

Tzeiner, A. and D. Eden (1985), 'Effects of crew composition on crew performance: does the whole equal the sum of its parts?', *Journal of Applied Psychology*, **70**, 85–93.

Van de Ven, A. and D.L. Ferry (1980), *Measuring and Assessing Organizations*, New York: John Wiley and Sons.

Williamson, O.E. (1975), *Markets and Hierarchies: Analysis and Antitrust Implications*, New York: Free Press.

Wrightsman, L.S. (1964), 'Measurement of philosophies of human nature', *Psychological Reports*, **14**, 743–51.

Zand, D.E. (1972), 'Trust and managerial problem solving', *Administrative Science Quarterly*, **17**, 229–39.

Zucker, L.G. (1986), 'Production of trust: institutional sources of economic structure, 1840–1920', *Research in Organizational Behavior*, **8**, 53–111.

# 7. Trusting others in organizations: leaders, management and co-workers

**Deanne den Hartog**

## INTRODUCTION

Trust seems important as a prerequisite for cooperation and has been described as an important feature in interpersonal relationships as well as in larger collectivities such as organizations or societies. From a sociological perspective, Misztal (1996) places trust and mutual obligations at the centre of the 'civil society' which reconciles the demands of individuality with those of the community. She states that the conventional bases for social cooperation, solidarity and consensus have eroded. The current search for new bases of integration has revived the interest in 'trust seen as a valuable asset, which develops in the mutually formative interplay of public institutions and individuals' (ibid., p. 3). Trust is also seen as related to people's motivation to cooperate as 'co-operation requires trust in the sense that the dependent parties need some degree of assurance that the other, non-dependent parties will not defect' (Williams, 1988, p. 8). According to Gambetta (1988, p. 235) 'trust uncovers dormant preferences for co-operation tucked under the seemingly safer blankets of defensive–aggressive revealed preferences'. Mayer *et al.* (1995) emphasize vulnerability, the willingness of a party to be vulnerable to the actions of another party, as an important part of trust. They propose a model of antecedents and outcomes of organizational trust, integrating research from multiple disciplines and differentiating trust from similar constructs such as cooperation, confidence and predictability.

Many different definitions of trust have been proposed from the context of individual expectations, interpersonal relationships, economic exchanges, social structures and ethical principles (see Hosmer, 1995). Creed and Miles (1996), for example, describe trust as both the specific expectation that another's actions will be beneficial rather than detrimental and the generalized ability to take for granted, or to take under trust, a vast array of features in the social order. This definition incorporates two of the above contexts or viewpoints, namely individual expectations and social structures. Cook and Wall (1980) take a somewhat different perspective. They define trust as the extent to which one is willing to ascribe good intentions to and have confidence in the words and actions of other people, viewing trust as a dimension of interpersonal relationships. They view trust between individuals and groups within an organization as a highly important ingredient in the long-term stability of the organization. The current chapter focuses on such interpersonal trust within organizations and especially on the relationship between leadership and trust. The proposed relationships between leadership and employees' trust in a focal leader, as well as their trust in two important groups of generalized others, namely management and co-workers, are described and a study among employees of two organizations is presented to test some of the proposed relationships.

## LEADERSHIP

Since its introduction over twenty years ago, transformational, charismatic, visionary or inspirational leadership has been strongly emphasized in the management literature (for example, Bass and Avolio, 1990; Burns, 1978; Den Hartog and Koopman, 2001; House, 1977, 1996; Shamir *et al.*, 1993). Charismatic or transformational leaders articulate a realistic vision of the future that can be shared, stimulate subordinates intellectually, and pay attention to the differences among the subordinates (Den Hartog *et al.*, 1997). Bass (1985) holds that inspirational or transformational leaders broaden and elevate the interests of followers, generate awareness and acceptance among the followers of the purposes and mission of the group and motivate followers to go beyond their self-interests for the good of the group. According to Bass (1985) the transformation of followers can be achieved by raising the awareness of the importance and value of desired outcomes, getting followers to transcend their own self-interests and altering or expanding followers' needs. Tichy and Devanna (1990) highlight the transforming effect these leaders can have on organizations as well as on individuals. By defining the need for change, creating new visions and mobilizing commitment to these visions, leaders can ultimately transform organizations.

Transformational or inspirational leaders articulate an ideological vision that describes a better future and is congruent with the dearly held values of followers. Through articulating such a vision, inspirational leaders are proposed to instil pride, gain respect and trust, and increase a sense of optimism (Shamir *et al.*, 1993). The leader's personal example serves as a model of the kind of behaviour required to attain the vision (House and

Podsakoff, 1994). These leaders also stimulate followers intellectually, providing them with a flow of challenging, new ideas that are supposed to stimulate rethinking of old ways of doing things (Bass, 1985). Furthermore, while a leader's charisma may attract subordinates to a vision or mission, the leader's individualized consideration also significantly contributes to individual subordinates achieving their fullest potential (Bass, 1985). In this vein, House (1977) emphasizes the importance of confidence building and expressing confidence in followers.

In the literature, transformational leadership is usually contrasted with transactional leadership. The transactional leadership perspective defines leader–follower relationships as based on implicit and/or explicit cost–benefit exchanges. Bass (1985) describes a transactional leader as one who recognizes what followers want to get from their work and tries to see that they get what they desire if their performance warrants it; exchanges (promises of) rewards for appropriate levels of effort; and responds to followers' self-interests as long as they are getting the job done. Thus transactional leadership theories are founded on the idea that leader–follower relations are based on a series of exchanges or implicit bargains between leaders and followers. According to House *et al.* (1988), the general notion in these theories is that, when the job and the environment of the follower fail to provide the necessary motivation, direction and satisfaction, the leader, through his or her behaviour, will be effective by compensating for the deficiencies. The leader clarifies the performance criteria, in other words what he expects from subordinates, and what they receive in return. Followers are rewarded for compliance. Research shows that such leader behaviour can indeed be effective (for example, Yukl, 1998). Transformational leadership goes beyond the cost–benefit exchange of transactional leadership by motivating and inspiring followers to perform beyond expectations (Bass, 1985). Hater and Bass (1988) point out that contrasting transactional and transformational leadership does not mean the models are unrelated. Burns (1978) thought of the two types of leadership as being at opposite ends of a continuum. Bass (1985), however, views them as separate dimensions, which would imply that a leader can be both transactional and transformational. He argues that transformational leadership builds on transactional leadership but not vice versa. Transformational leadership can be viewed as a special case of transactional leadership, inasmuch as both approaches are linked to the achievement of some goal or objective. The models differ on the process by which the leader motivates subordinates and on the types of goals set (Hater and Bass, 1988).

In measuring transactional leadership, two types of leader behaviour are often distinguished, namely contingent rewarding and management-by-exception (Bass, 1985). These two types of transactional leadership will also be distinguished in the study presented below. Contingent reward entails a positive exchange in which followers are rewarded for expending the necessary effort or attaining specified performance levels. Research shows that contingent reward positively affects subordinate performance and satisfaction (for example, Podsakoff *et al.*, 1982). Management by exception (MBE) entails a focus on corrective action and (preventing) mistakes and irregularities in follower performance. A leader intervenes when things go wrong or standards are not met (Bass, 1985). Although MBE is commonly referred to as 'transactional', it is less exchange-based than contingent-rewarding. It is perhaps best described as performance monitoring. Bass and associates distinguish between two forms of MBE, namely active and passive (for example, Bass and Avolio, 1990). The difference is that in the active form the leader searches for deviations and takes preventive action, whereas in the passive form the leader waits for problems to materialize (Hater and Bass, 1988). However, others hold that (at least in the way passive MBE is measured) it seems to have more in common with so-called 'passive' or 'laissez-faire' leadership. Passive leaders avoid taking action or decision making. Laissez-faire leadership and passive MBE usually correlate negatively with the more active leadership styles and can be combined into a single passive leadership factor (Den Hartog *et al.*, 1997). Passive leadership was not measured in the study presented in this chapter.

In general, inspirational leadership is expected and found to lead to more positive effects on subordinates than transactional leadership. Fiol *et al.* (1999) note that theories emphasizing transformational or charismatic leadership have been subjected to over a hundred empirical tests. Collectively, findings demonstrate that such leaders have positive effects on their organizations and followers, with effect sizes ranging from 0.35 to 0.50 for organizational performance effects, and from 0.40 to 0.80 for effects on follower satisfaction, commitment and organizational identification (ibid.). Meta-analytical studies of the literature support this conclusion (for example, Lowe *et al.*, 1996). In their meta-analysis, Lowe *et al.* find a 0.81 corrected correlation between charisma and subordinates' ratings of leader effectiveness and a 0.35 mean corrected correlation between such leadership and independent ratings of leader effectiveness. Although most work is cross-sectional, several longitudinal studies (for example, Howell and Avolio, 1993) and experimental studies (for example, Kirkpatrick and Locke, 1996) also support the conclusions reported above. Furthermore, there is evidence that both the positive endorsement and the positive effects of this type of leadership are found in a wide range of countries (Bass, 1997; Den Hartog *et al.*, 1999). The current study focuses on the relation between leadership, trust in the leader and trust in co-workers and management.

# INTERPERSONAL TRUST

Butler (1991) concluded that the literature on trust had converged on the beliefs that trust is an important aspect of interpersonal relationships, and that such trust is essential to the development of managerial careers. Although most of the literature on interpersonal trust focuses on trust in romantic or personal relationships, there are also authors focusing on the interpersonal nature of trust in organizations. Butler and Cantrell (1984), for instance, combined the interpersonal nature of trust as a condition for cooperation with the factor inequality in position. They proposed five specific components of trust (or characteristics of the people involved) and expected that the degree of each would differ according to the position (superior or subordinate) of the person: integrity, competence, consistency, loyalty and openness. Integrity refers to the reputation for honesty and truthfulness of the trusted party. Competence refers to the technical knowledge and interpersonal skills needed for job performance. Consistency refers to reliability, predictability and good judgment in handling situations. Openness refers to mental accessibility or the willingness to share ideas and information with others freely. Butler and Cantrell (1984) refer to loyalty as benevolence or the willingness to protect, support and encourage others. The dimension of loyalty was later refined. Rather than the proposed attitude of general benevolence, loyalty could also refer to an implicit promise from one party not to bring harm to the other (Butler, 1991; see also Hosmer, 1995).

Lewicki and Bunker (1996) propose three types of trust in professional relationships: calculus-based (or deterrence-based) trust, knowledge-based trust and identification-based trust. They hold that these three types are linked in a sequential iteration in which achieving trust at one level enables the development of trust at another level. The first type of trust which plays a role in professional relationships is calculus-based trust. This form of trust is based on assuring consistency of behaviour. In other words, individuals will do what they say because they fear the consequences of not doing what they say. Trust is sustained to the extent that the possible punishment is clear and likely to occur when the trust is violated. Calculus-based trust is not only deterrence-based, it could also be grounded in the rewards to be derived from preserving the trust. Thus calculus-based trust may be driven by both the value of benefits and the costs of cheating. An example is the negative effects that violating a trust may have on one's reputation in an organization or network versus the benefits of being perceived as trustworthy by others. At this stage, trust is partial and fragile. Lewicki and Bunker propose several conditions that need to be satisfied to make the threat of deterrence effective. First, the loss of future interaction must outweigh (be more threatening than) the profit potential that comes from defecting from the relationship or violating the trust. Deterrence requires both monitoring the other's behaviour and the exercise of behaviour control (a willingness to act in order to get the other party to do what the actor wants). Also the actors' orientation to risk will predispose either party to being exploited or overly suspicious.

The second type of trust Lewicki and Bunker (1996) describe is knowledge-based trust. 'This form of trust is grounded in the other's predictability – knowing the other sufficiently well so that the other's behaviour is anticipatable' (ibid., p. 121). This type of trust relies on information rather than deterrence. It develops over time as a function of the history of interaction between parties, that allows a generalized expectancy about the predictability and trustworthiness of the other party's behaviour to develop. Being able to understand and explain the behaviour of the other party makes it easier to accept the behaviour and react to it. Shapiro *et al.* (1992) hold that regular communication and 'courtship' are key processes in developing knowledge-based trust. Regular communication ensures a constant exchange of information about wants, needs and expectancies, and ensures that parties do not 'lose touch'. This increases predictability. 'Courtship' is behaviour that is specifically aimed at relationship development and learning more about the other party, again contributing to predictability (Lewicki and Bunker, 1996).

The third type of trust Lewicki and Bunker (1996, p. 122) describe is based on identification with the other's desires and intentions. At this level, 'trust exists because the parties effectively understand and appreciate the other's wants; this mutual understanding is developed to the point where they can effectively act for the other'. Increased identification enables one party to 'think, feel and respond like the other party'. People may empathize strongly with the other and incorporate ideas and ways of responding to this other into their own 'identity' (their needs, preferences, thoughts and behaviour patterns) as a collective identity develops. Kramer (1993), for example, argues that group-based trust is linked with group membership and develops through individuals' identification with the goals espoused by the group or organization. In these cases, salient group identification greatly enhances the frequency of cooperation.

## LEADERSHIP AND TRUST DEVELOPMENT

Both transactional and inspirational leader behaviours may help subordinates develop trust in their leader. The management-by-exception component of transactional leadership would probably primarily lead to calculus-based trust through the emphasis on monitoring and controlling whether subordinates perform as expected (performance monitoring). For example, Bass (1985, p. 137) states that 'management-by-exception follows directly from the emphasis on the manager as controller. (. . .) Management-by-exception is consistent with the cybernetics of negative feedback – feedback that signals the system to move back toward its steady-state base'. Standards are set and only when they are not (likely to be) met does the manager intervene. Bass also states that negative feedback 'can provide the novice subordinate with needed advice on what *not* to do' (ibid., p. 135).

Going beyond calculus-based trust, contingent rewarding and certain transformational leader behaviours may increase knowledge-based trust. Consistently practising contingent reward involves keeping promises made (for example, regarding extra pay or a promotion for work well done). At a higher level, contingent reward involves recognition of subordinates' performance. In time, both these dimensions should increase knowledge-based trust, in that subordinates come to rely upon the leader to reward them for their efforts. The transformational dimension of individualized consideration involves treating each subordinate differently according to their needs and capabilities, and giving them personal attention. Crucial are a mentoring and developmental orientation towards subordinates (Bass, 1985). This can take many forms, for instance, appreciating a job well done (much like higher levels of contingent reward), advising subordinates what to do in certain circumstances and providing feedback and constructive criticism to help subordinates improve their weak spots. Leaders can also, for instance, invite subordinates to accompany them on visits to clients or to participate in meetings to 'learn the ropes' (ibid.). Individualized consideration addresses the relationship development needed for knowledge-based trust and ensures the exchange of information on expectancies, needs and wants, another important element of this type of trust.

Finally, according to Lewicki and Bunker (1996, p. 123) many of the activities that increase the other forms of trust also serve to develop identification-based trust. Four types of activities that work more specifically to increase this type of trust are developing a collective identity; co-location (working in the same building or neighbourhood); creating joint products or goals; and committing oneself to commonly shared values. Articulating an attractive vision, accompanied by shared goals to strive for, committing oneself to shared values and developing a sense of collective identity are important components of inspirational leader behaviour and also seem likely to increase such trust. Several theories of inspirational leadership emphasize the importance of developing a collective identity and the importance of followers' identification with certain values and the collective (for example, Shamir *et al.*, 1993). Personal and social identification as well as value internalization play a role in this leadership process (Den Hartog, 1997). These processes also seem strongly linked to identification-based trust.

## TRUST IN THE LEADER, MANAGEMENT AND CO-WORKERS

A study by Podsakoff *et al.* (1990) examined subordinates' trust in the leader as a possible mediating variable in the relationship between transformational leadership and so-called 'organizational citizenship behaviours' (OCBs). OCBs describe employees' extra-role behaviour, including their civic virtue, courtesy and altruism. They show that, indeed, trust mediates this relationship. More specifically, they show that transformational leadership has a direct effect on both employee trust and satisfaction (but not on OCBs), and that trust (but not satisfaction) has a direct effect on OCBs. The operationalization of trust in the leader (six items) used by Podsakoff *et al.* incorporates three items referring to perceived fairness and integrity of the leader, two items regarding loyalty towards the leader, and one item which asks whether the follower would support the leader in almost any emergency. In their study these different aspects of trust are combined in a single scale. In the present study, we measured several aspects of trust in a leader separately in order to tease out the different components of trust in the leader. First, followers' faith in their leader and confidence in the leader's ability to overcome problems are assessed. In the remainder of this chapter we will refer to such follower's faith and confidence in the leader as 'trust in the leader'. Also included in the current study are items referring to perceived leader fairness and perceived ethical integrity.

As Craig and Gustafson (1998) point out, ethical integrity is an important aspect of leadership (which is not necessarily the same as having faith in the leader). They find high correlations between perceived leader integrity and employee job satisfaction. Such fairness and integrity were also measured in the current study. Inspirational or transformational leadership is expected to correlate more with the faith in the focal leader and leader integrity and fairness than transactional leadership. However, a certain degree of fairness and trustworthiness also seems important for transactional leadership, especially in cases of promised rewards for performance (such promises are only likely to be effective when employees trust they will receive what was promised).

Besides development of trust in the focal leader–follower relationship, employees can also develop more generalized trust in management and trust in colleagues or co-workers. Such trust or distrust is likely to influence employees' behaviour towards these groups and the amount of effort they are willing to expend on their behalf. Butler (1991) holds that trust in a specific person is more relevant in predicting certain outcomes than trust in generalized others. However, Hosmer (1995) states that the literature regarding trust in management has focused mostly on (the role of personal characteristics in) superior–subordinate relationships, whereas the literature on distrust in management has included generalized others. Also it follows from the different possible definitions that trust in specific others and trust in generalized others, groups and social systems can be important in the development and maintenance of cooperative attitudes towards those parties and the organization as a whole. Thus both trust in a focal leader and trust in general others (such as management) may be of importance in maintaining cooperation.

To measure trust in management and co-worker in the current study, the interpersonal trust scales as developed by Cook and Wall (1980) were used. The scales refer to two aspects of trust, namely having confidence in management/colleagues and having faith in management/colleagues. Clegg and Wall (1981) found that trust in management declines as one moves down the management, supervisory, white-collar and blue-collar hierarchy. Through its emphasis on values and processes of internalization, inspirational leadership is expected to increase a cooperative and trusting attitude towards management and co-workers. By increasing team spirit and the idea that the group works together as a collectivity, inspirational leaders could also positively affect trust in co-workers. Trusting one's own leader, feeling treated fairly, and the idea of pursuing a common organizational goal are also expected to increase a more generalized sense of trust in management. Thus inspirational leadership is expected to increase a cooperative and trusting attitude towards management and co-workers through its emphasis on values and processes of internalization. The relationship between inspirational leadership and generalized trust in management and colleagues is expected to be stronger than the relationship between transactional leadership and these types of trust. Trust in the leader, perceived fairness and integrity of the focal leader are also expected to increase trust in management and, following Podsakoff *et al.* (1990), trust in the leader (and possibly fairness and integrity) are expected to mediate the relationship between leader behaviours and generalized trust.

# METHOD

## Sample and Procedure

The sample in this study consisted of 330 employees of two very different organizations. The first was a utilities firm (in the process of being privatized), the second an organization in the entertainment industry. Respondents received questionnaires and cover letters in person at work and could send or hand in the questionnaire after completion. Researchers were available for answering questions. In total, 212 people returned (usable) questionnaires. The response was approximately 80 per cent in the public utility firm ($n = 145$) and 45 per cent in the entertainment company ($n = 67$). Eighty-two per cent of the respondents were male and 7.5 per cent had a (mostly lower-level) managerial position.

## Measures

The items used in the leadership scales were taken from a larger pool of items in the Inspirational Leadership in Organizations questionnaire (ILO) which was used in previous research (Den Hartog, 1997). The ILO is based on several other questionnaires tapping this type of leadership, namely the MLQ-8Y (Bass and Avolio, 1990), the Value-Based Leadership Questionnaire (House *et al.*, 1998) and to a lesser extent the questionnaire used by Podsakoff *et al.* (1990). For a description of the development of the ILO and the complete pool of items, see Den Hartog (1997). As stated, in the current study, only part of the ILO was used.

### Inspirational leadership

Nine items reflecting inspirational leadership were selected from the larger pool of items gathered by Den Hartog (1997). A principal components analysis yielded two factors, explaining a total of 64.9 per cent of the variance. The items and their factor loadings are presented in Table 7.1. The first component combines five items referring to vision, intellectual stimulation and motivating and will be labelled 'Visioning' (Cronbach α is 0.83). The second combines four items referring to individualized consideration and team building and is labelled 'Individualized consideration' (Cronbach α is 0.85). Only one item loads more than 0.4 on both factors; the loading on the first factor is higher (and the difference between the loadings is >0.2), thus the item is retained in the first factor.

### Performance monitoring

Seven items were used to assess performance monitoring (or management-by-exception). Examples are 'would indicate disapproval if I performed at

*Table 7.1    Factor loadings of the inspirational leadership items*

| Inspirational leadership | Factor 1: visioning | Factor 2: consideration |
| --- | --- | --- |
| 1. Articulates a vision of future opportunities . . . | 0.77 | |
| 2. Paints an exciting picture of the future of our unit/organization . . . | 0.82 | |
| 3. Makes me enthusiastic about my work assignments . . . | 0.68 | 0.41 |
| 4. Challenges me to think of old problems in new ways . . . | 0.66 | |
| 5. Has ideas that forced me to rethink some things that I have never questioned before | 0.70 | |
| 6. Looks out for my personal welfare . . . | | 0.78 |
| 7. Listens to my concerns . . . | | 0.84 |
| 8. Gets the group to work together for the same goal . . . | | 0.68 |
| 9. Shows confidence in my ability to contribute to the goals of the organization/unit . . . | | 0.84 |

*Note:*    Only loadings greater than 0.4 are printed.

a low level', 'points it out to me when my work is not up to par' and 'focuses attention on errors I make'. Cronbach $\alpha$ is 0.88.

**Contingent reward**

Four items were used to assess contingent reward behaviour. A sample item is 'tells me what to do to be rewarded for my efforts'. Cronbach $\alpha$ is 0.82.

**Integrity and fairness**

Twelve items referred to integrity and fairness on the part of the leader. A principal components analysis shows that three factors with an eigen value greater than 1 were found. The first two describe integrity and the third (a lack of) fairness. The first combines the positively worded items referring to ethical integrity and trustworthiness. The second factor combines the (recoded) negatively worded items, originally referring to a leader's manipulating behaviour, favouritism and a lack of integrity. The first will be labelled trustworthiness, the second integrity. Table 7.2 lists the items and shows their factor loadings. The three factors explain a total of 60.5 per cent of the variance. Cronbach $\alpha$ for the three scales were 0.85 for trustworthiness (five items), 0.71 for integrity (five items) and 0.70 for fairness (two items). One item loads greater than 0.4 on two factors. Again, as the difference between the loadings is sufficient, the item is retained.

*Table 7.2   Factor loadings of the integrity and trustworthiness items*

| | Factor 1: trustworthiness | Factor 2: integrity | Factor 3: fairness |
|---|---|---|---|
| 1.* Does not behave in a manner that is consistent with the values he/she expresses . . . | | 0.78 | |
| 2.* Manipulates subordinates . . . | | 0.50 | |
| 3.* Holds me responsible for things that are not my fault . . . | | | 0.86 |
| 4.* Clearly has favourites among subordinates . . . | | 0.54 | |
| 5.* Does not take things I propose seriously . . . | | 0.71 | |
| 6.* Holds me accountable for work I have no control over . . . | | | 0.82 |
| 7. He/she does what he/she says . . . | 0.76 | | |
| 8. Meets his/her obligations . . . | 0.75 | | |
| 9. Follows a definite moral code . . . | 0.80 | | |
| 10. Makes sure that his/her actions are always ethical . . . | 0.78 | | |
| 11. Is trustworthy (reliable) . . . | 0.68 | 0.43 | |
| 12.* Acts without considering my feelings . . . | | 0.66 | |

Note:   * Reverse coded items; only loadings greater than 0.4 are printed.

**Trust in the leader**

Two items were used to assess subordinates' faith and confidence in their focal leader, namely 'I have complete confidence in him/her' and 'I am ready to trust him/her to overcome any obstacle'. Cronbach $\alpha$ is 0.82.

**Trust in management and co-workers**

The interpersonal trust scales used in this study were translated: back-translated from Cook and Wall (1980). Six items assess trust in colleagues ($\alpha = 0.85$) and six assess trust in management ($\alpha = 0.87$) on a six-point scale. Sample items are 'One can trust management's ability to make the right decisions regarding the future of our organization' and 'I can rely on my co-workers to help me if necessary'.

**Analyses**

First, the pattern of correlations was calculated. Also the question whether leadership directly affects trust in generalized others or whether this relationship is mediated by trust in the focal leader and/or the variables describing leader integrity is answered using regression analyses. Baron and Kenny (1986) argue that mediation is demonstrated if three requirements are met. First, the independent variable (leadership) and the proposed mediators (trust in the focal leader, integrity) must each be significantly related to the dependent variable (that is, trust in management/colleagues) when considered separately. The second requirement for mediation states that the independent variable (leadership) should be significantly related to the proposed mediators (trust/integrity). The third requirement is that, when the dependent variable is regressed on both the independent variable and the mediator, the effect of the independent variable is less than when it is entered separately.

## RESULTS

Table 7.3 presents the scale means and intercorrelations between the scales used in this study. The first point of interest is the relationship between integrity and trust in the focal leader. As can be seen in the table, trust in the leader (measured as having faith and confidence in the leader) is significantly positively related to leader integrity (0.54), fairness (0.30) and trustworthiness (0.65).

Regression analyses show that these three integrity factors explained 48 per cent of the variance in trust in the leader. Both integrity and trustworthiness explain unique variance, fairness does not. Their respective standardized beta weights are 0.28\**, 0.51\** and 0.02. As stated, the question whether trust in the leader mediates the relationship between leader behaviour and trust in generalized others is of interest here. To meet the first requirement for mediation as described above, both the leadership variables and the mediators (trust in the leader/integrity) should be significantly related to trust in management and colleagues. Table 7.3 shows that trust in the leader is significantly positively related to trust in management (0.55) as well as trust in colleagues (0.27). As one would expect, the latter relationship is less strong. Table 7.3 also shows that the integrity variables (integrity, trustworthiness, fairness) are significantly positively related to trust in management (0.46, 0.45 and 0.32, respectively) and (again somewhat less so) to trust in colleagues (0.39, 0.26 and 0.18, respectively). Also Table 7.3 shows that both scales tapping inspirational leadership are significantly positively related to both trust in management (0.45 for visioning and 0.57 for individualized consideration) and trust in colleagues (0.22 for visioning and 0.29 for individualized consideration). The relationships are also (but barely) significant for performance monitoring (0.18 with trust

*Table 7.3  Scale means and intercorrelations between the scales*

|  | Mean | 1 | 2 | 3 | 4 | 5 | 6 | 7 | 8 | 9 | 10 |
|---|---|---|---|---|---|---|---|---|---|---|---|
| 1. Visioning | 2.42 | 1.00 | | | | | | | | | |
| 2. Consideration | 3.18 | 0.61** | 1.00 | | | | | | | | |
| 3. Contingent rew. | 1.65 | 0.56** | 0.45** | 1.00 | | | | | | | |
| 4. Perf. monitoring | 2.76 | 0.32** | 0.32** | 0.32** | 1.00 | | | | | | |
| 5. Trustworthiness | 3.49 | 0.55** | 0.71** | 0.29** | 0.41** | 1.00 | | | | | |
| 6. Integrity | 3.61 | 0.31** | 0.61** | 0.13 | 0.16* | 0.49** | 1.00 | | | | |
| 7. Fairness | 4.37 | 0.21** | 0.39** | 0.08 | 0.02 | 0.34** | 0.39** | 1.00 | | | |
| 8. Trust in leader | 2.94 | 0.54** | 0.70** | 0.39** | 0.42** | 0.65** | 0.54** | 0.30** | 1.00 | | |
| 9. Trust in mmt | 3.55 | 0.48** | 0.57** | 0.34** | 0.18* | 0.45** | 0.46** | 0.32** | 0.55** | 1.00 | |
| 10. Trust in coll. | 4.37 | 0.22** | 0.29** | 0.10 | 0.15* | 0.26** | 0.39** | 18* | 0.27** | 0.39** | 1.00 |

*Note:*  * Signif. <0.05. ** signif. <0.01

138

in management and 0.15 with trust in colleagues). As expected, contingent reward is significantly related to trust in management (0.34) but not to trust in colleagues (0.10). As shown here, the leadership skills (inspirational leadership as well as the transactional scales) all correlate positively with trust in management and all but one with trust in colleagues. The integrity variables as well as trust in the leader are also significantly positively related to both forms of trust in generalized others. Thus all relationships except the relationship between contingent reward and trust in colleagues meet Baron and Kenny's (1986) first requirement for mediation.

The second requirement states that the independent variable should be related to the proposed mediators. Here the relationship between the different leadership variables and trust in the leader and integrity are of interest. Table 7.3 shows that the two inspirational scales correlate positively with the mediators. The relationships are higher for individualized consideration than for visioning. Consideration is very highly positively related to the confidence/faith measure of trust in the leader (0.70), visioning slightly less so (0.54). Consideration is also related more strongly than visioning to integrity (0.61 versus 0.31), trustworthiness (0.71 versus 0.55) and to fairness (0.39 versus 0.21).

Finally, the third requirement is that, when the dependent variable (trust in management/colleagues) is regressed on both the independent variable (leadership) and mediator (trust in the leader/integrity), the effect of the independent variable is less than when it is entered separately. The regression analyses presented in Table 7.4 show such analysis for trust in the focal leader as a possible mediator and Table 7.5 for the integrity variables as possible mediators of the relationship between leadership and trust in generalized others. These analyses show that the different dimensions of trust in the leader do not fully mediate the relationship between inspirational leadership and generalized trust in others. Only partial rather than full mediation is found (that is, lower beta weights for leadership in the second step of the analysis, rather than non-significant weights). The leadership variables explain 34 per cent of the variance in trust in management (unadjusted; 33 per cent adjusted); adding trust in the leader into the regression equation increases the explained variance to 38 per cent (35 per cent adjusted). Adding faith, trustworthiness and integrity in the second step also increases the explained variance from 33 per cent to 38 per cent (36 per cent adjusted). These increases are all significant.

When the analysis includes inspirational leadership as a predictor (especially the individualized consideration factor), the effect of transactional leadership is not significant. However, when analysed separately, transactional leadership behaviours (that is, performance monitoring and contingent reward) explain 11 per cent of the variance in trust in management,

*Table 7.4    Hierarchical regression regarding the impact of leadership and trust in the leader on trust in generalized others*

| Dependent variables | Trust in management | | Trust in colleagues | |
|---|---|---|---|---|
| Added in step 1: | Step 1 | Step 2 | Step 1 | Step 2 |
| Contingent reward | β   0.05 | β   0.05 | β −0.11 | β −0.11 |
| Performance monitoring | β −0.03 | β −0.09 | β   0.07 | β   0.05 |
| Visioning | β   0.12 | β   0.08 | β   0.09 | β   0.08 |
| Individualized consideration | β   0.48** | β   0.33** | β   0.26** | β   0.21* |
| Added in step 2: | | | | |
| Trust in the leader | | β   0.29** | | β   0.09 |
| Adjusted (unadjusted) $R^2$ | 0.33 (0.34) | 0.35 (0.38) | 0.08 (0.10) | 0.08 (0.10) |
| F | 22.3** | 21.0** | 5.09** | 4.24** |
| Change in unadjusted $R^2$ | | 0.038 | | 0.00 |
| F | | 10.62** | | 0.82 |

*Note:*   * Signif. $\leq 0.05$; ** signif. $\leq 0.01$ (1-tailed); fully standardized (β) regression coefficients.

contingent reward being the significant predictor (as expected). Adding trust in the leader increases the explained variance to 31 per cent. Again, partial rather than full mediation is found. The same goes for integrity, trustworthiness and fairness as mediators.

For trust in colleagues, the two factors of inspirational leadership combined explain 9.4 per cent of the variance. Adding faith, trustworthiness and integrity in the second step increases the explained variance from to 10.3 per cent and, if in a third step trust in the leader is entered into the regression equation, the explained variance in trust in management increases slightly to 10.6 per cent. These two increases are not significant. Transactional leadership (that is, performance monitoring and contingent reward) as predictors of trust in colleagues only explain 2 per cent of the variance in such trust; this is not significant. Thus transactional leadership is not a significant predictor of trust in colleagues. In this study, the consideration factor of inspirational leadership acts as a predictor of trust in colleagues.

## DISCUSSION

The current study focuses on a specific area of interpersonal trust within organizations, namely how the behaviour of and relationship with one's supervisor affects trust in that supervisor as well as generalized others. In

*Table 7.5    Hierarchical regression predicting the impact of leadership, fairness, trustworthiness and integrity on trust in generalized others*

| Dependent variables | Trust in management | | Trust in colleagues | |
|---|---|---|---|---|
| | Step 1 | Step 2 | Step 1 | Step 2 |
| Added in step 1: | | | | |
| Contingent reward | β   0.06 | β   0.10 | β −0.09 | β −0.07 |
| Performance monitoring | β −0.04 | β   0.07 | β   0.05 | β   0.05 |
| Visioning | β   0.12 | β   0.12 | β   0.08 | β   0.07 |
| Individualized consideration | β   0.49** | β   0.31** | β   0.27** | β   0.20 |
| Added in step 2: | | | | |
| Integrity | | β   0.20* | | β   0.01 |
| Fairness | | β   0.09 | | β   0.08 |
| Trustworthiness | | β −0.01 | | β   0.05 |
| Adjusted (unadjusted) $R^2$ | 0.33 (0.34) | 0.36 (0.38) | 0.08(0.10) | 0.07 (0.10) |
| F | 22.7** | 14.8** | 5.04** | 3.06** |
| Change in unadjusted $R^2$ | | 0.034 | | 0.01 |
| F | | 3.15* | | 0.47 |

*Note:*    * Signif. $\leq 0.05$; ** signif. $\leq .001$ (1-tailed); fully standardized (β) regression coefficients.

the literature, trust is assumed to be very important for inspirational leadership (for example, Bennis and Nanus, 1985). The results of this study support this notion. As was seen above, both scales measuring inspirational leadership were positively related to the different forms of trust measured in this study. In previous studies, trust in the leader was operationalized as a combination of elements such as faith and confidence in the leader as well as leader fairness and integrity. This study shows there are differences between these elements that deserve further attention. Similarly, in some studies faith and confidence in the leader have been measured as part of transformational leadership (for example, Bass and Avolio, 1990). Although the relationship between this type of leadership and trust is high, items tapping trust in the leader are measures of outcomes rather than leader behaviour, which supports separating the two. This seems especially true given the results found here that the relationship between trust and some aspects of inspirational leadership (individualized consideration and team building) is stronger than between trust and other such aspects (visioning, intellectual stimulation), even though these inspirational leader behaviours are found to be highly correlated.

The inspirational leadership scale tapping individualized consideration and team building was very strongly related to trust in the leader, integrity and trustworthiness and somewhat less so to fairness. The relationships found here were slightly less strong (but still substantial) for the scale tapping the visioning, intellectually stimulating, motivating side of inspirational leadership. Given the nature of the behaviours these factors capture, it does not seem surprising that consideration is linked most strongly to trust. Other important outcomes such as organizational commitment or performance may be more strongly related to the visioning component. Another factor that may be of influence in the current study is that the leaders who were rated were mostly first-line supervisors and lower-level managers. Research shows that at lower levels being sensitive to subordinate needs and team building are seen as more important for leaders than for top managers and, conversely, visioning is seen as more important for top-level than for lower-level managers (Den Hartog *et al.*, 1999). An interesting question for future research is therefore how these relationships would play out at higher levels in the organization. Visioning may be more important for trust than consideration at such higher levels.

In line with previous research, the relationships found in this study between trust in the focal leader and transactional leadership are less strong than those involving inspirational leadership. Both transactional scales (contingent reward) were related to trust in the leader and trustworthiness of the leader, but barely or not at all to fairness and integrity. Similarly, as expected, both inspirational leadership scales were positively related to trust in management and colleagues (again, the relationships were stronger for individualized consideration) and these relationships were less strong for transactional leadership.

The mediation hypothesis was not supported in this study. The relationship between inspirational leadership and trust in generalized others was only very partially (and not strongly or fully) mediated by the different aspects of trust in the leader that were measured. The same goes for transactional leadership. In other words, leadership explains unique variance in such trust in management and colleagues over and above the variance explained by trust in the leader. Again, looking at the separate components of leadership, the relationships are stronger for inspirational leadership than for transactional leadership. In even more detail, the individualized consideration component is more important as a predictor of trust than the visioning component, and contingent reward more than performance monitoring.

The major limitation of this study lies in the cross-sectional nature of the research design which prevents testing for causal relationships. Thus, although the different trust variables are treated here mostly as outcomes of leadership, the results of this study do not preclude reverse causation. For instance, trusting individuals may perceive their leader as more inspirational. More research into leadership development and the nature of cause–effect relationships is necessary.

Also the relationship between inspirational leadership and commitment has been characterized as a 'double edged sword' (Shamir *et al.*, 1993). This also holds for the relationship between inspirational leadership and trust in management. When a leader's vision is in line with organizational goals and he or she is seen as *representative* of management, inspirational leadership is likely to increase trust in management. However, when such a vision goes *against* organizational values or strategies, such trust in management may well decrease. Thus, conceptually, such inspirational leadership may result in either increased or decreased trust in management. In organizations, however, the latter process is constrained by selection and performance evaluation processes (certain types of people are hired and dissonant managers can be replaced or fired). Also, especially at lower levels, leaders will often not have enough discretion or resources to pursue visions that are highly discrepant with basic organizational goals or those proposed by higher management.

A final limitation of this study is that it is based on single source survey data. Both leader behaviour and trust were measured through the eyes of subordinates using questionnaires. More research using multiple methods and sources of data is needed. The relatively high intercorrelations between the leadership scales that were found here are also commonly found in other studies using these types of questionnaires. Development of more sophisticated questionnaires or even entirely different methods to assess these types of leadership is desirable.

The results of this study seem to underline the importance of trust-building processes in leader–follower relationships. As described above, the development of trust in the workplace is a complicated process, involving different stages and bases (Lewicki and Bunker 1996; Sheppard and Tuchinsky, 1996). Longitudinal research on the trust development process and the role of leadership in this process is needed.

The results also suggest several other interesting future studies on leadership and trust. Besides the possible stages of development in trust in the leader and generalized others and the relationship between leadership styles and forms of trust (possible consequences of) leaders' violations of subordinates' trust also seem like an important area for future research. Although much research to date focuses on the positive influence leaders may have on organizational as well as individual outcomes, anecdotal evidence and popular opinion polls suggest employees are very often not happy with their supervisors and the way they are treated by them. Similarly, leaders may trust but also distrust their subordinates. The role of violations of trust by both leaders and followers, and when these result in distrust between them, have not received much attention in the leadership field. However, the literature on the violation of the psychological contract (for example, Robinson, 1996) and interactional justice (for example, Colquitt, 2001) may help theory building in this area. As a result of unethical or unfair treatment by a supervisor, one would expect that trust in that supervisor decreases (especially when the violations of trust are grave or repeated). As a result, trust in management and cooperative attitudes towards the organization may also decrease (and cynicism and hostility may increase). Such violations and distrust may be more likely to spill over (from trust in the focal leader to more general attitudes towards management and the organization) under certain circumstances. For instance, this seems more likely when employees not only feel badly or unfairly treated in a grave or prolonged manner, but also feel that this is (or should be) known to others (especially those in managerial positions) and that these others take insufficient measures to correct the situation. More theoretical and empirical work is needed to integrate the knowledge gained in the different streams of literature and to develop further insight in this area.

The current study aimed to explore several aspects of the relationship between leadership and trust. The dynamics of trust and distrust between leaders and followers and the antecedents and consequences of such trust and distrust seem a worthwhile area for further exploration, and increased insight in this area will yield both scientific and practical merit.

## REFERENCES

Baron, R.M. and D.A. Kenny (1986), 'The moderator–mediator variable distinction in social psychological research: conceptual, strategic and statistical considerations', *Journal of Personality and Social Psychology*, **51**, 1173–82.

Bass, B.M. (1985), *Leadership and Performance Beyond Expectations*, New York: Free Press.

Bass, B.M. (1997), 'Does the transactional–transformational paradigm transcend organizational and national boundaries?', *American Psychologist*, **52**(2), 130–39.

Bass, B.M. and B.J. Avolio (1990), 'The implications of transactional and transformational leadership for individual, team, and organizational development', *Research in Organizational Change and Development*, **4**, 231–72.

Bennis, W.G. and B. Nanus (1985), *Leaders: The Strategies for Taking Charge*, New York: Harper Perennial.

Burns, J.M. (1978), *Leadership*, New York: Harper & Row.

Butler, J.K. (1991), 'Toward understanding and measuring trust: evolution of a conditions of trust inventory', *Journal of Management*, **17**, 643–63.

Butler, J.K. and R.S. Cantrell (1984), 'A behavioral decision theory approach to modelling dyadic trust in superiors and subordinates', *Psychological Reports*, **55**, 19–28.

Clegg, C.W. and T.D. Wall (1981), 'Notes on some new scales for measuring aspects of psychological well-being', *Journal of Occupational Psychology*, **52**, 221–28.

Colquitt, J.A. (2001), 'On the dimensionality of organizational justice: a construct validation of a measure', *Journal of Applied Psychology*, 386–99.

Cook, J.D. and T.D. Wall (1980), 'New work attitude measures of trust, organizational commitment and personal need non-fulfilment', *Journal of Occupational Psychology*, **53**, 39–52.

Craig, S.B. and S.B. Gustafson (1998), 'Perceived leader integrity: an instrument for assessing employee perceptions of leader integrity', *Leadership Quarterly*, **9**, 127–45.

Creed, W.E.D. and R.E. Miles (1996), 'Trust in organizations: a conceptual framework linking organizational forms, managerial philosophies and the opportunity costs of controls', in R.M. Kramer and T.R. Tyler (eds), *Trust in Organizations: Frontiers of Theory and Research,* London: Sage, pp. 16–38.

Den Hartog, D.N. (1997), '*Inspirational leadership*', VU doctoral dissertation, KLI-dissertation series, 1997-nr 2, Enschede: Ipskamp.

Den Hartog, D.N. and P.L. Koopman (2001), 'Leadership in organizations', in N. Anderson, D.S. Ones, H. Kepir-Sinangil and C. Viswesvaran (eds), *International Handbook of Industrial, Work and Organizational Psychology*, vol. 2, London: Sage, pp. 166–87.

Den Hartog, D.N., J.J. Van Muijen and P.L. Koopman (1997), 'Transactional versus transformational leadership: an analysis of the MLQ', *Journal of Occupational and Organizational Psychology*, **70**(1), 19–34.

Den Hartog, D.N., R.J. House, P. Hanges, P. Dorfman, Ruiz-Quintanilla, A., and 159 co-authors (1999), 'Culture-specific and cross-culturally endorsed implicit leadership theories: are attributes of charismatic/transformational leadership universally endorsed?', *Leadership Quarterly*, **10**(2), 219–56.

Fiol, C.M., D. Harris and R.J. House (1999), 'Charismatic leadership: strategies for effecting social change', *Leadership Quarterly*, 449–82.

Fuller, J.B., C.P. Patterson, K. Hester and D.Y. Stringer (1996), 'A quantitative review of research on charismatic leadership', *Psychological Reports*, **78**, 271–87.

Gambetta, D. (ed.) (1988), *Trust: Making and Breaking Cooperative Relationships*, New York: Basil Blackwell.

Hater, J.J. and B.M. Bass (1988), 'Superiors' evaluations and subordinates' perceptions of transformational and transactional leadership', *Journal of Applied Psychology*, **73**, 695–702.

Hosmer, L.T. (1995), 'Trust: the connecting link between organizational theory and philosophical ethics', *Academy of Management Review*, **20**, 379–403.

House, R.J. (1977), 'A 1976 theory of charismatic leadership', in J.G. Hunt and L.L. Larson (eds), *Leadership: the Cutting Edge*, Carbondale, IL: Southern Illinois University Press, pp. 189–204.

House, R.J. (1996), 'Path-goal theory of leadership: lessons, legacy and a reformulated theory', *Leadership Quarterly,* **7**(3), 323–52.

House, R.J. and P.M. Podsakoff (1994), 'Leadership effectiveness: past perspectives and future directions for research', in J. Greenberg (ed.), *Organizational Behavior: The State of the Science,* pp. 45–82.

House, R.J., A. Delbecq and T.W. Taris (1998), 'Value based leadership: an integrated theory and an empirical test', working paper.

House, R.J., J. Woycke and E.M. Fodor (1988), 'Charismatic and noncharismatic leaders: differences in behavior and effectiveness', in J.A. Conger and R.N.

Kanungo (eds), *Charismatic Leadership: The Elusive Factor in Organizational Effectiveness*, San Francisco: Jossey-Bass, pp. 98–121.

Howell, J.M. and B.J. Avolio (1993), 'Transformational leadership, transactional leadership, locus of control and support for innovation', *Journal of Applied Psychology*, **78**, 891–902.

Kirkpatrick, S.A. and E.A. Locke (1996), 'Direct and indirect effects of three core charismatic leadership components on performance and attitudes', *Journal of Applied Psychology*, **81**(1), 36–51.

Kramer, R.M. (1993), 'Cooperation and organizational identification', in K. Murnighan (ed.), *Social Psychology in Organizations: Advances in Theory and Research*, Englewood Cliffs, NJ: Prentice-Hall.

Lewicki, R.J. and B.B. Bunker (1996), 'Developing and maintaining trust in work relationships', in R.M. Kramer and T.R. Tyler (eds), *Trust in Organizations: Frontiers of Theory and Research*, London: Sage, pp. 114–39.

Lowe, K.B., K. Galen Kroek and N. Sivasubramaniam (1996), 'Effectiveness correlates of transformational and transactional leadership: a meta-analytic review', *Leadership Quarterly,* **7**, 385–425.

Mayer, R.C., J.H. Davis and F.D. Schoorman (1995), 'An integrative model of organizational trust', *Academy of Management Review*, **20**, 709–34.

Misztal, B.A. (1996), *Trust in Modern Societies*, Cambridge: Polity Press.

Podsakoff, P.M., W.D. Todor and R. Skov (1982), 'Effects of leader contingent and non-contingent reward and punishment behaviors on subordinate performance and satisfaction', *Academy of Management Journal*, **25**, 810–21.

Podsakoff, P.M., S.B. MacKenzie, R.H. Moorman and R. Fetter (1990), 'Transformational leader behaviors and their effects on followers' trust in leader, satisfaction and organizational citizenship behaviors', *Leadership Quarterly*, **1**(2), 107–42.

Robinson, S.L. (1996), 'Trust and breach of the psychological contract', *Administrative Science Quarterly*, **41**, 574–99.

Shamir, B., R.J. House and M.B. Arthur (1993), 'The motivational effects of charismatic leadership: a self-concept based theory', *Organization Science*, **4**, 1–17.

Shapiro, D., B.H. Sheppard and L. Cheraskin (1992), 'Business on a handshake', *Negotiation Journal*, **8**, 365–77.

Sheppard, B.H. and M. Tuchinsky (1996), 'Micro-OB and the network organization', in R.M. Kramer and T.R. Tyler (eds), *Trust in Organizations: Frontiers of Theory and Research*, London: Sage.

Tichy, N.M. and M.A. Devanna (1990), *The Transformational Leader*, 2nd edn (1st edn 1986), New York: Wiley.

Williams, B. (1988), 'Formal structures and social reality', in D. Gambetta (ed.), *Trust: Making and Breaking Cooperative Relations*, New York: Basil Blackwell, pp. 3–13.

Yukl, G. (1998), *Leadership in Organizations*, 4th edn, Englewood Cliffs, NJ: Prentice-Hall.

# 8. Trust building inside the 'epistemic community': an investigation with an empirical case study

**Nathalie Lazaric**

## INTRODUCTION

Trust does not occur spontaneously inside organizations but is linked to individual and collective learning. It arises out of the need to determine whether mutual expectations regarding trust are fulfilled and is the outcome of direct interactions between the actors involved in the process (Luhmann, 1979; Lazaric and Lorenz, 1998; Moingeon and Edmonson, 1998; Sako, 1998). Trust, in this sense, is inherently linked to a process of risk taking, because learning is costly and uncertain and its success cannot be guaranteed a priori (see Bart Nooteboom, Chapter 2, this volume). Nevertheless, trust may be an important ingredient in any attempt to stabilize mutual expectations. It can also generate positive feedback and interpretations in a context of uncertainty as long as the individuals or organization in question are able to provide reliable and fair signals or organizational procedures.

We will illustrate this process with the aid of an extensive case study carried out over the period 1996–2000. The project revolved around a French company, Usinor, that had launched an important programme of knowledge capitalization for the steel industry. An 'epistemic community' was created as a result of this project in order to articulate and validate all practices the company felt might face extinction following the disruption of traditional knowledge transfer patterns which had hitherto been carried out primarily via an apprenticeship system. The changes introduced by the programme, therefore, had an impact on the social status and prestige of many of the company's practitioners, notably the blast furnace experts whose practices had to be reviewed following the disclosure of their know-how. Securing the cooperation of the company's employees was extremely difficult in the circumstances and depended to a very large extent on the discretion of practitioners, but also on the implicit signals the hierarchy had put out to stabilize mutual expectations.

The first section of this chapter will deal with the problem of trust in the 'epistemic community' at a conceptual level. The second section will introduce the sectoral and historical contexts which formed the background to the case study, in order to identify the background to the trust-building exercise. The third section will deal with Usinor's Sachem project in more detail as this will help identify the different stages of the process of knowledge articulation and codification. The fourth section will explain how cooperation can emerge in a context of drastic change, and will also show how some organizational rules appear to have played a crucial role in the trust-building exercise (notably the validation rule). The fifth section will examine the role a training policy can have in a context of cooperation between employers and employees. Finally, we will derive some general conclusions from this case study and draw out the elements that emerge as crucial to the establishment of trust and collective learning.

## THE 'EPISTEMIC COMMUNITY' AND TRUST BUILDING: SOME THEORETICAL AND ANALYTICAL DEBATES

We begin this section by examining the notion of an 'epistemic community' in order to understand the reasons for which it played a crucial role in the process of trust building within the Usinor group. In this context, the role assumed by this community is quite distinct from the traditional 'communities of practice' described by Brown and Duguit (1991) and Wenger (1998). The 'epistemic community's' cognitive function is not limited to the exchange of tacit knowledge but extends to the validation and dissemination of this knowledge to the group of practitioners. It is this fundamental difference between knowledge exchange and knowledge validation that distinguishes a 'community of practice' from an 'epistemic community'. In fact,

> an 'epistemic community' is a network of professionals with recognized expertise and competence in a particular domain and an authoritative claim to policy-relevant knowledge within domain or issue-area (...) This network has (1) a shared set of normative and principled beliefs, which provide a value-based rationale for the social action of community members; (2) shared causal beliefs, which are derived from their analysis of practices leading or contributing to a central set of problems in their domain and which then serve as the basis for elucidating the multiple linkages between possible actions and desired outcomes; (3) shared notions of validity – that is, intersubjective, internally defined criteria for weighing and validating knowledge in the domain of their expertise; and (4) a common policy enterprise – that is, a set of common practices associated with a set of problems to which their professional competence is directed, presumably out of the conviction that human welfare will be enhanced as a consequence. (Haas, 1992, p. 3)

The 'epistemic community' has an important role to play as it has substantial authority and can therefore exercise significant pressure on any attempt to validate or invalidate a particular practice within the company. Such pressure is present at different levels: at an organizational level it can affect the selection of particular practices by reviewing them and acknowledging them as relevant to both the company and its organizational memory; on the other hand the pressure is also evident at an individual level, as this community can play a role in the selection of the shared beliefs and values that evolve through the use of a particular technology and by generating a new *episteme* inside the company, which can eventually lead to an entirely new cognitive representation of the technology itself. This process of selection is extremely delicate and cannot be implemented in the absence of trust. As Steinmueller (2000) recognizes:

> The availability of collective memory within an 'epistemic community' also allows the reduction of remembering solutions to problems that have been previously discovered and documented. This permits a reduction in effort devoted to re-invention. For such gains to be realised the codification of solutions need not to be complete. Instead the purpose of the collective memory is to 'signal' the availability of the previous work and a solution that might arise again within the community. The gains from this process are both collective and individual and therefore are incentive compatible with efforts to contribute to the group memory project. *Note that it is important for the group to have some degree of trust and mutual regard for such system to work. Otherwise individuals will not regard the 'solutions' or 'ideas' of others to be worth the time it takes to become aware of and evaluate them in a new context.* (pp. 19–20, emphasis added.)

Trust building here comes into play at different levels. First, trust is a fundamental prerequisite for free discussion. This point is far from trivial in the context of the steel industry, where knowledge tends to be local and distributed between different plants and where the causal mechanisms underlying different technical events are not readily identifiable. The working of a blast furnace is a case in point: the knowledge required for its operation has to be acquired empirically as scientific models to date have failed to provide other than a poor theoretical understanding of its operation (Allen, 1983; Rosenberg, 1982; Steiler and Schneider, 1994). As a result of this kind of problem, any attempt to extract and then articulate the relevant empirical knowledge requires lengthy interactions with the blast furnace experts and usually involves an extensive study of their respective cognitive representations. Discussions on and exchanges of tacit knowledge are, however, time-consuming. As a result, in the absence of a truly motivated workforce, any such process has a very small chance of succeeding. At the same time, such discussions are necessary, given the inevitable disruption produced by the introduction of any new technological support mechanism for the memorization of knowledge (for a general discussion of this point, see Frédérique Six, Chapter 10 this volume). The disruption is caused by the change imposed on the habitual expectations formed by the workers when carrying out their daily tasks. In short, the introduction of an expert system changes routine behaviour and imposes a process of learning on practitioners who have to learn to deal with the new and therefore more uncertain environment.

Secondly, any process of articulation and codification inevitably results in an extraction of knowledge that goes well beyond the remit of the preliminary exchange. Knowledge is defined here as being 'articulated' when the knowledge of a person or an organization has been made explicit by means of natural language. It follows that 'articulable knowledge' is any knowledge that can be rendered explicit through ordinary language. Language in this context refers to a system of signs and conventions that allows the reproduction and storage of knowledge in such a way that it can be communicated to and transferred between individuals.[1] Articulation is more concerned with the stage of 'explicitation' with natural language and metaphors (see Nonaka and Tackeuchi, 1995 for more details) and codification is more oriented through the diffusion of knowledge via technical tools (see also Winter, 1987; Mangolte, 1997; Divry and Lazaric, 1998; Lazaric and Mangolte, 1999). Articulation, however, is distinct from knowledge codification[2] and may be considered as a product of this preliminary step:

> Knowledge codification, in fact, is a more restrictive notion with respect to knowledge articulation processes. The latter is required in order to achieve the former, while the opposite is obviously not true. Actually the fact that in most cases articulated knowledge is never codified bears witness to the argument of increasing costs to be incurred when scaling up the effort from simply sharing individual experience to developing written reports, manuals or process-specific tools. (Zollo and Winter, 2001, p. 17)

A company's members can feel threatened by a process of articulation, as they may sense that, following its implementation, their vulnerability vis-à-vis the company's hierarchy is likely to increase. In fact, any extraction of knowledge implies a process of knowledge disclosure on behalf of the different 'communities of practice'. This sense of vulnerability and uncertainty is enhanced by the loss of control over well-established routines and may affect the population of blast furnace experts to different degrees. Moreover, this kind of uncertainty may be associated with different parts of the process and is directly related to the problems of 'competence trust'[3] (will the blast furnace experts be able to solve new problems with this new tool?) and 'goodwill trust'/'intentional trust' (what are the real motives of the management underlying this knowledge management programme?).

Thirdly, employees must be both motivated and confident in the results of the process in order to build a shared representation of the technology. Indeed, the maintenance of collective knowledge through the articulation and memorization of 'best practices' is not neutral because the creation of specific assets renders the product of human experience more 'manageable' by affecting the selection of routines and practices that are stored in the organization's memory: 'The degree of articulation of anything that is "articulable" is partially controllable' (Winter, 1987, p. 174). This means that any attempt to create an 'epistemic community' through the establishment of a centralized organizational memory may be difficult to implement successfully because the process might be perceived by a company's members as a purely authoritarian attempt to eliminate part of the existing expertise. Since the process involves the articulation of knowledge accumulated through dealing with unanticipated contingencies, it is not clear how to establish a priori rules which can ensure that the actions of both the hierarchy and the 'epistemic community' will be perceived as being fair by the company's members. Given that the sources of the uncertainty associated with this process are varied and that the uncertainty (whether technical, human or organizational) itself is very high, it is as likely that the process will result in a virtuous circle of trust building as it is that it will embark on a vicious circle of distrust, and no one can predict the outcome of such a collective experiment.

In fact, the prevailing social climate may produce a series of minor events and/or collective rules that can work towards enabling or hindering the process of trust building (Lazaric and Lorenz, 1998). The interpretation of any event associated with articulation, although highly subjective and personal, can prove crucial in paving the way towards the acceptance of organizational change. Trust is also crucial to this process because the context is one of bounded rationality, where the contracts between the employers and the employees are incomplete and where the nature of industrial relations and the space for cooperation offer different courses of action for each of the actors involved. In this context, the hierarchy can opt for a monitoring solution, the employees for either a passive or an innovative one (for more details on the motivation of individuals, see Leibenstein, 1987; and for examples of these different situations see Lazaric and Denis, 2001): a careful identification of the key actors in this process is essential for its success. Mansell and Steinmueller (2000) emphasize that, in a knowledge-based economy, the nature of skills has to be reconsidered and can lead to a 'creative destruction' that relocates the interactions between individuals and shared community perceptions of social honour:

these trends are being experienced in the forms of labour adjustments and skill competency mismatches; fears of displacement and new patterns and categories of adjustment and adaptation; new languages to describe interactions with technology; and new occupational definitions for who does what and why. They entail new strategies of management control and reinforcement of hierarchy, new rules of governance and use of old technologies, and new policies for organizations to provide some basis for managing widespread changes in how, why, and when social groups communicate with each other. The derivation of social status may, as Neice (1996) suggests, be an emergent property of this complex pattern of interaction and change. A new vocabulary may be needed to describe this process of alignment, coincidence, and complementary that collectively are coming to define social status. (Mansell and Steinmueller, 2000, p. 58)

Fourthly, the way in which the expert system itself is built is also crucial, as it can either be seen as an inert 'black box' used to encode selected practices or as an 'open box' with which to encode expertise and update it. The way in which users relate to the technology affects the degree to which they are likely to accept the diffusion of their private knowledge (itself a part of local knowledge) and will cooperate in updating the system. However, this relation can also be affected by the organization itself and the communication rules that prevail within it. Given that articulation and codification can never be complete, because they are based on live expertise that cannot be entirely codified, the 'epistemic community' plays an important role in determining certain 'reliable beliefs' but also in preventing knowledge fossilization. The way in which articulation is perceived at the beginning of the process can lead to a number of minor events that increase in importance during the maintenance stage – after all, any notion of an update implies the successful completion of an original articulation stage. Finally, the temptation to distrust the new tool might be strong as the expert system may modify a part of prior beliefs about technology. Furthermore, a lack of confidence in the structure and implementation of the system in question can prevent it from running smoothly. In practice, the expert system itself can affect the ways in which operators and blast furnace experts will interact with the technology. Before consenting to a review of prior beliefs, workers must be sufficiently confident about the hierarchy's motives and a new cognitive representation must prevail in order to avoid the potential disaster that can follow widespread lack of cooperation and distrust (for some examples of failures in expert system implementations, see de Terssac, 1997).

# THE HISTORICAL AND SECTORAL CONTEXT OF THE CASE STUDY

Most companies in the steel industry are very keen to improve the workings of the blast furnace. They are therefore attracted by the idea of using technical tools, such as an expert system, that are capable of transforming the knowledge stored in the company, including its past repertoires, and which thus raise questions about organizational memory, the knowledge holders and knowledge storage.

The need to articulate and codify Usinor's know-how emerged at the end of the 1970s, a time of serious economic difficulty for the French steel industry. Shrinking markets and the emergence of new competitors made substantive improvements in productivity and product quality crucial to the survival of the industry. The steel sector in both France and other countries faced a prolonged period of structural excess capacity during the first half of the 1980s. This led to a process of company selection in the first instance and later to a series of mergers amongst the survivors aimed at strengthening existing industrial positions. In this context, Usinor absorbed a large number of existing French steel companies with the help of the French government. So, for example, Sacilor, an old rival, became part of the group in 1986. The French government, Usinor's majority shareholder at the time, progressively disengaged from the company (a process that was concluded in 1995), thus enabling Usinor to absorb foreign companies, such as Arvedi in 1998, and Ekosthal and Cockeril in 1999.

By the mid-1980s, the group's main problem was to create an effective organizational entity and to reach a degree of mutual understanding between experts with different practices and routines. Decentralized plants and forms of knowledge associated with the experience of working with individual blast furnaces led to the continued existence of different ways of understanding the same problem. Although both articulated and tacit knowledge were present, they were distributed across the various plants and different communities of practice coexisted. Consequently, the company incorporated different dialects and, with them, different beliefs and know-how about the blast furnace. Each plant depended on the personal vision of its blast furnace experts, the authoritative figures that discussed, articulated, transmitted and validated knowledge. These experts were a lot more powerful than their hierarchical grade and status inside the plant warranted. As Godelier (1997) insists, Usinor relied on an internal market where credibility depended on length of service rather than seniority. The elders, in fact, were the repositories of the company's memory and were the only people capable of introducing younger employees into the company and providing them with 'on-the-job training'. Another crucial problem was the memorization of the company's knowledge in a context of rapidly declining manpower.

Overall, four major reasons prompted Usinor to articulate and codify its knowledge.

1.  It was necessary to create capabilities and articulated knowledge inside the group and to channel all local knowledge into a common project in order to create shared semantics between experts ('to be sure that we are talking about the same thing'). In other words, the company had to unify the different dialects present in the various 'communities of practice'.
2.  The company made 98000 employees redundant between 1977 and 1990 (mainly through a retirement policy). Few employees have been hired in recent years and the group is confronted with an ageing population (around 50 per cent of Usinor's employees will have retired by 2010). In this context, the need to save the collective knowledge is crucial, given that most of its human holders will disappear in the near future.
3.  It was necessary to improve the quality of the process by introducing real-time intervention, thus ensuring the rapid resolution of problems occurring during the early stages of metal fusion (the cost of guiding the blast furnace in a plant like Sollac represents 56 per cent of the total costs of steel production).
4.  Usinor's merger and acquisition activity also led to a concentration of R&D centres. For example, IRSID,[4] which was meant to carry out fundamental research for all French firms in the steel industry, became, in practice, an integrated Usinor R&D centre and a de facto private R&D centre. This large laboratory, which had wide-ranging expertise in artificial intelligence, played an active role in the implementation of the Sachem project.

## BUILDING AN 'EPISTEMIC COMMUNITY' IN USINOR: THE SACHEM PROJECT

The company began building its 'epistemic community' by carrying out a horizontal coordination exercise aimed at identifying the different ways in which the various communities of practice carried out similar tasks. The stage was concluded with the compilation of Xperdoc, which was put together during the articulation and codification phase by a small group of experts, knowledge engineers and technicians.

**Finding a Shared Vocabulary: Xperdoc Writing**

The tradition of memorizing long-standing practices in order to improve processes is not new in the steel industry. In France, many books provide descriptions of the empirical practices associated with the blast furnace (see Thierry, 1940). More recently, the need to articulate know-how has seen the light with Corbion's compilation of a kind of dictionary of the steel industry's long-evolving language during the 1980s, in an attempt to make it more explicit (Corbion, 1989).[5] In the case of Usinor, knowledge was articulated through the launch of 'Xperdoc' in 1989. This established a common word list for the creation of a shared vocabulary among blast furnace experts. Shared semantics were seen as the first step in the process of harmonizing different practices, beliefs and repertoires and were meant to constitute a common reference for the group. This 'handbook' was used by the experts and created an 'epistemic community', which, in turn, generated discussion and the mutual acknowledgment of different practices. 'Xperdoc' had the following objectives: (a) to bring the experts together by giving them the opportunity to meet ('Xperdoc' in this way gave them a chance to exchange views and discuss their practices), and (b) to establish an acknowledgment of different practices and help institute personal trust between experts. This latter point was far from trivial: the creation of a 'common reference' depended on a prior selection of 'best practices', which was difficult to implement. The company needed to establish a climate of trust before it could achieve a real acknowledgment of practices among experts. In effect, 'Xperdoc' brought changes to the usual ways of doing things and was understood in different ways by the experts who had shaped their personal vision through their own experience of the workings of the blast furnace. Moreover, 'Xperdoc' produced a radical change in organizational memory, and in the knowledge activated daily in the company, by questioning old repertoires and the social links surrounding the activation of these repertoires.

**Finding Shared Knowledge: the Sachem Project**

In 1987, the Sachem initiative came to light, mainly owing to the efforts of a part of the staff who believed that artificial intelligence could help memorize a large part of the knowledge held by experts. This idea was only implemented in 1990, under the supervision of Francis Mer, the company's top manager, who took a particular interest in this new tool in his efforts to improve Usinor's productivity. Over the course of a year, more than a hundred artificial intelligence applications were tested in collaboration with Usinor's R&D centre, IRSID. The implementation of artificial intelligence benefited from European subsidies and a 40-strong team spent five years working towards the creation of systems and their diffusion inside the group. Following this first stage, 17 technical solutions were selected, one of which was the Sachem project.[6] This was first implemented in October 1996, following a long period of discussion within the company, which focused mainly on the following crucial questions. What kinds of knowledge should be articulated and stored? How should practices be selected? How can such practices be transposed into a new tool? How can the loss of tacit knowledge be avoided as the importance of articulated knowledge increases?

In order to identify the 'best practices' and key 'know-how', 13 experts were chosen among those who had cooperated in writing 'Xperdoc'. Experts were selected according to know-how and location, in order to ensure a 'fair' representation of the various types of knowledge prevailing in the different plants (Sollac Fos, Dunkerque, Lorfonte Patural and so on). The team worked with six 'knowledge engineers' in order to extract the 'core know-how' and articulate it (400 interviews were conducted).

It was this team that created Usinor's 'epistemic community' and in the process ensured that the new community was representative of all the different types of know-how found in the group in order to avoid the emergence of a climate of distrust towards the ways in which knowledge was being articulated.

Before the extraction process took place, an interpretative model[7] was created in order to gain an understanding of expert know-how. Blast furnace experts based this interpretative model on a collection of representative case studies. The samples exemplified the different ways in which experts understood the blast furnace and the ways in which they solved problems. This preliminary work took 10 months (from September 1991 to June 1992) and allowed the identification of the crucial know-how activated daily. Consequently, the perimeter of expertise was delimited and the 'relevant' expertise was diffused among the experts. This process of disclosure also entailed a selection of knowledge from the daily activated know-how. Two important conditions had to be fulfilled before knowledge could be selected, validated and eventually codified. First, knowledge had to be generic; that is to say, it had to be sufficiently broad to remain meaningful once it had been dissociated from its local context and its specific use. The variety among experts and their associated expertise, which stemmed from different plants, helped identify the broader strand of knowledge. Second, the knowledge had to be identified and acknowledged as 'true' by all the experts involved. The knowledge had to be deemed useful to and employable by operators before it was codified. A knowledge manager clearly recognized this point: 'the automation of knowledge is the transformation of true expertise into useful expertise'. Consequently, at this stage, parts of the pre-existing knowledge were lost while others were accentuated (validation reinforces the parts collectively judged as crucial, to the detriment of those deemed too tacit or local to be selected).

The selected know-how was classified and indexed between April 1992 and May 1995. During this stage, called AED,[8] key concepts and their articulation were registered in order to introduce consistent problem solving. For example, 150 potential blast furnace phenomena were identified and classified according to their position in the steel-making process (quality, gas, wall, temperature decline, permeability and so on). On the basis of this knowledge, specific problems (notably an unusual temperature increase) could be identified systematically, operators alerted and specific recommendations made on the actions to be implemented.

Following the process of translating words into codes, the stage of knowledge acknowledgment and validation was launched.[9] Blast furnace experts had to recognize their codified know-how, which had been radically transformed by computation. This stage was crucial, as it allowed experts to verify whether the codes did in fact represent what they had intended to articulate in the first place. Knowledge validation was a long and difficult stage as consensus had to be reached before it could be concluded. Individual meetings, which saw experts having one-to-one discussions with knowledge engineers, and a collective one, including all the experts, took place. Local know-how had been radically transformed as the 'knowledge engineers' had changed the way experts represented their own expertise. As it happened, parts of the general knowledge codified in the expert system had ceased to be meaningful to some of the experts and the knowledge engineers designed a linguistic model (in natural language) in order to translate the code. The experts were thus able to recognize their own expertise and acknowledge it collectively. Similarly to the interpretative model, which had translated the experts' articulated knowledge into codes, the linguistic model converted codes into words. Different models had to be created because different levels of abstraction and local knowledge were required, depending on their use. The different levels of knowledge created by Sachem are depicted in Figure 8.1, which also shows the rupture introduced by the automation of knowledge.[10]

## BUILDING COOPERATION IN ORDER TO COPE WITH THE COGNITIVE AND ORGANIZATIONAL CHANGES INTRODUCED BY THE SACHEM PROJECT

The consequences of articulation and codification were very important because actual knowledge content changed drastically, forcing some blast

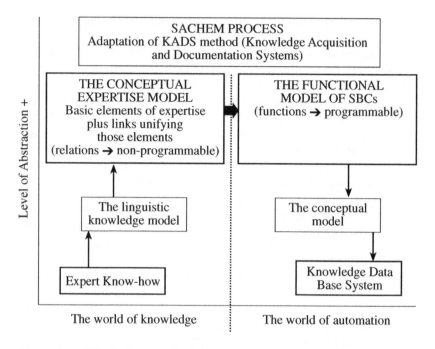

*Figure 8.1    The Sachem methodology*

furnace experts to modify long-standing beliefs and their usual interpretation of technical phenomena. One would expect some degree of resistance
to this process. In fact, cooperation in the knowledge identification was successful partly because the blast furnace experts were acknowledged as the
organizational knowledge carriers and their existing expertise was validated by the 'epistemic community'. The company also allowed the experts
to play an active role in the adaptation and updating of the system in order
to integrate minor changes and improve its daily performance. Below we
explain this process in more detail.

### Rule of Validation or the Acknowledgment of Drastic Changes in the Content of Knowledge

Articulation and codification entail a radical change in knowledge because
they involve the selection of parts of all available know-how. Moreover,
they affect the content of knowledge, as, in practice, the traditional expertise anchored in an expert's routines is alive. A first transformation occurs
when experts put their practices and parts of their tacit know-how into
words. This 'explicitation' creates articulated knowledge, which entails a

first selection of know-how. Parts of know-how are too dependent on practices prevailing in local plants: these cannot be articulated and resist extraction because of their ambiguity and fragility (deeply tacit knowledge and personal judgment may defy codification by virtue of being too personal). Consequently, knowledge may be difficult to disembody:

> Experts generally know what to do because they have a mature and practiced understanding. When deeply involved in coping with their environment, they do not see problems in some detached way and consciously work at solving them. The skills of experts have become so much a part of them that they need be no more aware of them than they are of their own bodies. (Dreyfus and Dreyfus, 1986, p. 44)

A second transformation takes place when articulated knowledge is turned into code as technicians have their own ways of representing and selecting knowledge: parts of knowledge may be deemed useful simply because of the nature of particular technical parameters embedded in the expert system. In other words, the nature of the container is far from neutral and can in fact change knowledge content by including unnecessary bits of know-how while excluding others. Consequently, the outcome is not a simple translation of existing knowledge into code but also a reformulation produced by the knowledge engineers and validated by the experts. Each stage of the transformation, which takes place in the hand-over of live expertise and activated knowledge to the memory of an outsider and from one outsider to another, entails a change in the preserved knowledge. This is neither a perfect equivalent nor a total substitute for the knowledge carried in the different memories. As a knowledge engineer recognized: 'It is the same relation that the painter has with the nature he observes. He magnifies it. The knowledge engineer describes the know-how of the expert; his art is to capture live expertise in order to reveal it and make it consistent outside of him.' Hatchuel and Weil (1992) argue that the container transforms knowledge content because each language has its very own ways of representing things. Repeated transmission through a variety of languages will always involve some losses as codes differ radically across languages. Moreover, articulation and codification are largely unpredictable in a way because they are largely based on individuals' willingness to participate in a process that is likely to depart from their initial experience because most implemented codes differ substantially from the original individual representations of their particular technical problems.

This is the reason why the translation into natural language and the validation by the experts that took place following the codification process was crucial to the project: it prevented experts from feeling they had lost their original know-how after they had passed it on to the knowledge engineer.

As was acknowledged by one blast furnace expert: 'The validation procedure implemented with the knowledge engineer prevented us from becoming frustrated and helped us understand why our know-how remained important even in its human form.' The rule of validation built inside the 'epistemic community' paved the way for trust building. In effect, the way experts cooperated in the construction of Sachem and their involvement in the process of extraction and articulation of their own expertise may appear curious to external observers. Two arguments can explain their cooperation.

First, experts and operators were sensitized to the fact that part of their own memory had to be preserved and communicated to others. Most of them were also encouraged to transfer their know-how before reaching retirement and were proud to participate in the passing of knowledge to younger employees. Second, operators, technicians and blast furnace experts in the steel industry belong to the same 'community of practice', and blast furnace experts in particular are very powerful because of their long-standing experience. Their own legitimacy is entirely based on their personal knowledge and not their hierarchical grade. To the experts, participation in the Sachem project meant that the company acknowledged their empirical knowledge and validated their extensive work. The rule of validation was, in this context, perceived as a signal: an implicit acknowledgment of local knowledge and a formal validation of live expertise present in the company that had not always been clearly identified by the hierarchy before. However, although this process helped some experts get a better understanding of the power of their personal knowledge, it also highlighted the limits of their local know-how, because a part of their beliefs turned out to be either insufficiently reliable or only partially true. The beliefs concerning fluidization are an example of the kind of knowledge that suffered from the selection process.

### An Unexpected Event: the Revision of Collective Beliefs on Some Technical Events

The process of collective learning inevitably led to an individual and collective revision of the way in which a number of technical events were understood. In this context, it makes sense to use the notion of an 'epistemic community' as the process involved the gradual implementation of new representations of the relevant technical knowledge and therefore a revision of prior shared beliefs relating to the interpretation and solution of problems. An important contribution of the Sachem project was that it brought about a change in the way operators and experts themselves understood the blast furnace process. As has already been emphasized, the blast furnace experts' know-how is generally empirical and has yet to be captured in its entirety by a scientific model. Implementation of the Sachem codes meant that parts of the pre-existing know-how were validated and acknowledged whereas other prior beliefs were first discussed and then collectively rejected.

For example, before Sachem was set up, a phenomenon called 'fluidization' was observed: this involved an increase in temperature above the ores. It was connected to the suspension of coke iron ore and limestone flux and was associated with a fall in different ores. In the 'Fos sur Mer' plant two beliefs prevailed about this phenomenon: (a) experts believed that fluidization never occurred in Fos sur Mer; (b) when descending ores and fluidization were detected, experts did not associate it with fluidization and the temperature increase was attributed to a different phenomenon.

After Sachem came into use, prior beliefs were revised; notably, people came to believe that (a) fluidization did take place in Fos sur Mer; and (b) when fluidization occurred, it had preceded the descent of ores by an hour.

In this context, prior beliefs have come to be slowly redefined as a matter of course: what had been known to be true starts to appear as being only partly so (especially through the discovery of new causal links between technical events). The causal links connecting separate technical events, which used to be tacit and intuitive, are now tested and systematically proven. The articulation process is not conducive to a scientifically grounded vision of the blast furnace (still to be achieved), but does provide the company with more robust beliefs and unquestionable know-how by changing the experts' and operators' local cognitive representations. Without enough confidence in this process of articulation and without sufficient discussion and cooperation between the experts, this change of prior individual and collective beliefs would have been difficult to implement and get accepted, as habitual beliefs had to be called into question and be selected by the 'epistemic community' attesting to their reliability.

## COOPERATION FOLLOWING THE INTRODUCTION OF THE EXPERT SYSTEM, OR HOW TO AVOID THE FOSSILIZATION OF CODIFIED KNOWLEDGE

The Sachem project led to the creation of generic knowledge. This latter was not only based on technical parameters but depended vitally on the social cooperation of the blast furnace experts, the main holders of this knowledge. In practice, the value of this tool is determined in large part by the way it is used and therefore usage becomes crucial to its survival. Usinor's management was aware of these fundamental issues and let the experts play an active role in this process by implementing an active training policy aimed at improving the use of the system and ensuring its regular update. In a virtuous cycle, the policy itself came to be perceived by the employees as a further signal of the will to cooperate, thereby, in turn, increasing the willingness of workers to master the new technology and to learn to interact with it. Given the importance of this point, we examine it in greater detail in the following paragraphs.

**The Training Policy or Managerial Investment in Human Capital**

Sachem is a tool that can actually collect systematic data (with the aid of over 1000 sensors placed inside the blast furnace), interpret and qualify them. The system continuously compares the collected information with a reference situation and can, in this way, make certain predictions by interpreting data, detecting problems and making recommendations to operators. It provides a global vision in real time, a selection of interesting indicators and some solutions. Operators retain a certain amount of autonomy in decision making, as they are able to ask the system to provide explanations on a number of the phenomena it detects. The system has been set up in this way in order to avoid automatic guidance, which would risk reducing operators to a passive role and thereby undermine their ability to solve problems. In order to stimulate the operators' energy and attention, the company introduced an important training policy ('off-the-job training'). This was put in place in 1995, before Sachem had begun operating effectively. In 1995, a team of operators and blast furnace experts was put together in order to anticipate potential problems with Sachem and encourage interaction with the new technological artifact. The training policy put an end to the old apprenticeship system and particularly affected the transmission of know-how from experts to newcomers.[11] Prior to the introduction of the expert system, it took 10 years of 'on-the-job training' to become a confirmed operator. Now only three years of work within the company are required to reach operational status and five to become a confirmed operator. The new training policy has forced both experts and operators to reflect on their own know-how, as they now need to understand the ways in which they solve problems and justify their repertoires. This has transformed their knowledge and expertise, hitherto largely based on 'know-how', and has activated new pieces of detached knowledge, predominantly based on 'know-that'.[12]

The training policy contributed to the trust-building exercise in a further important way, in that it broadened the range of workers' skills and generalized them by preventing operators from reacting passively to the data produced by Sachem and by helping them understand their meaning. This process had the added effect of increasing the degree of cooperation between different generations of practitioners operating within the company and helping disseminate knowledge that was previously open only to those partaking in the long-established apprenticeship system. Finally, the fact that the workforce interpreted the management's efforts as a positive signal that helped engage different parts of the company in the process of collective learning, and that the effort encouraged the formation of a provisional but positive perception of the hierarchy's intentions, were two factors that proved crucial to the success of the process. In short, the training policy was extremely well perceived by the company's employees and played a crucial role in stabilizing mutual expectations in a context of high uncertainty.

### The Preservation of the Blast Furnace Experts' Legitimacy: the Maintenance and Updating Stage

The training policy was also implemented in order to avoid a 'cognitive prosthesis syndrome'. In other words, management had to *ensure that both operators and experts remained constantly vigilant and active and did not become too confident in the new technological artifact.* An operator recognizes this point: 'We are not going to systematically listen to its recommendations, we are not going to be blind, we have our experience and our practice as "hand-rail". As the system is not locked in, we can interact with it, otherwise [. . . when the system is locked in], I will not use it.'

In fact, *the system requires a feedback from its users and the blast furnace experts in order to be updated.* As a result, the system's recommendations, which stem from its interpretation of the data (especially the identification of causal links between different events), and the operators' ultimate decisions are compared and scrutinized on a regular basis. All discrepancies between the system's commendations and the operators' ultimate decisions are systematically deconstructed in order to detect divergences. This analysis allows the database to be enriched and updated. Parts of the tacit know-how that were not articulated by the operators and blast furnace experts and were considered insignificant during the first stage of articulation (in 1992) are gradually incorporated into the system. Updates are formalized in an annual meeting with the operators, foremen and experts. Experts play a crucial role in this context as they formalize and systematize the divergence analysis of users (operators) and introduce the new articulated knowledge later turned into codes by the knowledge managers. In this way, the system's knowledge base is constantly enhanced by new articulated knowledge, a process that prevents it from rapidly becoming obsolete. The constant activation of human skills is very important because, as Dreyfus and Dreyfus (1986) remind us, the coupling of human skills and machine capacity is crucial in order to trigger all the expert system's potentialities. Indeed, the expert system is not able to deal with new situations or solve new problems. Its ability is limited to the knowledge that has been already articulated. Without integrating new pieces of knowledge and codifying them, the system would rapidly become obsolete in the long run. All this means that the legitimacy of the blast furnace experts and their social status within the company are reinforced rather than diminished by the new technological tool and that the power of their expertise remains a key component of the new 'epistemic community' (see Fleck, 1998, for a similar discussion of this point).

## CONCLUSION

In this case study, trust has played a fundamental role in stabilizing the 'epistemic community's' mutual expectations. The process of knowledge articulation and codification was confronted by important uncertainties because it entailed a profound change for the old 'communities of practices'. Trust and cooperation, in this context, were primarily achieved through tangible signals, notably the importance attributed to the training policy and the elaboration of organizational rules. For example, the rule of validation that was established following the process of codification and the practice of examining any divergence between the expert system's recommendations and the operators' decisions acted as such signals and created a climate of collective learning that gave an active role to the blast furnace experts. Such experts realized that the new system not only validated their existing empirical know-how, but also helped disseminate parts of their knowledge, thereby further enhancing their legitimacy. This process was also successful because the management did not impose a strict monitoring system and opted instead to create an 'epistemic community', a decentralized team that had a high degree of autonomy with respect to the hierarchy itself and that was accepted by the practitioners (despite the fact that it was precisely this team that was responsible for the substantial centralization of existing know-how through codification).

After a period of uncertainty that prevailed following the introduction of the new technological tool, a degree of confidence was restored, thus allowing operators to revise their prior beliefs about the technology itself. Also, paradoxically, this situation led to a degree of comfort that soon verged on overconfidence, thereby forcing the management to introduce procedures that required the staff to review and question the formalized data regularly. This means that routinized behaviour carries a risk: when not confronted by novelty it can lead to excessive trust and therefore generate a degree of inertia that can prove detrimental to its own evolution (see also Bart Nooteboom in Chapter 2, this volume, for a similar point of view).

## NOTES

1. For a discussion on natural language and the role of grammar producing a certain degree of consistency between the various signs, see Chomsky (1988), Piaget (1970) and Polanyi (1958).
2. For a debate on codification, see Cowan and Foray (1997), Cowan *et al.* (2000) and the reply by Nightingale (2001). The latter argues that tacit and codified are not substitutes and expresses doubts to the effect that codification may precede articulation in some cases, notably via a 'codebook'.
3. For a general definition of the different notions of trust, see notably Sako (1998) and Chapter 1 this volume.
4. The acronym stands for 'Institut de Recherche de la Sidérurgie Française' (the French Steel Industry Research Institute).
5. Corbion started off with 730 words but many additions were gradually made to the original so that by the mid-1980s the dictionary contained 1760 words. By the end of the 1990s, the figure had reached 12000. The aim of this glossary was of course to articulate the industry's language and to record different dialects and expressions. This initiative began during a period of recovery for the French steel industry. In this context, the glossary attempted to create a collective memory as, according to its author, each word referred to different semantic layers that had evolved since the origin of iron production and was the deposit of prior know-how. It was also intended to preserve the ancient dialects that had developed over time and risked disappearing with their human owners: 'the more a group loses the use of its own language the more it loses its own identity' (ibid., p. 8).
6. The acronym that gives its name to the project stands for 'Système d'Aide à la Conduite des Hauts fourneaux En Marche' (aid system for the control of a working blast furnace).
7. This was called AEG (the acronym stands for 'general analysis of expertise').
8. The acronym stands for 'detailed analysis of expertise'.
9. For a description of a similar way of knowledge acknowledgment and validation during the implementation of a knowledge-based system, see de Jongh *et al.* (1994).
10. More specific and technical details about KADS (Knowledge Acquisition and Documentation Systems) are reviewed in a recent article by Shabolt (1998).
11. It is now impossible to hire unskilled operators, as all newcomers must already be endowed with a technical diploma called BTS (brevet de technicien supérieur), which can only be obtained after the completion of secondary school.
12. 'Know-how' usually refers to the sum of both unconscious and conscious knowledge. 'Know-that' refers to the conscious level and to knowledge that can be articulated. For a longer discussion on this distinction, introduced by Ryle (1949), see Loasby (1998).

## REFERENCES

Allen, R.C. (1983), 'Collective invention', *Journal of Economic Behavior and Organization*, **4**, 1–24.

Brown, S. and P. Duguid (1991), 'Organizational learning and communities of practice: towards a unified view of working, learning and innovation', *Organization Science*, **2**, 40–57.

Chomsky, N. (1988), *Language and Problems of Knowledge: The Managua Lectures*, Cambridge, MA: MIT Press.

Corbion, J. (1989), *Le savoir-fer, glossaire du haut fourneau,* Sérémange-Erzange: Presses du Nord.

Cowan, R. and D. Foray (1997), 'The economics of codification and the diffusion of knowledge', *Industrial and Corporate Change*, **6** (3), 595–622.

Cowan, R., P.A. David and D. Foray (2000), 'The explicit economics of codification and tacitness', *Industrial and Corporate Change*, **10** (2), 211–53.

Divry, C. and N. Lazaric (1998), 'Mémoire organizationnelle et codification des connaissances', *Revue Internationale de Systémique*, **12**, 3–11.

Dreyfus, H. and S. Dreyfus (1986), 'Why computers may never think like people', *Technology Review*, **89**, 20–42.

Fleck, J. (1998), 'Expertise: knowledge power and tradeability', in R. Faulkner Williams and J. Fleck (eds), *Exploring Expertise*, London: Macmillan Press, pp. 143–72.

Godelier, E. (1997), 'De la stratégie des sites à la stratégie de groupe: contingence et changement chez Usinor', *Gérer et comprendre, Annales des mines*, June, 79–92.

Haas, P.M. (1992), 'Introduction : epistemic communities and international policy coordination', *International Organization*, **46** (1), 1–35.

Hatchuel, A. and B. Weil (1992), *L'expert et le système,* Paris: Economica.

de Jongh, P.J. *et al.* (1994), 'Future: a knowledge based system for threat assessment', *Interfaces*, **24**, 261–72.

Lazaric, N. and B. Denis (2001), 'Implementing a new effort convention when routines change: some lessons from two case studies', working paper presented to the Nelson and Winter conference Aalborg, June; published in T. Knudsen and S. Winter (eds), *Firm, Organization and Routines*, Oxford: Oxford University Press.

Lazaric, N. and E. Lorenz (1998), 'The learning dynamics of trust reputation and confidence', in N. Lazaric and E. Lorenz (eds), *Trust and Economic Learning*, Cheltenham, UK and Lyme, US: Edward Elgar, pp. 1–20.

Lazaric, N. and P.A. Mangolte (1999), 'Routines in theory and in practice: some criticism of cognitive perspective', *Rivista di Economia Contemporanea*, **5**, 7–35.

Leibenstein, H. (1987), *Inside the Firm: The Inefficiencies of Hierarchy*, Cambridge, MA: Harvard University Press.

Loasby, B. (1998), 'The organization of capabilities', *Journal of Economic Behaviour and Organization*, **35**, 139–60.

Luhmann, N. (1979), *Trust and Power: Two Works of Niklas Luhmann*, Chichester: Wiley.

Mangolte, P.-A. (1997), 'La dynamique des connaissances tacites et articulées: une approche socio-cognitive', *Economie Appliquée*, **2**, 105–34.

Mansell, R. and E. Steinmueller (2000), *Mobilizing the Information Society*, Oxford: Oxford University Press.

Moingeon, B. and A. Edmonson (1998), 'Trust and organizational learning', in N. Lazaric and E. Lorenz (eds), *Trust and Economic Learning*, Cheltenham, UK and Lyme, US: Edward Elgar, pp. 228–47.

Nightingale, P. (2001), 'If Nelson and Winter are only half right about tacit knowledge, Which half ? a reply to David Foray and Cowan', working paper presented to the Nelson and Winter conference, Aalborg, June.

Nonaka, I. and H. Tackeuchi (1995), *The Knowledge-Creating Company*, Oxford: Oxford University Press.

Piaget, J. (1970), *L'epistémologie génétique*, Paris:Presses Universitaires de France.
Polanyi, M. (1958), *Personal Knowledge. Towards a Post-critical Philosophy*, London: Routledge & Kegan Paul.
Rosenberg, N. (1982), *Inside the Black Box, Technology and Economics*, Oxford: Oxford University Press.
Ryle, G. (1949), *The Concept of the Mind*, London: Hutchinson.
Sako, M. (1998), 'The information requirements of trust in supplier relations: evidence from Japan, Europe and the United States', in N. Lazaric and E. Lorenz (eds), *Trust and Economic Learning*, Cheltenham, UK and Lyme, US: Edward Elgar, pp. 23–47.
Shabolt, N. (1998), 'Building models of expertise', in R. Faulkner Williams and J. Fleck (eds), *Exploring Expertise*, London: Macmillan Press, pp. 101–20.
Steiler, J.M. and M. Schneider (1994), 'L'élaboration de la fonte', in J.M. Steiler and M. Schneider (eds), *Le livre de l'acier*, Paris: Technique & Documentation – Lavoisier, pp. 1187–1229.
Steinmueller, W.E. (2000), 'Will information and communication technologies improve the "codification" of knowledge?', *Industrial and Corporate Change*, **10** (2), 361–76.
Terssac, de G. (1997), *Autonomie dans le travail*, Paris: Presses Universitaires de France.
Thierry, P. (1940), *La pratique du haut-fourneau*, Paris. Liège: Librairie Polytechnique, C. Béranger.
Wenger, E. (1998), *Communities of Practice: Learning, Meaning and Identity*, Cambridge: Cambridge University Press.
Winter, S. (1987), 'Knowledge and competence as strategic assets', in D.J. Teece (ed.), *The Competitive Challenge: Strategies for Industrial Innovation and Renewal*, Cambridge: Ballinger, pp. 159–83.
Zollo, M. and S.G. Winter (2002), 'Deliberate learning and the evolution of dynamic capabilities', *Organization Science*, **13**, 339–51.

# 9. Norm violations and informal control in organizations: a relational signalling perspective

**Rafael Wittek**

## INTRODUCTION

Processes of informal social control play a crucial role in the functioning of organizations. This is particularly relevant for so-called 'high-trust' settings in which governance of the employment relationship is achieved primarily through mutual adjustment in teams rather than by hierarchy. Consequently, organizational scholars have allocated much attention to the question of how informal control and peer pressure come about and what are the consequences both for the behaviour of individuals in organizations and for organizational performance. Informal control is conceived by many as the ultimate remedy for the flexible and efficient resolution of problems, whether caused by external (market) forces or by work-related processes inside the organization (Pennings and Woiceshyn, 1987). However, the question of which types of problems occur and how members of such high-trust organizations actually deal with them has, surprisingly, received little attention. The few studies which do tackle the role of grievances distinguish between the type, scope, seriousness and frequency of grievances and have found mixed effects on control strategy choice (for a brief review, see Wittek, 1999, pp. 40–42). More generally, previous research focusing on the link between grievances and informal control behaviour has three major flaws.

First, it is highly *undertheorized* when it comes to modelling sanction strength. Many researchers seem to assume implicitly that informal sanctions can be ordered according to their 'strength', but despite this hardly any efforts have been made to model the choice of different sanctioning levels. This is particularly disappointing since sanction strength is an essential explanatory variable in much formal work on the provision of collective goods and social dilemmas. These studies search for conditions that might stimulate or inhibit actors to bear the costs of sanctioning a co-worker. Variation concerning sanction strength enters these models in the form of an abstract interval scale from zero to one (Flache and Macy, 1996; Heckathorn, 1990, 1993; Kandel and Lazear, 1992; Macy, 1993).

Second, despite a flourishing literature on influence tactics and compliance-gaining strategies inside and outside organizations (Kellerman and Cole, 1994), virtually no efforts have been made to operationalize the notion of sanction strength by linking it to the variety of compliance-gaining behaviours as they are found in real life. The bulk of the compliance-gaining literature generates nominal classifications of different types of sanctioning strategies, without modelling or measuring which of the strategies can be expected to be more 'severe' than the other. This leaves the research community in a highly ambiguous situation (for example, should we consider shouting angrily at a colleague in private a stronger sanction than calmly pointing out the mistake to the colleague during a company meeting?).

Finally, there is a gap between the theoretical literature on collective goods and informal control on the one hand and the vast social–psychological literature on influence strategies on the other. The former shows a strong emphasis on the second-order free-rider problem, that is, the fact that it is individually rational but collectively detrimental not to invest in sanctions, but makes little effort to operationalize the theoretical construct of 'sanction strength'. The latter offers a huge body of literature on influence strategy choice and classifications of compliance-gaining behaviour (ibid.), but most of this fails to incorporate the option of not sanctioning as a possible behavioural alternative.

As a result, the link between variations in the type of trouble, the willingness to sanction, and sanction strength, so far remains largely unexplored. It is the purpose of the present study to address this gap. Its goal is twofold: first, to develop an instrument to measure sanction strength; second, to model the impact of different types of trouble or grievances on informal control behaviour in high-trust organizations. The research problem that will be addressed can be stated as follows: how can the willingness to sanction and the choice of a sanction level in organizations be explained by differences in the severity, frequency and scope of grievances?

In what follows, we will first sketch a theoretical framework and, from this, derive some empirically testable hypotheses. A description of the research design and method, and a preliminary exploratory empirical test of the hypotheses, follow this. The chapter concludes with some observations for future research.

## MODELLING SANCTIONING BEHAVIOUR: INCENTIVES OR SIGNALS?

At first sight, modelling the link between types of grievances and sanction strength seems to be a straightforward issue. Following the economic theory of incentives, one could argue that the willingness to perform a particular action or to refrain from it is a linear function of the size of rewards or punishments. One could call this the *incentive approach* to sanctions: (a) it assumes a single continuum of sanction strength, ranging from negative (punishments) to positive (rewards); (b) it assumes that the stronger the grievance (in terms of costs or losses), the stronger the (negative) sanction will be.

Like most theoretical frameworks inspired by neoclassical economic reasoning, the incentive interpretation of the link between grievance size and sanction strength has the advantage of being both parsimonious and rooted in a well elaborated micro-theory of action. The incentive approach therefore provides a useful starting point for theorizing about sanctions. Yet as research in (neoinstitutional) economics and other social sciences has repeatedly shown, empirical studies often yield results that are at odds with the predictions following from neoclassical economics. Many scholars in the social sciences therefore propose discarding economic reasoning as a whole. Others suggest retaining the theoretical core of the rational choice framework of economics, but to extend it with a theoretical framework which models individual actors as boundedly rational and socially embedded. The present chapter is an attempt to contribute to the development of such an extended theoretical framework.

Research in the bounded rationality framework suggests limitations to the straightforward incentive interpretation as it was outlined above. The first limitation is related to the single-continuum assumption of sanction strength. Evidence suggesting that it is not only the strength of a sanction that matters goes as far as the experiments related to operational behaviourism in the 1930s and reinforcement theory in the 1950s. Another shortcoming of the single-continuum assumption is that individuals are assumed to treat punishments and rewards similarly. An overwhelming body of research on the role of loss frames (Kahnemann and Tversky, 1979) and retributive justice (Griffith, 1989) shows that this assumption is questionable, to say the least. Thus there is reason to believe that people categorize negative and positive sanctions differently.

The second limitation of the incentive approach relates to the fact that the salient feature of a grievance is, above all, its severity in terms of costs to the offended person. The problem with this assumption is that it does not take into consideration various cognitive and attribution processes that were found to fundamentally influence the interpretation of events (for a succinct overview, see, for example, Augoustinos and Walker 1995, pp. 60–96). As a result, the incentive approach cannot explain why grievances, despite being minor, nevertheless cause surprisingly high levels of escalation and emotional reactions. Likewise, it has difficulties in explaining why behaviour that causes considerable trouble often either is not sanctioned or only elicits a comparatively weak punishment (for ethnographic examples of such situations, see, for example, Wittek, 1999, pp. 105–109). Hence there is reason to believe that the incentive approach neglects some important factors that are considered to affect the perception of grievances and their severity.

In what follows, an alternative approach will be developed which is able to tackle these two problems. We will refer to this perspective as the relational signalling approach (see also Siegwart Lindenberg, 1997, 1998, in Chapter 3, this volume; Mühlau, 2000; Wielers, 1997). In a nutshell, it argues (a) that the crucial quality of grievances as well as of informal sanctions is not their seriousness, or their strength, respectively, but whether or not they convey relational signals; and (b) that individuals categorize negative sanctions into two independent cognitive dimensions, depending on whether the sanction conveys negative or positive relational signals.

Relational signals are cues in the behaviour of other persons that tell us something about the salience of their solidarity frame; that is, their willingness to maintain a mutually rewarding relationship with us in the future. Given the important role that social relations play in achieving our goals, we not only constantly screen the actions of others for their potential relational signalling character, but we also anticipate the potential relational signalling aspects of our own behaviour. This implies that, when we are evaluating each other's behaviour, the human mind classifies it into one of three cognitive categories: behaviour that conveys positive relational signals, behaviour that conveys negative relational signals, and behaviour that has no signalling character. Consequently, it can be hypothesized that negative sanctions will not be perceived along a single continuum, ranging from weak to strong – as the incentive approach would argue – but rather will be cognitively represented along two mutually exclusive dimensions representing positive, negative or no relational signals. That is, negative sanctions are first evaluated according to their quality (positive or negative relational signal). It is within these qualitative dimensions that their strength or intensity will be assessed. The hypotheses of both approaches can be summarized as follows.

*Unidimensional sanction hierarchy hypothesis (IN-1):* negative sanctions represent a single latent hierarchy of escalation, ranging from weak to strong.

*Multidimensional sanctioning hierarchy hypothesis ( RS-1 ):*    negative sanctions represent two latent hierarchies of escalation, one reflecting positive and the other negative relational signals.

If sanctions convey relational signals, rational actors can be assumed to anticipate the signalling character of their sanctions. This implies that models of sanctioning behaviour need to predict under which circumstances an individual selects sanctions with a negative or a positive relational signalling character in order to react to a grievance. Attribution research (Hewstone, 1983; Jaspars *et al.*, 1983; Augoustinos and Walker, 1995) has shown that the interpretation of events and behaviour of others is subject to numerous biases, and that the related attribution processes matter in terms of how we behave towards others. However, despite its accomplishments, attribution theory is still criticized because 'The model ignores how individuals may differ in how they attribute, and ignores how interpersonal relations, affect and evaluate . . . and the relative group memberships of the attributer and the object of attribution all might affect the attribution process' (Augoustinos and Walker, 1995, p. 93). Thus, though attribution theory points to the importance of incorporating cognitive processes that filter our interpretations of other people's behaviours and thereby are likely to shape our subsequent behavioural responses, it still offers little guidance for the development of hypotheses on how interpersonal relations and relational signals might affect sanctioning behaviour.

A more promising solution to this problem can be found in a closer examination of framing processes. Relational signalling theory assumes that individuals define ('frame') the situation in terms of only one overriding goal (Lindenberg, 1993; Braspenning, 1992). This goal is called the salient goal. Other goals may be present at the same time. However, such background goals do not define the situation, but have a negative or positive influence on the salience of the main goal. The stronger the background goal becomes, the more likely it is that it will replace the main goal. Such a situation is called a frame switch. Though the number of possible frames may be unlimited, framing theorists have concentrated much of their efforts on the study of two interrelated classes of frames: gain and loss frames on the one hand and relational frames on the other.

In a number of experiments concerning the loss frame, it could be shown that actors tend to take more risks in situations described in terms of losses rather than gains. In other words, people weigh losses as being heavier than gains of the same amount. Two important conclusions have been drawn from research on the loss frame. They have been summarized in the so-called 'loss hypothesis', which states (Lindenberg, 1993, p. 24): '(a) the likelihood that avoidance of uncompensated loss dominates other possible frames in any given situation grows disproportionately with the size of the loss; and (b) the costs incurred in pursuing this goal may be higher than the (subjective) value of the assets before the loss occurred'.

Studies dealing with the effects of relational frames on economic transactions have been mainly interested in how different solidarity frames reduce the salience of the gain frame (Ligthart, 1995; Ligthart and Lindenberg, 1994). This branch of framing theory distinguishes two different types of solidarity frames (Lindenberg, 1988). If norms of strong solidarity are present, the salient goal of an actor is to conform to group norms. In the case of weak solidarity, gain seeking is the dominant frame, but it is tempered by norms of strong solidarity. In both cases, 'keeping the relationship going' will be present as a goal. However, whereas in strong solidarity the obligation of individuals will be to the group rather than to a specific other individual actor, in weak solidarity obligation is bilaterally defined. Finally, opportunism is a situation where the goal of pure gain seeking is not tempered by solidarity considerations.

While the link between solidarity relations and the gain frame has received much attention, this does not hold for the interrelationship between losses and solidarity relations. However, it is exactly this combination which provides the key for modelling the interrelationship between grievances and sanctioning behaviour. A solidarity relationship will sensitize both transacting parties not to inflict losses on each other. Moreover, in a functioning solidarity relationship, each party will constantly screen the other's behaviour for cues that tell them something about the other party's intentions to maintain the relationship and to refrain from opportunistic behaviour. Nevertheless, owing to incomplete information and complex interdependencies, negative externalities may actually occur even within very strong solidarity relationships. Negative externalities create losses for the affected person. Consequently, one would expect that the salient frame of the offended party would be the loss frame. If the loss hypothesis is correct, relatively small increases in the size of the loss will trigger disproportionately harsh reactions. In the extreme case, the affected individual will be willing to invest more resources to reach compensation than the value of the lost assets. However, within a solidarity relation, two conditions hold: (a) the solidarity frame tempers the gain frame. Therefore, actors are strongly inclined and expected to avoid actions that could produce losses for the other party; (b) the solidarity frame tempers the loss frame. As long as an externality is not seen as evidence for a decreased general inclination of its producer towards loss avoidance, losses are less likely to produce a loss frame. That is, he or she will receive the 'benefit of the doubt'.

From these assumptions the following conclusions can be drawn. First, in a functioning solidarity relationship, the person confronted by a loss caused by an externality of the other actor will assess whether the behaviour is an accident or an indication of a decreasing solidarity frame of the offender – a negative relational signal. In the first case, solidarity considerations will temper the loss frame, and consequently the offended party will take care that any subsequent sanctioning does not convey a negative relational signal. In the second case, solidarity considerations will switch into the background, so that relational signalling considerations will be less salient in the selection of a sanction. Sanctioning behaviour is thus likely to escalate.

Second, where the offender and the offended do not have a functioning solidarity relationship, they will not screen each other's behaviour for relational signals. This implies that an offended person will evaluate the grievance purely according to the losses it causes. Since there are no solidarity considerations to temper the evaluation, the likelihood that the offended party will experience a loss frame increases, and so does the tendency to use disproportionately harsh sanctions with a high negative relational signalling value. Figure 9.1 gives a simplified graphical representation of the proportionality and the escalation hypothesis.

*Proportionality hypothesis (IN-2):* the larger the perceived loss, (a) the more likely active sanctioning becomes, and (b) the higher the level of negative sanctions, independent of the signalling character of the loss.
*Escalation hypothesis (RS-2):* The stronger the negative relational signalling character of a loss, (a) the more likely active sanctioning becomes, and (b) the higher the level of negative sanctions, independent of the strength of the loss.

Finally, the incentive approach and the signalling approach yield different predictions about losses that affect the group as a whole and losses that are limited to a single individual. In the incentive approach, individuals are considered as calculating how particular events or decisions will affect their cost–benefit equation. From this perspective, the fact that somebody else may be confronted by a similar problem or loss does not feature. The person affected by a negative externality will evaluate whether it pays to sanction the offender, and to select the type of sanction that will yield the highest net benefit. However, this reasoning can be refined. Building on insights from economic theories of collective action, it can be argued that, in settings where more than one person is affected by the negative externality of a third party, the collectivity has to solve the second-order free-rider problem, that is, the dilemma that everybody hopes that somebody else will allocate a sanction. Thus it can be argued that compared to situations in

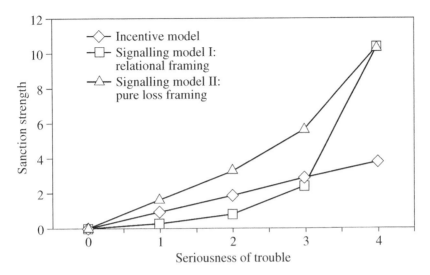

*Figure 9.1  Incentive and signalling models of sanctioning behaviour*

which only a single individual is confronted by an externality, losses affecting a group will less often lead to active sanctioning efforts, and the strength of the sanction will be weaker.

Relational signalling theory yields a different prediction. Here it is assumed that in settings in which, owing to high levels of functional interdependence, individuals are likely to be confronted with negative externalities that simultaneously affect more than only a single person, strong solidarity norms will emerge in order to prevent the production of these negative externalities (Lindenberg, 1993). Norms of strong solidarity favour a collectivist orientation by putting a premium on generalized exchange and limiting restricted exchange. Because of the vital role that norm conformity plays in avoiding the production of negative externalities, members of such strongly solidary groups have an interest in maintaining their own frame stability. Opportunity costs of sanctioning are pushed into the background. Since active social control will also yield peer approval, it will actually become an attractive alternative to passivity. Hence relational signalling theory predicts that problematic behaviour that troubles a whole group will be more likely to result in active sanctioning efforts and higher levels of escalation than problems that only affect a single individual.

*Free-rider hypothesis (IN-3):*  Losses affecting the whole group will (a) either have no effect on sanctioning behaviour or be less likely to evoke active sanctioning efforts, and (b) result in weaker sanctions than losses that only affect a single individual.

*Group obligation hypothesis (RS-3):*    Losses affecting the whole group will (a) be more likely to evoke active sanctioning efforts, and (b) result in stronger negative sanctions than losses that only affect a single individual.

Note that the group obligation hypothesis holds only in settings in which strong solidarity defines the relationships in a group. In business and organizational settings, strong solidarity is probably the exception rather than the rule. The group does not play a role in weak solidarity relationships, the latter being far more common in business settings. In such cases, group-level externalities will have no effect on the willingness and strength of sanctioning behaviour.

Table 9.1 provides an overview of the hypotheses of the signalling and the incentive approaches.

*Table 9.1    Overview of hypotheses*

| Variable | Incentive approach | Signalling approach |
|---|---|---|
| Sanctions | Unidimensional | Multidimensional |
|  | Proportionality | Escalation |
| Grievance severity | + | 0 |
| Grievance frequency | 0 | + |
|  | Free-rider | Group obligation |
| Grievance scope | − | + |

## DATA AND METHOD

Given that previous attempts to assess the cognitive dimensions and signalling character of grievances and sanctions are scarce, the empirical part of this study is exploratory in nature. A research design was needed that could capture *intra*-individual variations in the perception of grievances and subsequent behavioural choices. Vignette analysis (Rossi, 1979) fulfils this requirement. The data consist of the aggregated responses from 19 managers, each of whom indicated for eight hypothetical grievance situations to what degree he considers using 12 different types of sanctions. Thus the study should be considered as an attempt to uncover the cognitive representations of sanctions and grievances through an in-depth investigation of a single group, rather than as an effort to achieve generalizable conclusions.

## The Organization

Data were gathered from all members of the management team of a German paper factory (Wittek, 1999). The 19 managers described their team as a 'trust culture'. The factory is situated in a village with 800 inhabitants in southern Germany. When fieldwork started in 1995, the organization had 170 employees and two paper machines. After a bankruptcy in 1993, the company was taken over by a German multinational, which decided to invest 40 million German Marks to enlarge the site by adding a new production hall and a third paper machine. During the observation period this project – and the realization of the deadline of 1 September 1995 – comprised the most central event in the factory. During this phase the managers had to cope with a double workload. Besides their individual function in the daily production process, they were now also responsible for the successful realization of the project. Interdependence between them and the necessity to coordinate and cooperate reached heights that, heretofore, were unknown. Stable membership, frequent unscheduled lateral and vertical communication, and weekly meetings characterize the team in which most of the managers participated on a regular basis. The average team member was 41 years old (SD 10.9) and had worked 13.2 years (SD 11.8) for the factory. All of them were male. Two-thirds of the managers had a degree in engineering. There were seven departments: production, the chemical lab, maintenance, logistics, personnel, technical customer service and a project department. Data collection was carried out when the joint project was in full operation. Evidence from participant observation and a survey confirms the self-perceptions of the team members as a highly solidary work unit operating on the basis of trust rather than hierarchical control (see Wittek, 1999, pp. 86–100, 122–34).

### Independent Variables

Vignette analysis (Rossi, 1979) was used to gather data on grievances and sanctioning. Eight vignettes, each one printed on a separate card, were distributed to 19 managers. Each vignette contained a hypothetical situation. They had in common that a hypothetical member of the team made a mistake.

The situations, though hypothetical, should reflect events that could happen in real life. They were based on background knowledge gathered during the first three months of participant observation. Four types of events were chosen:

*Situations 1 and 2 ('Passed over in Decision', strong bilateral externality)*
A group member (once/repeatedly) has been passed over in the decision-

making process by another colleague. The passed colleague, consequently, has to cancel a booked holiday.

*Situations 3 and 4 ('Delayed Information', weak bilateral externality)*    A group member (once/repeatedly) failed to receive, in sufficient time, relevant information from another colleague. He therefore has to cancel a long-planned personal date.

*Situations 5 and 6 ('Breach of Trust', strong group externality)*    A group member (once/repeatedly) passed confidential information to a person outside the group. This created conflicts in every department and (once/repeatedly) culminated in the refusal of the workers to work during the Easter holiday.

*Situations 7 and 8 ('Collective Decision', weak group externality)*    A group member (once/repeatedly) took a decision that should have been a collective decision. The result is that two additional meetings had to be held, lasting long into the night.

The situations sketched in the vignettes varied along three dimensions, which represent the three independent variables of this study.

**Grievance severity**
This is the major variable used to test the predictions of the incentive approach. It covers whether the consequences of the problem were relatively serious or relatively trivial. Two situations were assumed to be experienced as relatively serious. The first one – having to cancel a booked holiday because a colleague took an important decision without consulting you – was considered by the managers to be a very extreme situation which would most probably affect only the highest ranks of the company. They did not, however, consider it a completely impossible scenario. The second – a team member passing confidential management team information to the shopfloor, and this resulting in a factory-wide conflict with the shopfloor refusing to work overtime during Easter holiday – was considered to be much closer to real life, since the union representative and the chief operating officer were actually negotiating this issue during the observation period. The remaining two situations – having to cancel a long-planned personal appointment, and having to attend two additional evening meetings – were assumed to represent relatively less severe grievances, since they were found to occur frequently during the observation period.

**Grievance frequency**
Each of the four situations was presented twice. The text was identical and differed only in the use of the word 'once' or 'repeatedly'. The former

denotes that it was the first time that the member had caused the problem, whereas the latter indicates that the same person had caused the same trouble at least once in the past. This factor intends to manipulate the relational signalling character of the grievance. It is based on the idea that the repeated production of the same type of externality by the same person will be seen as evidence that the actor's willingness to avoid the production of losses is decreasing. The actor violates the rule of loss avoidance despite earlier sanctions; that is, he is aware of the negative consequences of his action for others but nevertheless makes no effort to change his behaviour. Hence, in the present study, the repeated occurrence of the same type of troublesome behaviour is seen as a negative relational signal, whereas a single incidence is seen as not having a negative relational signalling value.

### Grievance scope
The third dimension covers whether the mistake had negative consequences only for a single group member (situations 1–4) or for the group as a whole (situations 5–8).

### Dependent Variables

### Control strategy choice
Having looked at the eight cards with the vignettes, respondents then received a questionnaire. In randomized order, each page contained one of the eight situations, followed by the list of 12 control strategies, again in randomized order. Each respondent was asked to imagine that the situation at the top of the page had recently occurred in their team, and that he was playing the role of the victim or one of the victims. For each control strategy the respondent then had to rate on a scale from one to five whether he regarded this reaction as being very likely, likely, unlikely, very unlikely or nearly impossible to occur in such a situation.[1] Thus, for eight different types of grievances, each of the 19 respondents indicated his inclination to make use of 12 different sanctions, resulting in $n = 1824$ observations. The complete list of control strategies and the items are listed in Table 9.2.

### Control Variable

To control for the potential influence of position in the hierarchy, the formal position of a manager is included as a control variable. It has two levels: superior (applying to department heads) and subordinate (applying to their subordinates and assistants).

*Table 9.2    Typology of control strategies*

| Type | Label | Translation of item |
|---|---|---|
| Public | Public negotiation | Soberly discussing the problem during a meeting |
| | Public arguing | Accusing deviator during a meeting |
| Formal | Vertical mediation | Asking the superior to talk to deviator |
| | Authority enforcement | Complaining to superior about deviator |
| Indirect | Information seeking | Asking opinion of colleagues |
| | Lateral mediation | Asking a colleague to talk to the deviator |
| | Gossip | Complaining to a colleague |
| Direct | Bilateral negotiation | Personally asking deviator to change behaviour |
| | Bilateral arguing | Personally complaining to the deviator |
| Unilateral | Retaliation | Retaliating, when the opportunity arises |
| | Avoidance | Avoiding interaction |
| No sanction | Resignation | Keeping one's temper and doing nothing |

## Manipulation Checks

### Grievance severity

In order to assess the perceived severity of the eight types of grievances, after completing the questionnaire respondents were again given the cards with the vignettes and asked to rank the eight situations according to the severity they attached to each event. They were then asked to rate every situation on an interval scale. For that purpose the situation with rank number 1 was fixed as 100 per cent 'severe' on a unipolar scale. The mean ratings of the eight situations in Figure 9.2 give a first indication of the relative weight attached to each type of grievance. The events 'repeated breach of trust' and 'repeatedly being passed when a decision was taken' received the highest scores. Ranks three and four are occupied by their unique equivalents. Repeatedly withholding information is regarded as being a worse offence than that of repeatedly making a decision based only on one's own authority. For further analysis, the first four strategies are considered as strong externalities, the last four as weak externalities.

### Appropriateness of sanctioning strategy

In order to assess the relational signalling character of sanctions, respondents were also handed cards with the 12 control strategies, which they first

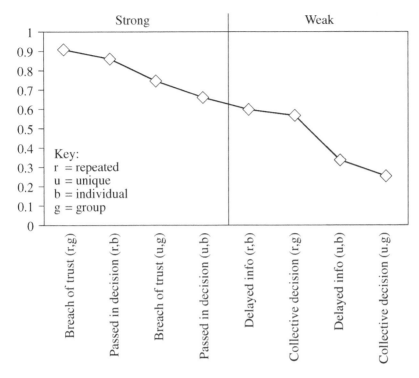

*Figure 9.2  Severity of grievances*

ranked according to the criterion, in general, how appropriate were each of the strategies to their work context. They were then asked to rate the appropriateness of each strategy on an interval scale. For that purpose, the strategies with rank number 1 and rank number 12 were fixed at +100 per cent 'appropriate' and −100 per cent 'inappropriate', respectively, on a bipolar scale. The mean appropriateness ratings are represented in Figure 9.3.

## ANALYSES AND RESULTS

### Unidimensional versus Multidimensional Sanctioning Hierarchy

Technically speaking, the existence of a sanctioning hierarchy implies that it is possible to represent the preferred reactions of all members of the population on at least one latent dimension. Though there are different ways to test this assumption, multidimensional unfolding was chosen (van Schuur and Post, 1990). The rationale underlying this choice is a theoretical one.

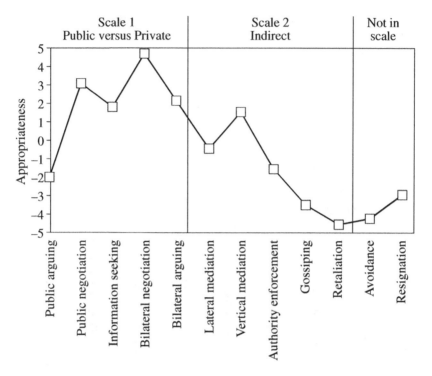

*Figure 9.3    Appropriateness of sanctions*

First, the theory predicts that under certain circumstances, such as the repeated occurrence of a loss, actors will not consider positive strategies to be adequate, but will immediately prefer negative ones. In a cumulative model like that of Mokken, actors choosing negative strategies will first have to 'pass' positive control strategies. Second, the technique has to be able to identify more than only one latent dimension in the data. Multidimensional unfolding satisfies both conditions.

The eight matrices (one for each situation) containing the 12 responses of 19 subjects were stacked, so that each respondent appears eight times in the data set. Values 1 (very likely) and 2 (likely) were coded as preferred values. MUDFOLD detected two scales (see Tables 9.3 and 9.4). The algorithm dropped the items 'Avoidance' (preferred in 5 per cent of the cases) and 'Resignation' (preferred in 7 per cent of the cases); that is, they do not form part of the scales.

The first scale consists of five items. It clearly shows the transition from public to private modes of sanctioning. That is, public control is perceived as representing a lower level of escalation than private strategies. Scale two

*Table 9.3    MUDFOLD scale 1, 'Public versus Private Control'*

| Control strategy with scale score | P(I) | H(I) | OBS. | EXP. Error | SD(H) Error | T(H) |
|---|---|---|---|---|---|---|
| 1  Public arguing | 0.23 | 0.80 | 10 | 49.3 | 0.1434 | 5.5613 |
| 2  Public negotiation | 0.68 | 0.55 | 44 | 97.5 | 0.0863 | 6.3536 |
| 3  Information search | 0.61 | 0.51 | 49 | 100.5 | 0.0799 | 6.4158 |
| 4  Bilateral negotiation | 0.87 | 0.55 | 35 | 77.6 | 0.0813 | 6.7505 |
| 5  Bilateral arguing | 0.70 | 0.64 | 24 | 65.9 | 0.0948 | 6.7065 |

*Note:*   N = 152, H = 0.59, T(H) = 7.51; P(I) = percentage of respondents who mentioned stimulus; H(I) = scalability value for stimulus.

*Table 9.4    MUDFOLD scale 2, 'Indirect Control'*

| Control strategy with scale score | P(I) | H(I) | OBS. | EXP. Error | SD(H) Error | T(H) |
|---|---|---|---|---|---|---|
| 1  Lateral mediation | 0.14 | 0.88 | 1 | 8.6 | 0.3686 | 2.3981 |
| 2  Vertical mediation | 0.58 | 0.95 | 1 | 19.7 | 0.1874 | 5.0673 |
| 3  Authority enforcement | 0.37 | 0.90 | 2 | 19.4 | 0.1794 | 4.9994 |
| 4  Gossiping | 0.16 | 0.89 | 2 | 18.6 | 0.1965 | 4.5411 |
| 5  Retaliation | 0.05 | 1.00 | 0 | 10.0 | 0.2867 | 3.4874 |

*Note:*   N = 152 responses (19 subjects rating 8 situations), H = 0.92, T(H) = 5.20; P(I) = percentage of responses in which stimulus was mentioned; H(I) = scalability value for stimulus.

also consists of five items. Four of them represent strategies of indirect social control, where the controller makes use of a third person to bring the target back into line.

The two-dimensional solution provides supporting evidence for the first relational signalling hypothesis (RS-1), and disconfirms the hypothesized unidimensional sanction hierarchy of the incentive approach (IN-1). This conclusion is further strengthened by the fact that four of the five strategies in the public–private control scale are regarded as appropriate, while four of the five strategies in the indirect control scale are perceived as inappropriate reactions.

Note that in the overall rating of the appropriateness of the strategies in the public–private scale, only public arguing received a negative score. This strategy occupies one extreme of the scale. At the other extreme one finds the analogous confrontational strategy for the private context, bilateral arguing. Both strategies are followed by their positive equivalent: soberly discussing the problem during a meeting and discussing the problem personally with the trouble maker. The latter is also the most preferred stimulus in the whole set of reactions (87 per cent mentioned it as likely or very likely). The centre of the scale is occupied by the strategy 'asking colleagues for their opinion'.

As in the first scale, there is a gradual transition in the indirect control scale from strategies rated as appropriate to a final strategy that is rated as inappropriate. The first two items represent the activation of a mediator. In the first case, the mediator is a colleague at the same hierarchical level. In the second case, it is the superior. Note that vertical mediation is much more frequently chosen than lateral mediation: 58 per cent of the respondents mentioned the invocation of the boss as very likely or likely, compared to 14 per cent who regard lateral mediation as a viable option. Further, while lateral mediation received a slightly negative overall rating, vertical mediation is generally accepted as an appropriate strategy. From the items in scale two, vertical mediation is by far the most preferred control strategy. The last three items of the scale contain forms of indirect control that have a clearly negative character: complaining to the superior or to colleagues about the deviator, as well as retaliation. The latter is situated at the lowest end of the scale: only 5 per cent of the respondents mentioned it as a reaction that would be likely.

Two items have been dropped by the scaling algorithm: 'Avoiding further interaction with the trouble maker', and 'Keeping one's temper and doing nothing'. Both items are mentioned by only a very small fraction as likely reactions (5 per cent and 7 per cent, respectively). This is a significant finding because resignation reflects the absence of a control effort, and avoidance represents a unilateral action – and both strategies represent behaviour which, compared to the other items in the list, is not easily visible or recognizable, and therefore has no relational signalling value.

In sum, there are at least two latent dimensions underlying sanctioning behaviour, as predicted by the signalling approach (RS-1): one continuum ranging from public to private forms of social control, and another one ranging from constructive forms of indirect social control in the form of third party mediation to rather destructive manifestations like gossiping and retaliation. There seems to be a shared conception concerning the rank order of control strategies according to their appropriateness. However, these form not one but two unidimensional scales, dominated by either negatively or positively evaluated strategies. Overall, these results favour the relational signalling approach, and disconfirm the predictions of the incentive approach (IN-1).

**Proportionality Effect versus Escalation Effect**

In order to test the remaining hypotheses, the scale values of the two unfolding scales as well as the variables 'resignation' and 'avoidance' were used as the dependent variables in a multivariate analysis of variance.[2] A 'one between, three within' design was chosen. It contains the following factors and factor levels: (a) the first within subjects factor was the *severity* of the grievance (weak versus strong); (b) the second within subjects factor represents the *frequency* of the grievance (unique versus repeated); (c) the third within subject factor covers the *scope* of the grievance (affecting only a single individual or the whole group); (d) formal *rank* is included as a between subject control variable (superior versus subordinate).

Generally, the null hypothesis that the mean likelihood of choosing a strategy will be the same for each of the eight situations can be rejected for both scales and the item 'resignation', whereas no significant effects were detected for the item 'avoidance'. The results of the analysis are summarized in Tables 9.5–9.7.

The *proportionality hypothesis* of the incentive approach predicted that the likelihood of sanctioning as well as the sanction level are a direct function of the severity of the grievance, independent of the relational signalling character of the grievance. Translated into the current research design, this would require that grievance severity have (a) a negative main effect on resignation and (b) a positive main effect on both sanctioning hierarchies. Note that, from an incentive perspective, one would also expect that the repeated production of trouble by the same person will not have an impact on sanctioning behaviour: what counts for a rational actor is purely the costs that result from the current externalities produced by somebody else. Externalities that have occurred in the past and that have been sanctioned are irrelevant for the cost–benefit calculation of whether or not and how to react to a current grievance, since it does not matter who produced them.

The results provide only partial support for the *proportionality hypothesis*. First, the likelihood of resignation is in fact significantly lower for strong compared to weak grievances, as predicted by IN-2a. Second, grievance severity also has a significant impact on the public–private continuum of social control: the stronger the grievance, the more likely the choice of private control strategies becomes. However, no significant relationship could be detected between grievance severity and the continuum of indirect control. Thus, the second half of the proportionality hypothesis (IN-2b) could only partially be supported by the data.

The *escalation hypothesis* of the relational signalling approach predicted that the likelihood of sanctioning and the level of negative sanctions increase with the negative relational signalling character of the

*The trust process in organizations*

*Table 9.5   Results of MANOVA*

| Independent variable | Scale 1 Public– private | | Scale 2 Indirect | | Item Resignation | |
|---|---|---|---|---|---|---|
| | F | p | F | p | F | p |
| Hierarchy (between subjects) | 0.00 | 1.000 | 0.03 | 0.872 | 1.45 | 0.245 |
| Severity | **6.63** | **0.020** | 0.30 | 0.593 | **13.69** | **0.002** |
| Hierarchy * Severity | 0.41 | 0.528 | 0.30 | 0.593 | 3.85 | 0.066 |
| Frequency | 0.01 | 0.914 | **16.22** | **0.001** | **13.37** | **0.002** |
| Hierarchy * Frequency | **5.07** | **0.038** | 2.03 | 0.172 | **13.37** | **0.002** |
| Group | 0.56 | 0.466 | 0.28 | 0.603 | 0.43 | 0.523 |
| Hierarchy * Group | 0.01 | 0.927 | 0.28 | 0.603 | 0.16 | 0.690 |
| Severity * Frequency | **5.23** | **0.035** | 2.14 | 0.162 | 0.81 | 0.381 |
| Hierarchy * Severity * Frequency | 0.66 | 0.428 | 1.34 | 0.263 | 2.34 | 0.144 |
| Severity * Group | 1.37 | 0.258 | 0.10 | 0.760 | **9.84** | **0.006** |
| Hierarchy * Severity * Group | 0.18 | 0.675 | 0.10 | 0.760 | 0.08 | 0.779 |
| Frequency *Group | 0.40 | 0.538 | 0.16 | 0.698 | 1.01 | 0.330 |
| Hierarchy * Frequency * Group | 0.08 | 0.785 | 0.97 | 0.338 | 2.88 | 0.108 |
| Severity * Frequency * Group | 0.00 | 0.981 | 2.42 | 0.139 | 1.28 | 0.274 |
| Hierarchy * Severity * Frequency * Group | 0.09 | 0.763 | 0.75 | 0.400 | 1.96 | 0.179 |

*Notes:*   Between subjects factor: hierarchy (high v. low); within subjects factor: grievance severity (strong v. weak), grievance frequency (repeated v. unique), grievance scope (group v. individual); df = 1, n = 152 observations on each dependent variable (based on the responses of 19 respondents to 8 situations). Bold figures represent significant results (p <= 0.05). Convention for degrees of freedom represented by df. Asterisks indicate interaction effects.

grievance, but do so independent of the size of the loss. This implies that the repeated occurrence of a grievance should have (a) a significant negative main effect on resignation, and (b) a significant positive main effect on the continuum of indirect control. The factor should either have no affect on the continuum of public–private control or be negatively associated with this variable, since it represents sanctions conveying positive relational signals.

The results lend support to both parts of the escalation hypothesis (RS-2a and RS-2b). The repeated occurrence of an externality decreases the likelihood of resignation and increases the likelihood of indirect control, indicating a stronger inclination to switch from mediation (the lower part of the scale) towards more confrontational indirect strategies and retaliation (the upper part of the scale). In fact, grievance frequency is the only factor that has a significant effect on the continuum of indirect control, which implies that the severity of the grievance does not affect the use of

*Table 9.6    Means for the effects on scale 1 (public versus private control)*

|  | Strong | Weak | Superior | Subordinate |
|---|---|---|---|---|
| Repeated | 2.583 | 3.500 | 2.979 | 3.286 |
| Unique | 3.250 | 3.000 | 3.271 | 2.964 |
| Total | 2.917 | 3.250 | 3.125 | 3.125 |

*Table 9.7    Means for the interaction effects on the item 'Resignation'*

|  | Strong | Weak |  | Repeated | Unique |
|---|---|---|---|---|---|
| Group | 4.111 | 3.429 | Superior | 4.313 | 4.313 |
| Bilateral | 4.500 | 3.857 | Subordinate | 4.321 | 3.643 |
| Total | 4.306 | 3.643 | Total | 4.317 | 3.978 |

sanctioning strategies that are generally evaluated as inappropriate. This supports the claim made by relational signalling theory that forms of indirect control like gossiping or retaliation are activated by a different mechanism than direct bilateral or public sanctions.

The repeated production of trouble by the same individual does not have a direct effect on the public–private continuum of sanctioning, but there is a significant interaction effect between grievance severity and grievance frequency (see Figure 9.4). That is, repeated grievances that are perceived as *weak* elicit a *higher* level of escalation on this scale (that is, private, bilateral sanctions rather than public sanctions) than unique grievances of the same level of low severity. This finding is unexpected both from an incentive perspective (which predicted no association between the two variables) and from a relational signalling perspective, which predicted that grievance frequency, being an indicator of the negative relational signalling character of grievance, would have a negative or no impact on the public–private control continuum (since the latter measures sanctions with positive relational signalling value). While both predictions are correct in so far as the main effect of grievance frequency is not significant, the positive interaction with grievance severity is inconsistent with both theoretical explanations.

Overall, the results seem to be slightly in favour of the signalling approach, given the fact that grievance severity does not affect indirect control, and grievance frequency does increase the likelihood of sanctioning.

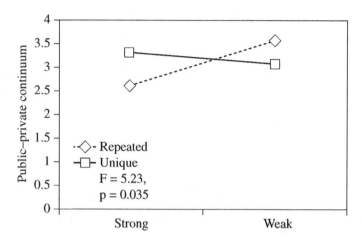

*Figure 9.4   Impact of grievance severity and frequency on public–private control*

### Free-rider Effect versus Group Obligation Effect

The incentive approach argued that grievance scope has (a) either a negative or no effect on the likelihood of sanctioning, and (b) that group-related grievances would elicit weaker sanctions than grievances limited to a single individual. The signalling approach predicted that group-related grievances would increase both the likelihood and the strength of the sanction.

As can be seen in Table 9.5, grievance scope does not have a significant main effect on any of the dependent variables. However, there is a significant interaction effect between grievance scope and grievance severity on the item 'resignation': strong individual grievances are more likely to increase the willingness to allocate a sanction than weak group-related grievances. These results clearly confirm the first part of the *free-rider hypothesis* (IN-3a), and disconfirm the first part of the *group obligation hypothesis* (RS-3a). The fact that grievance scope does not have an impact on the other two dependent variables leads to the conclusion that the second part of both hypotheses (IN-3b and RS-3b) is not supported by the data.

Overall, the findings presented in this section are in favour of the incentive approach and contradict the relational signalling approach, since group-related grievances seem to decrease rather than to increase the willingness to sanction.

**Formal Rank**

The between-subject variable 'rank' has no main effect on the dependent variables. However, significant interactions were found between rank and grievance frequency on public–private control and resignation. When confronted by a repeated loss, superiors are both more likely to become active as agents of social control and to use public control strategies than subordinates (see Figures 9.5 and 9.6).

## DISCUSSION AND CONCLUSION

The present research contributes to the study of informal control in two ways. First, theoretically, there is a disentangling of two alternative micro foundations of a theory of social control in organizations which link types of trouble and sanction strength. Second, empirically, the study develops a theoretically grounded instrument for the measurement of sanctioning hierarchies and provides further insight into the way grievances are handled in so-called 'trust cultures'. More specifically, a first comparative test of two alternative theories of informal control behaviour was conducted, the incentive approach and the relational signalling approach. Empirically, the major results of the analysis can be summarized as follows: (a) sanctions should be conceived in terms of at least two latent dimensions or escalation hierarchies; (b) the stronger and the more frequent the grievance, the more

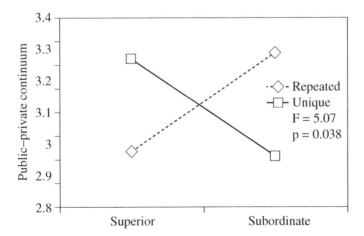

*Figure 9.5*   *Impact of grievance frequency and rank on public–private control*

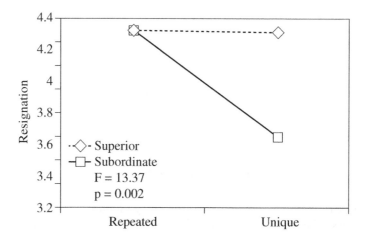

*Figure 9.6   Impact of grievance frequency and rank on resignation*

likely active control efforts become; (c) escalation from public to private control is primarily a function of grievance severity; (d) escalation from constructive to destructive forms of indirect control is exclusively a function of grievance frequency; (e) grievance scope and formal position of the controller have no independent impact on sanctioning behaviour, but they do interact with grievance severity and frequency, respectively.

The empirical results of this study are summarized in Figures 9.7–9.9. It should be stressed that these results are based on data that were gathered in a team that was in a phase of high interdependence and trust, where solidarity was strong and the group goal salient.

On a theoretical level, these results lead to the following conclusions. First, they point towards the need to revise thoroughly the (often implicit) assumption of a *unidimensional* sanctioning hierarchy as made by incentive theories. Sanctions are evaluated not only in terms of their strength, but also according to some other criteria. They are cognitively *multidimensional* constructs. It was argued that the most important candidate for identifying these constructs is relational signals. This implies that there are at least two types of negative sanctions: those that convey negative relational signals, and those that do not. In the first case, the actor allocating a sanction not only punishes the offender by communicating behavioural disapproval, but also signals that he or she is increasingly less willing to view the relationship with the target as one of solidarity. In the second case, the sanction communicates disapproval, but at the same time signals to the offender that the person allocating the sanction is still interested in maintaining the status quo in the relationship and complying with solidarity norms.

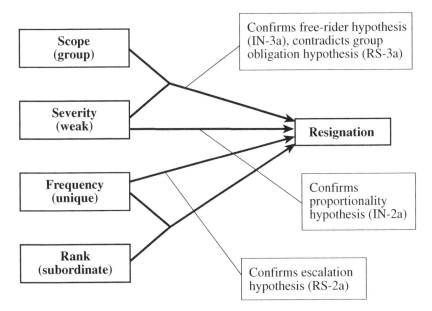

*Figure 9.7   Empirical predictors of absence of control efforts*

Second, the results provide mixed evidence for the incentive approach and the relational signalling approach. On the one hand, the confirmation of the *escalation hypothesis* favours the claim made by relational signalling theory that sanction strength is not a simple linear function of grievance strength, as argued in the *proportionality hypothesis* of the incentive approach, but is contingent upon the relational signalling character of the grievance. On the other hand, the negative impact of group-related grievances on the willingness to sanction and on the strength of sanctions clearly favours the *free-rider hypothesis* of the incentive approach and contradicts the *group identification hypothesis* of the signalling approach.

Taken together, this evidence shows that, while the social mechanisms underlying sanctioning behaviour are more complex than assumed by the incentive approach, the relational signalling approach only partially succeeded in generating empirical support for its refined perspective.

In this context, some shortcomings of the present study should be pointed out. First, the operationalization of sanctioning hierarchies and the measurement of the signalling character of grievances as well as that of sanctions are far from perfect. Though the application of multidimensional unfolding techniques produced interesting insights into the cognitive representation of sanctions, more systematic efforts need to be made to assess the robustness of the final scales.

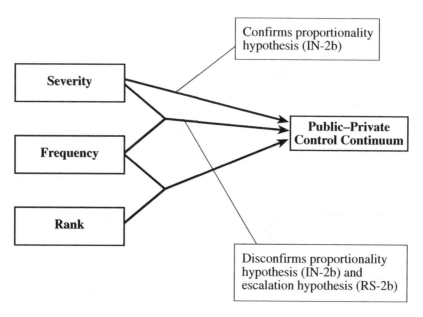

*Figure 9.8    Empirical predictors of private–public control*

At least five promising areas for future research emerge from these conclusions. First, it seems worth while to investigate the perception of grievances, in particular the degree to which they affect a whole group or only a single individual, and whether they are attributed to intentional norm violations or accidents. In the present study, the measurement of these perceptions in the form of manipulation checks remained very crude, as was the operationalization of the signalling value of grievances by distinguishing between repeated and unique misbehaviour. Second, by specifying how interpersonal relations affect the evaluation of behaviour of others, the relational signalling approach might contribute to tackling one of the major shortcomings of attribution theory. Both approaches might benefit from a more thorough exploration of the potential interrelationships between framing, signalling and attribution processes. Third, far more insights are needed regarding the cognitive representation of sanctioning strategies and their potential signalling character. The comparison with a general appropriateness rating as used in the present study yields only imperfect information about this dimension. Fourth, more theoretical work needs to be done to link aspects of grievances with the quality of the relationship between the offender and the person allocating a sanction. Here one could build on recent insights from studies linking social network characteristics to control behaviour (Black, 1984; Burt, 1992; Flap, 1988;

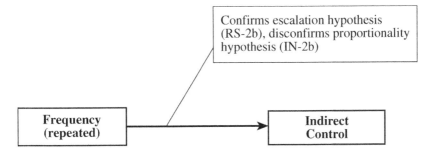

*Figure 9.9    Empirical predictors of indirect control*

Friedkin, 1983; Gargiulo, 1993; Lazega, 1992; Wittek *et al.*, 2001). Finally, more attention needs to be paid to forms, causes and consequences of indirect control.

In sum, it seems that the signalling approach offers a promising extension to the study of social control in small groups because it provides an explanation for effects that would be difficult to account for with the incentive perspective. Though far from complete, the evidence presented suggests that the idea that relational signals are a layer that will significantly influence how we interpret misbehaviour and how we react to it might be a fruitful way of extending our knowledge on informal social control and the functioning of workgroups in organizational settings.

## NOTES

1. In order to minimize effects of social desirability, it was initially planned to ask respondents to judge what they would expect their colleagues to do. Most respondents had said that they would have difficulties with such an evaluation. Consequently, the instruction was changed and the respondents were asked to indicate how they, personally, would react in such a situation.
2. Note that each actor has 16 scale values: one for each of the eight situations on the 'public–private control' scale and the 'indirect control' scale.

## REFERENCES

Augoustinos, M. and I. Walker (1995), *Social Cognition: An Integrated Introduction*, London: Sage.
Black, D. (1984), 'Social control as a dependent variable', in Donald Black (ed.), *Toward a General Theory of Social Control. Vol. 1: Fundamentals*, Orlando: Academic Press, pp. 1–36.
Braspenning, J. (1992), 'Framing: De Prospecttheorie en het Discriminatiemodel', doctoral dissertation, University of Groningen.

Burt, R. (1992), *Structural Holes. The Social Structure of Competition*, Cambridge, MA: Harvard University Press.

Erickson, B. and T. Nosanchuk (1984), 'The allocation of esteem and disesteem: a test of Goode's theory', *American Sociological Review*, **49**, 648–58.

Flache, A. and M. Macy (1996), 'The weakness of strong ties: collective action failure in a highly cohesive group', *Journal of Mathematical Sociology*, **21**, 3–28.

Flap, H. (1988), *Conflict, Loyalty and Violence. The Effects of Social Networks on Behaviour*, Frankfurt am Main: Peter Lang.

Freidson, E. (1975), *Doctoring Together. A Study of Professional Social Control*, New York: Elsevier.

Friedkin, N. (1983), 'Horizons of observability and limits of informal control in organizations', *Social Forces*, **62** (1), 54–77.

Gargiulo, M. (1993), 'Two-step leverage: managing constraint in organizational politics', *Administrative Science Quarterly*, **38**, 1–19.

Griffith, W. (1989), 'The allocation of negative outcomes,' *Advances in Group Processes*, **6**, 107–37.

Heckathorn, D. (1990), 'Collective sanctions and compliance norms: a formal theory of group-mediated social control', *American Sociological Review*, **55**, 366–84.

Heckathorn, D. (1993), 'Collective action and group heterogeneity: voluntary provision versus selective incentives', *American Sociological Review*, **58**, 329–50.

Hewstone, M. (1983), *Attribution Theory. Social and Functional Extensions*, Oxford: Basil Blackwell.

Jaspars, J., F. Fincham and M. Hewstone (eds) (1983), *Attribution Theory and Research: Conceptual, Developmental and Social Dimensions*, London: Academic Press.

Kahnemann, D. and A. Tversky (1979), 'Prospect theory: an analysis of decision under risk', *Econometrica*, **47**, 263–91.

Kandel, E. and E. Lazear (1992), 'Peer pressure and partnerships', *Journal of Political Economy*, **100** (41), 801–17.

Kellermann, K. and T. Cole (1994), 'Classifying compliance gaining messages: taxonomic disorder and strategic confusion', *Communication Theory*, **4** (1), 3–60.

Kipnis, D., S. Schmidt and I. Wilkinson (1980), 'Intraorganizational influence tactics: explorations in getting one's way', *Journal of Applied Psychology*, **65** (4), 440–52.

Lange, E. (1975), *Strukturprobleme einfacher Interaktionssysteme. Eine empirische Untersuchung über Informationsdefizite, Nonkonformität, Dissens und ihre Abwicklung*, Berlin: Duncker & Humblot.

Lazega, E. (1992), 'Analyse de réseaux d'une organization collégiale: les avocats d'affaires', *Revue française de sociologie*, **XXXIII**, 559–89.

Ligthart, P. (1995), *Solidarity in Economic Transactions. An Experimental Study of Framing Effects in Bargaining and Contracting*, Amsterdam: Thesis Publishers.

Ligthart, P. and S. Lindenberg (1994), 'Ethical regulation of economic transactions: solidarity frame versus gain-maximization frame', in K. Wärneryd and A. Lewis (eds), *Ethics and Economic Affairs*, London: Routledge.

Lindenberg, S. (1982), 'Sharing groups: theory and suggested applications', *Journal of Mathematical Sociology*, **9**, 33–62.

Lindenberg, S. (1988), 'Contractual relations and weak solidarity: the behavioural basis of restraints on gain-maximization', *Journal of Institutional and Theoretical Economics*, **144**, 39–58.

Lindenberg, S. (1992), 'An extended theory of institutions and contractual discipline', *Journal of Institutional and Theoretical Economics*, **148**, 125–54.

Lindenberg, S. (1993), 'Framing, empirical evidence and applications', *Jahrbuch für Neue Politische Ökonomie*, Tübingen: Mohr (Siebeck), pp. 11–35.

Lindenberg, S. (1994), 'Norms and the power of loss: Ellickson's theory and beyond', *Journal of Theoretical and Institutional Economics*, **150** (1), 101–13.

Lindenberg, S. (1997), 'Grounding groups in theory: functional, structural and cognitive interdependencies', *Advances in Group Processes*, **14**, 281–331.

Lindenberg, S. (1998), 'Solidarity: its microfoundations and macrodependence. a framing approach', in P. Doreian and T. Fararo (eds), *The Problem of Solidarity. Theories and Models,* Gordon and Breach, pp. 61–112.

Macy, M. (1993), 'Backward-looking social control', *American Sociological Review*, **58**, 819–36.

Marwell, G. and D. Schmitt (1967), 'Dimensions of compliance-gaining behaviour: an empirical analysis', *Sociometry*, **30**, 350–64.

Morey, N. and F. Luthans (1991), 'The use of dyadic alliances in informal organization: an ethnographic study', *Human Relations*, **44** (6), 597–618.

Morrill, C. (1989), 'The management of managers: disputing in an executive hierarchy', *Sociological Forum*, **4** (3), 387–407.

Morrill, C. (1991), 'The customs of conflict management among corporate executives', *American Anthropologist*, **93** (4), 871–93.

Mühlau, P. (2000), '*The governance of the employment relation. A relational signalling perspective*', doctoral dissertation, University of Groningen.

Noon, M. and R. Delbridge (1993), 'News from behind my hand: gossip in organizations', *Organization Studies*, **14** (1), 23–36.

Pennings, J. and J. Woiceshyn (1987), 'A typology of organizational control and its metaphors', *Research in the Sociology of Organizations*, **5**, 73–104.

Richmond, V., L. Davis, K. Saylor and J. McCroskey (1984), 'Power strategies in organizations. Communication techniques and messages', *Human Communication Research*, **11** (1), 85–108.

Rossi, P. (1979), 'Vignette analysis: uncovering the normative structure of complex judgements', in R. Merton, J. S. Coleman and P. Rossi, *Qualitative and Quantitative Social Research. Papers in Honour of Paul L. Lazarsfeld*, New York: Free Press, pp. 176–86.

Thurman, B. (1979), 'In the office: networks and coalitions', *Social Networks*, **2**, 47–63.

Van Schuur, W. (1993), '*The nonparametric proximity model*', manuscript.

Van Schuur, W. and W.J. Post (1990), *MUDFOLD Users Manual*, Groningen: iec ProGamma.

Wielers, R. (1997), 'The wages of trust: the case of child minders', *Rationality and Society*, **9** (3), 351–71.

Wittek, R. (1999). '*Interdependence and informal control in organizations*', doctoral dissertation, University of Groningen.

Wittek, R., M. van Duijn and T. Snijders (2001), 'Informele netwerken en sociale escalatie van conflicten in ccn managementteam', *Sociale Wetenschappen*, **44** (1), 48–67.

# 10. The dynamics of trust and trouble
## Frédérique Six

## INTRODUCTION

This chapter reports on the exploration of the dynamics of trust and trouble in a professional services firm in the Netherlands. The aim of the research is to identify how people deal with trust and trouble. How is trust developed and maintained? How does trouble influence this process? We argue that trust and trouble are inextricably linked in organizational life. Both trust and trouble deal with patterns of expectations. With trust the pattern is confirmed; with trouble the pattern is disrupted. Furthermore, in relationships where cooperation is desired, trust is an important quality. Yet, since the world is unpredictable and people do not always behave rationally, patterns of expectations, or trust, are inevitably disrupted. Hence trouble, an unpleasant surprise, is inevitable.

Our quest for improving our understanding of the dynamics of trust and trouble is driven by our belief that, the better our ability to deal with trust and trouble, the better we are at building and maintaining the network of generative relationships out of which novel resource deployments can be created: that is, innovation. Future research will make the connections between the current research and this innovative ability.

The Living Company (TLC) is an international professional services firm in the field of human resource management and professional development. It provides consulting, coaching and training services. TLC may be characterized by the strong culture it has built and the explicit vision, mission, values and principles it has formulated. The business processes are characterized by the many explicit rules and procedures laid down in quality handbooks. New recruits are subjected to an intensive socialization process to learn and internalize what TLC is about, how it operates and what is expected of those working within it. Every single person working within the Dutch office has a coach for her/his professional and personal development. In the autumn of 2000, TLC had over 200 employees worldwide of which more than one-third were part of the Dutch office. Within the Dutch office, the consultants and commercial assistants form operational units. The six units meet once a month to discuss and exchange views on operational matters. The heads of the support departments also meet once a month to discuss operational matters. The usual support departments can be distinguished such as finance, personnel, IT and reception. Through the structure of the work within TLC, there is a high risk of fragmentation: the consultants carry out the work for clients on their own and most of the acquisition and sales is done alone. They often only visit the office once a month for the monthly meeting. This risk of fragmentation may be illustrated by the regular spin-offs of groups of consultants: both internationally and in Holland, the organization went through some crises as groups of people split off from the core to start their own firm. To counteract this risk, a system has been introduced whereby the operational units are rotated every year to avoid separate kingdoms being created. This results in a situation where a consultant (or commercial assistant) who has been with the firm for several years will have had a functional relationship with most of his or her colleagues within that office.

The structure of the chapter is as follows: after a brief description of the data collection methods, we first investigate how trust is developed, defining trust and exploring trust processes and the strategies for building trust within TLC. Next, we investigate how trouble influences the trust process, exploring how trouble is dealt with and what the impact is on the relationship. Finally, we draw conclusions and formulate avenues for further research.

## DATA COLLECTION

The data on which this chapter is based are the trust and trouble events, called cases, collected during exploratory research within the Dutch office of The Living Company. People were interviewed and meetings were observed, yielding a total of 52 hours of recorded material. Of the 197 cases collected, 80 cases (41 per cent) were labelled as trouble, 63 cases (32 per cent) as trust and 54 cases (27 per cent) as trust and trouble.[1] A total of 122 cases are based on interviews (62 per cent) and 75 are based on observations (38 per cent). All cases were entered into a database and coded along several dimensions. The codification was carried out by the person who had provided the case (interviews) or who was directly involved (observations). The researcher had independently coded the cases on the basis of the case description, and had checked whether the participant had chosen the correct perspective and had understood the questions. In a selection of the cases, the other person involved was also asked to codify the case. Not all cases were coded by the person directly involved: in eight cases the person involved was no longer in active service with the organization; 39

concerned a straightforward compliment given to a colleague for a particular job well done, which was not checked in order to reduce the burden for the codifiers. Some 89 per cent of the people involved returned the forms with codifications. A total of 27 interviews (over one-third of the office) were conducted: 14 in-depth interviews (face-to-face) of on average one and a half hours, and 13 telephone interviews, usually of half an hour. All interviews involved asking the interviewee to recall events in which he or she was conscious that trust and/or trouble was involved. The in-depth interviews also focused on getting a sense of how trust is developed, and on getting a sense of the organizational context – the culture and structure of the organization. Finally, a range of meetings were observed.

# DEVELOPING TRUST

Many authors emphasize the importance of trust as a quality of cooperative relationships (among others, Argyris, 1970; Nooteboom, 2000; Deutsch, 1973; Isaacs, 1999; Zand, 1972, 1997; Ghoshal and Bartlett, 1997). For example, 'trust frees people to be open, lifting relationships to new heights of achievements; mistrust shrivels people, destroying their relationship through frustration and rage' (Zand, 1997, p. 97). Does that make trust the be-all and end-all of cooperation? No, trust is a more complex phenomenon. There are limits to trust; trust is situation-specific and person-specific. Blind trust is naïve. Therefore there are valid reasons and occasions for distrust.

In this section we define trust, look at the dimensions of trustworthiness, and explore the processes for developing trust.

## Defining Trust

Defining trust requires a decision on what perspective you want to take: are you looking at the noun 'the trust' or at the verb 'to trust'? The first approach focuses on the disposition to engage in trusting behaviour, while the second approach focuses on the trusting behaviour itself. Both approaches can be found in the literature on trust, although the dispositional approach appears to dominate (for example, Zucker, 1986; Bradach and Eccles, 1989; Boon and Holmes, 1991; Barney and Hansen, 1994; Mayer *et al.*, 1995; McAllister, 1995, 1997; Fukuyama, 1995; Tyler and Kramer, 1996; Shaw, 1997; Nooteboom, 2000). Other authors focus on the enactment of trust, although many implicitly translate 'to trust' as 'to cooperate'. Deutsch (1973), Zand (1972, 1997), Lewis and Weigert (1985) and Ghoshal and Bartlett (1997) do not make that implicit translation, yet stress the behavioural dimension. For example, 'to trust is to live *as if* certain rationally possible futures will not occur' (Lewis and Weigert, 1985, p. 969). We also focus on the action, that is the enactment of trust. Adapting from Mayer *et al.* (1995, who incidentally follow the dispositional approach), we will use the following definition: to trust is to make yourself vulnerable to the actions of another party in the expectation that the other will perform a particular action which is important to you. This comes close to Zand's description: to trust is to 'increase one's vulnerability to others whose behavior one cannot control' (Zand, 1972, p. 231). In this approach, a disposition or willingness to trust becomes a willingness to make yourself vulnerable to the actions of the other party. It incorporates the factors grounding trust, that is, the perceived trustworthiness of the trustee and the trustor's general propensity to trust. The contextual factors of the specific situation in which you face the question of behaving in a trusting way (or not), that is, the risks involved and the alternatives available, will determine whether you will turn that willingness into actual trusting behaviour (Mayer *et al.*, 1995). Important also in this approach is the use of the notion of vulnerability. Making yourself vulnerable implies that you can get hurt. This is exactly the dilemma you face when considering whether to take a trusting action or not. You will only open yourself up to this chance of damage when the upside is worth it, or when the action you want the other to take is important to you. Finally, the role of expectations needs to be stressed. Trust is about having a particular pattern of expectations in which the other person does what you want him to do, even though you cannot control his behaviour.

Why this focus on the action? First, Lewis and Weigert argue that the enactment is part and parcel of the trust phenomenon, which consists of three dimensions: the cognitive process, the emotional base and the behavioural enactment of trust: 'The behavioural content of trust is the undertaking of a risky course of action on the confident expectation that all persons involved in the action will act competently and dutifully. [. . .] Behavioural displays of trust-implying actions help to create the cognitive platform of trust [and] help to establish or reinforce the emotional sentiment of trust' (1985, p. 971). Furthermore, Hardin (1993) also stresses the importance of the action as he develops Luhmann's (1979, p. 27) statement that 'trust has to be learned, just like any other kind of generalization'. He argues from a Bayesian learning perspective that excessive trusters, those who err on the side of too much trust in others, will enter far more interactions than the distrusters, who err on the side of too much distrust, and will therefore have many more direct opportunities to correct their judgment of the 'correct level' of trustworthiness. He concludes that, even in only modestly supportive worlds, adopting not only the attitude but also the behaviour of an optimistic truster may be beneficial, since that behaviour opens up the possibility of discovering the trustworthy. Finally, this choice best fits the topic of this research: the *dynamics* of trust and trouble and the impact of trust and trouble on relationships.

## Dimensions of Trustworthiness

What can we have trust in? In the literature, many different dimensions of trustworthiness are distinguished. Mayer *et al.* have studied over 20 sources to analyse which dimensions of trustworthiness are used. They then propose three dimensions which in their opinion 'explain a major portion of trustworthiness' (Mayer *et al.*, 1995, p. 717): ability, benevolence and integrity (both personal and moral). On the basis of our own analysis, which appears to be supported by the empirical evidence at TLC, we use the following categories: ability, benevolence, dedication and ethics.

*Ability* (or competence) is 'that group of skills, competencies and characteristics that enable a party to have influence within some specific domain' (ibid.). It is situation- and domain-specific. Does the trustee have the skills, experience, means and position to perform as I want? A person may be highly competent, and therefore worthy of my trust, in one area, for example finance, but inexperienced or incompetent in another area, such as personnel. Also a person may simply not be in a position to influence or even control the situation in the direction desired by the trustor. For example, a superior promises you that you will be able to follow a particular career path within the organization. That person, however, is not in a position to deliver on that promise as he does not control the resources; nor does he have the decision-making power required to deliver.

*Benevolence* is 'the extent to which the trustee is believed to want to do good to the trustor, aside from an egocentric profit motive' (ibid., p. 718). It is person-specific. Benevolence only appears relevant when the trustee has opportunities for opportunistic behaviour. And there are limits to the occasions when people will forgo opportunistic opportunities: everyone has a price (Nooteboom, 2000).

*Dedication* is the extent to which the trustee is believed to make the effort to meet the expectations of the trustor. Dedication as a dimension of trustworthiness is about commitment, punctuality, making the effort and reliability. If the trustee fails, despite making the effort, this may be because of his inability to meet the expectations of the trustor in the specific situation; and since the trustee tried but failed, the trustor was not aware of his inability. Or the failure despite the effort may be due to changed circumstances which have led the trustee to change his priorities to opportunistic behaviour after all. The distinction between benevolence and dedication may be illustrated by the situation in which the trustee really means well – is benevolent towards the trustor – but he cannot be bothered to make the effort. One could possibly argue that, if you cannot be bothered, you are not really benevolent, since your egocentric laziness dominates. But, in real life, these situations occur regularly, hence the distinction is found to be useful. The trustee can also be found to be dedicated without being benevolent. This occurs when the particular action that the trustor trusts the trustee to take is also in the trustee's own interest; that is, he has an egocentric profit motive. Is trust relevant in that situation? Yes, because the trustee's self-interest may be weak and he may therefore not bother. The trustor has to consider how dedicated the trustee is, whether he will bother to make the effort. Perceived lack of dedication needs to be evaluated carefully. It can simply be due to the natural occurrence of inconsistent behaviour. Even though many of us make an effort to 'practise what we preach' or 'walk our talk', we will never be perfect. Mayer *et al.*'s third dimension includes personal integrity or one's adherence to a set of principles. This has to do with making the effort and being dedicated.

*Ethics* is the acceptability of the trustee's set of values and principles. Since it is rare for two individuals to have complete value-congruence, occasions for violations of trust, that is, trouble, exist whenever we find the other's principles unacceptable. Someone can be highly capable, benevolent towards me and dedicated, yet I may want to have nothing to do with him. He may be benevolent to me but, in wanting to help me, hurt others. He may not behave opportunistically towards me, but take every chance he gets to take what he can from others. This is likely to happen when I belong to his 'clan' and the other person does not. If someone helps me by behaving in ways that I consider unethical, I will not ask this person to help me. I may even avoid contact because I do not want this person to volunteer to help me. For example, he may steal, commit fraud, lie or otherwise harm others or break rules. He may consider that fair play while I do not. The emphasis is thus on the trustee's behaviour towards others: whether that is acceptable to the trustor.

Within TLC, in two-thirds of the trust cases the most relevant dimension of trustworthiness is ability, while almost three-quarters of the trouble cases deal with a perceived lack of dedication and ability (Table 10.1). It may be surprising to see such a low occurrence of ethics as the most relevant dimension of trustworthiness. In general, an organization can reduce the chances of experiencing trouble because of lack of acceptability of the other's values and principles through the explicit definition of those values and principles relevant for operating within its organization. This facilitates value-congruence occurring on those dimensions. TLC has done exactly that: it is very explicit in its vision, mission, values and principles. This not only reduces the chances of trouble due to unacceptable values and principles, but it also enhances the resolution of trouble when, inevitably, it does occur. In almost two-thirds of the cases in which trouble occurred, a reference was made to values, principles, rules or procedures. In three-quarters of the trust cases, no such reference was made – there appears to be no need. This appears to fit the ambitious, almost idealistic, attitude that many people in the organization exhibit.

*Table 10.1   Dimensions of trustworthiness, by type of case*

| Number of cases (n = 197) | Trust cases (n = 63) | Trust and trouble cases (n = 54) | Trouble cases (n = 80) |
|---|---|---|---|
| Ability (n = 83) | 41 | 19 | 23 |
| Benevolence (n = 31) | 5 | 10 | 16 |
| Dedication (n = 65) | 16 | 15 | 34 |
| Ethics (n = 17) | 1 | 10 | 6 |
| Not coded (n = 1) | — | — | 1 |

**Trust Processes**

Trust is best conceived as a dynamic process that develops as the parties involved interact. As the parties interact, trust or distrust, as the case may be, may develop. Zucker *et al.* (1996, p. 92) observe, 'trust production can occur when an individual is *open to social influence* from another individual or when a third party with whom both individuals are open to social influence intervenes to mediate'. McAllister (1995) proposes two stages of trust development: (a) cognition-based trust is trust grounded in the individual's beliefs about the other's reliability and professionalism; (b) affect-based trust is trust grounded in the emotional bonds connecting people. People make emotional investments in trust relationships, express genuine care and concern for the welfare of partners, believe in the intrinsic virtue of such relationships and believe that their sentiments are reciprocated.

He observes that affect-based trust only appears after a certain level of cognition-based trust is established. Lewicki and Bunker's (1996) three consecutive stages of trust development are comparable to McAllister's stages: calculus-based trust, knowledge-based trust and identification-based trust. In the first stage, cognition is the main basis for trust; in the second it is a mixture; and, in the third, affection is the main basis for trust. The authors point out that, as one moves from one stage to the next, the frame of reference changes: As one moves from calculus-based trust to knowledge-based trust, the frame changes from the perceptual sensitivity to *contrasts* between self and other to the perceptual sensitivity to the *assimilation* between self and other. And as one moves from knowledge-based trust to identification-based trust, the frame changes from extending one's *knowledge* about the other to the personal *identification* with the other.

Relationships within TLC appear to develop beyond a pure cognition-based and functional stage. In roughly one-third of the cases, the main basis for the trust was affect-based; in the other two-thirds of the cases it was cognition-based. Almost two-thirds of the trust cases are about giving public compliments. These nearly all have a cognitive basis. Affect-based trust cases are nearly always dealt with in private. Roughly two-thirds of the trouble cases are cognition-based. When looking at the way people within TLC tend to interact and talk about their relationships with their colleagues, the dominant frame appears to be about extending one's knowledge about the other and the perceptual sensitivity to the assimilation between self and other. In the closer personal relationships, personal identification with the other may occur. And in some instances perceptual sensitivity to contrasts between self and other dominates.

Does the development of trust always follow this sequence? Probably, but not necessarily. As Bart Nooteboom (Chapter 2 in this volume) points out, one can imagine situations in which the order is reversed. Within TLC, with its intensive selection and socialization process for consultants and commercial assistants, the frame of perceptual sensitivity to contrasts between self and other is usually only felt during the initial socialization period. New recruits who have finished their initial socialization are generally considered by other colleagues as sufficiently socialized to be approached with a frame of perceptual sensitivity to the assimilation between self and others. Only in situations where trouble leads to a downward recalibration of the relationship will the frame of perceptual sensitivity to contrasts between self and other become dominant. So, in fact, the order is reversed in these instances.

What actions are effective when one wants consciously to build trust? Building on Zand (1972, 1997), we identify the following key actions:

- *information*: disclose information in an accurate and timely fashion, give both positive and negative feedback;
- *influence*: initiate and accept changes to your decisions, seek and accept the counsel of other people;
- *control*: make yourself dependent on the other person, delegate tasks, give responsibility to other people.

All these actions are observed regularly within TLC. In addition, people within TLC appear very strong on giving compliments to each other, both privately and in public. Private compliments can be considered as part of 'information' as it is about giving feedback to the other person. Public compliments serve this role as well and have another important role. Public compliments help build experience-based trust with people who have as yet little direct experience with the recipient of the compliment. It is a strong and effective way to use third parties in building trust within an organization. Finally, in general, compliments help build the self-confidence of the recipient of the compliment. Self-confidence is often considered to be an important prerequisite for being trusting and trustworthy.

The categories identified as relevant for TLC (the percentages give the relative frequency of occurrence) are:

- giving a public compliment (62 per cent);
- informing the other person about the situation and asking for advice (13 per cent);
- informing the other person about the situation (11 per cent);
- giving responsibility to another player (8 per cent);
- other (6 per cent).

The main trust development strategy that TLC adopts as an institution is the intensive socialization process to which newcomers in the organization are 'subjected'. During this socialization process, newcomers are told about the vision, mission, values and principles of TLC. This gives them many clues on how to interact within the organization. The socialization process also gives them an intensive training for the tasks they are expected to perform; they are taught explicitly what is expected of them. Thus they can build the confidence that they can do their job in the way that TLC expects of them. And, finally, they are taught the common TLC language and conceptual categories. TLC appears to be quite explicit about words that are relevant to its operations and interpersonal behaviour. The meanings of many words depict strong cultural aspects.[2] Principles such as confrontation – saying 'yes' to the person, and 'no' to the behaviour – and no gossip (we talk with people, not about them) help build the confidence to ask and inquire into behaviour and motives in situations where trust is necessary or trouble occurs. Another crucial element in building trust is the fact that everyone has a coach with whom they can discuss anything. If, for whatever reason, the coach–coachee relationship is troubled, the consultants and the commercial assistants always have other people who have helped them socialize and who can usually be trusted enough to discuss sensitive issues.

So far we have looked at ways in which newcomers to the organization can build trust in the organization and their colleagues. How do people learn to trust newcomers? Again, the socialization process is crucial. You can trust the socialization process to deliver people who know the basics of what they are expected to do. If newcomers are not up to it, they will not be 'released' into the organization. Also, after the initial introduction, newcomers receive close coaching and on-the-job training to continue practising what they have been taught and to develop new skills and experience. Basically, you can be sure that a person will not be allowed to perform a particular task alone, unless someone more experienced has checked that that person is able and ready to perform that task alone. And, as one interviewee describes it: 'The attitude is "go on, do it!", yet there is always someone checking, ready to offer support when needed.'

In general, many opportunities to celebrate success are taken within TLC, but this is especially the case with newcomers. This helps to build the trust others can have in the newcomer and helps to build the self-confidence of the newcomer. For example, during a unit meeting, the coach of a newcomer asks him to tell the unit his first commercial experience. After he has done so, the coach gives him a big public compliment. Later in the day, the coach tells this first success of the newcomer to all the partners in a partner meeting, again giving him a big compliment (in his absence).

## THE INFLUENCE OF TROUBLE ON TRUST MAINTENANCE

The models at the end of the previous section describe the development and deepening of trust over time through positive experiences. However, the trust experience is not necessarily always positive. There are limits to trust. Furthermore, since the world is unpredictable and people do not always behave rationally, unexpected events or surprises are inevitable. Hence an unpleasant surprise, or trouble, is inevitable. We define trouble as the disruption of the flow of expectations, which is, at least initially, experienced as unpleasant. Thus both trust and trouble deal with patterns of expectations. With trust, the pattern is confirmed; with trouble, the pattern is disrupted.

Dealing with trouble is something we would rather avoid. Three basic human tendencies are those towards consistency or balance, attribution and evaluation (Argyris, 1970). Yet the way to deal effectively with trouble requires us to do the opposite: to suspend our judgment (evaluation) and attributions and inquire into the causes of the troubling experience. After all, there are many possible causes behind a troubling experience, for example, a mishap, a misunderstanding, a disagreement, incompetence or malicious intent. Only some of these causes need lead to distrust. A violation of expectations 'produces a sense of disruption of trust, or profound confusion, but not of distrust. Distrust only emerges when the suspicion arises that the disruption of expectations in one exchange is likely to generalize to other transactions. To distrust, then, implies an attribution of intentionality that continues throughout all interactions or exchanges, at least of a particular type' (Zucker, 1986, p. 59).

It is this dynamic interplay between trust and trouble that ultimately determines the quality of a particular relationship and its effectiveness, or the degree to which it is sustainable and generative.

## Trouble Strategies

What strategy is used to deal with the trouble? From Wittek's (1999) perspective, social control is about bringing colleagues back into line after they have caused us trouble. He puts forward three aspects for becoming an active controller. First, there is the *informational* aspect of control. 'According to this view, the sanction provides corrective feedback information helping the target to adjust her behavior so that it is congruent with the behavioral expectations defined by the controller.' Second, there is the *damaging* aspect of sanctions as propagated by rational choice sociologists. 'They argue that humans break rules and defect if the benefits of this behavior outweigh its costs. Therefore, the costs of negative sanctions must outweigh the benefits of defection, in order that compliance to the rules be a more attractive option than their violation.' The third aspect is the *relational signalling* character of the corrective action. 'Relational signals are behavioral cues that allow us to make inferences about other people's interest in maintaining a mutually rewarding social relationship with us' (ibid., pp. 7–8).

Wittek distinguishes different social control strategies based on the person with whom the lead player communicates: no one (passive), the other player (private), a third party (indirect), a formal boss (formal), or both the other player and a third party (public). The way he approaches social control is very much one-way: the controller makes up his mind and takes action. This implicitly assumes that the controller has all the relevant information and has made an accurate assessment of the other's motives and intentions. Our interest goes beyond that. We also want to make a distinction regarding *whether or not the controller includes an inquiry step before executing a sanction*, and whether he executes a sanction at all. In other words, does the controller suspend his judgment until he has more relevant information to determine the cause behind a troubling experience? We believe that, for most of these causes, an approach that includes an open inquiry and an emphasis on the (mutual) informational and relational signalling aspects of social control would be most effective. This kind of behaviour, however, is not self-evident. As we have noted above, the three basic human tendencies are towards consistency or balance, attribution and evaluation.

We first analysed TLC cases along the five dimensions Wittek distinguished: to whom does the lead player talk? In almost half of the cases where trouble was relevant, the lead player talked directly to the other player in private; in just under one-third of these cases the lead player addressed the other player in public. In one-third of the trust cases, the lead player talked directly to the other player in private; in almost two-thirds of these cases the lead player addressed the other player in public. Talking formally to a superior is very rare. In some instances, two actions were taken by the lead player in succession. Both these actions were recorded when recounted to or observed by the researcher. Table 10.2 shows the succession of actions split up by type of case.

Table 10.2   *To whom the lead player talks, in first and second instance, by type of case*

| Number of cases (n = 197) | | Trust cases (n = 63) | Trust and trouble cases (n = 54) | Trouble cases (n = 80) |
|---|---|---|---|---|
| First action | Second action | | | |
| Privately to the other player (n = 83) | Privately | — | 1 | 1 |
| | Publicly | 1 | 3 | — |
| | Formally | 1 | 4 | 4 |
| | Indirectly | — | 5 | 10 |
| | No one | — | — | 1 |
| | Not applicable | 19 | 18 | 15 |
| In public to other player and colleagues (n = 80) | Privately | — | 3 | 5 |
| | Publicly | — | 4 | 2 |
| | Indirectly | — | — | 1 |
| | Not applicable | 39 | 8 | 19 |
| No one (n = 18) | Privately | — | 2 | 2 |
| | Publicly | — | 1 | — |
| | Indirectly | — | — | 1 |
| | Not applicable | 3 | — | 9 |
| Indirectly to a colleague (n = 13) | Privately | — | 4 | 4 |
| | Indirectly | — | — | 1 |
| | Formally | — | 1 | — |
| | Not applicable | — | — | 3 |
| Formally to a superior (n = 3) | Privately | — | — | 1 |
| | Publicly | — | — | 1 |
| | No one | — | — | 1 |

Bart Nooteboom (Chapter 2 in this volume) points us to the concept of 'voice' versus 'exit' as introduced by Hirschman (1970). Does an experience of trouble or trust violation lead you to 'exit' the relationship or do you 'voice' your concerns, needs and expectations? Our underlying assumption in the larger context of this research is that the better each of us is at voicing our side of the relationship in a constructive manner, the better our chances for a sustainable relationship. But, again, there are limits to voice and, when you reach them, you need to seriously consider exit if the trouble exceeds the benefit of the relationship. However, the more people who choose exit, the thinner the relationship networks for value creation.

When analysing the TLC cases, voice appears to be the dominant reaction when encountering trouble. Trouble is usually dealt with in direct interaction with the other player. Three-quarters of the cases in which trouble is relevant are in the first instance dealt with by talking directly to the other player, whether in private or in public. Furthermore, of those events where the lead player did not address the other player directly and there was a second action, this action nearly always involved addressing the other player directly (in private and in public). This yields a total of more than four-fifths of the cases in which the lead player voices his concern and trouble to the other person. Of the cases where the lead player initially talks to no one, this remains the case in most of the purely trouble cases. In all but one of the trust and trouble cases, the lead player in the first or second instance talks directly to the other player, thus enabling trust to unfold: voice, no exit.

Next we analysed whether the lead player suspends his judgment and inquires into the situation or whether he jumps to a conclusion about the motives of the other player. In the cases where trouble is relevant, just over one-third of the cases showed suspension and inquiry while the remainder showed immediate judgment. Jumping to a conclusion does not necessarily imply also imposing a sanction to seek redress. In the cases where trouble was relevant, far fewer cases showed that a sanction was applied than that the lead player immediately made judgments. In fact, in all the cases in which trouble occurred, sanctions were applied in just under a quarter of the cases.

Then an analysis was carried out to see whether third party mediation was sought. This happened in only a few cases. People within TLC appear to take their own responsibility and address trouble themselves, as shown above, usually directly to the other person. They do, however, seek advice from people they trust and who know the other player in a trouble situation. This is an interesting and important distinction to make: whether you ask someone's advice, but act yourself, or whether you ask someone to act on your behalf.

Within his five main trouble strategies, Wittek (1999) identified 15 different types of action that the lead player could take to address his trouble. We have added one based on our empirical findings and have split them along the dimensions identified above. This results in the matrix of possible actions by the lead player shown in Table 10.3. The possible actions (the percentages refer to the occurrence of the action in those cases in which trouble occurs) are as follows:

- resignation: keep anger to yourself and do nothing (10 per cent);
- avoidance: avoid meeting the person (1 per cent);
- retaliation: give the person a taste of his own medicine if the opportunity arises (1 per cent);
- confrontation: tell the person about trouble in a private discussion, expecting a reaction (16 per cent);
- direct complaint: complain to the person in a private discussion (8 per cent);
- direct inquiry: ask the person about his behaviour (12 per cent);
- private negotiation: as kindly as possible ask the person, in private, to change his behaviour (5 per cent);
- gossip: complain to colleagues about the person (4 per cent);
- indirect inquiry: ask other colleagues' opinion about the person's behaviour (4 per cent);
- leverage: ask a colleague to talk to the person (1 per cent);
- formal complaint: complain to a superior about the person (1 per cent);
- formal inquiry: ask a superior about the person's behaviour (1 per cent);
- arbitration: ask a superior to talk to the person (0 per cent);
- public complaint: complain in public about the person (with him present) (20 per cent);
- dialogue: ask about the person's behaviour and explain your experience in a group (4 per cent);
- public negotiation: as kindly as possible ask the person, in public, to change his behaviour (2 per cent);
- other, not coded (10 per cent).

In the categories in which the lead player inquires and explains or asks for mediation, he expresses a desire to continue, if possible deepen, the relationship. In the category where a sanction is applied immediately, ambivalence about the relationship is expressed. Avoidance signals an attitude to end the relationship, whereas resignation suggests ambivalence.

The most frequent action taken is 'public complaint'. This can range

*Table 10.3   Actions of the lead player*

| Talk to | No action | Immediately sanction | Inquire and explain | First inquire, then sanction | Ask for mediation |
|---|---|---|---|---|---|
| No one | • avoidance<br>• resignation | retaliation | — | — | — |
| Private to other player | — | direct complaint | • confrontation<br>• direct inquiry | private negotiation | — |
| Indirect to colleagues | — | gossip | indirect iniquiry | — | leverage |
| Formal to boss | — | formal complaint | formal inquiry | — | arbitration |
| Public to all at once | — | public complaint | dialogue | public negotiation | dialogue |

←——→  ←————————————————→
Ambivalent about relationship          Wants to continue, if possible deepen, relationship

from making a comment, almost in passing, when someone arrives late for a meeting to a 'serious' complaint about someone's behaviour in the discussion, often a fierce disagreement. The next most frequent action is 'confrontation'. This is not surprising, given the culture of TLC that expects you to confront the other person when he acts in a way that you do not like or that is not in line with the values and principles of TLC. Confrontation in this way does not entail sanctioning the other person. It is a clear and direct way to voice your trouble while indicating a desire to continue the relationship. The third most frequent action is 'direct inquiry'. This also entails voicing your trouble directly to the other person involved, only now it is done by asking a question and suspending your judgment. It is less strong than confrontation. Mediation, as shown before, is hardly ever sought. As mentioned earlier, TLC has a principle that 'we do not talk about people, but with people'. This implies that they do not gossip. As shown, gossip does occur, though rarely. Several cases showed, however, that when someone gossiped to another person about a third person not present, the other person confronted him or her with the fact that he or she was gossiping.

Another conclusion that emerges is that, wherever possible, within TLC compliments are given in public and trouble is dealt with privately. As said earlier, every opportunity to celebrate a success is taken, especially with newcomers. Almost two-thirds of the trust cases are dealt with publicly and are about giving a public compliment. Only one-third of the trouble cases are dealt with publicly. In three-quarters of the cases in which trouble was relevant, this was dealt with directly in private, in the first or second instance. People within TLC would probably say, 'So what? Isn't that normal behaviour?' According to Wittek's research, it is not. He researched the 16-man management team of a German paper factory during several periods in which trouble was addressed in different ways. The first period, in which trouble was dealt with privately in roughly 40 per cent of the cases and publicly in roughly 30 per cent of the cases, he labelled strong solidarity. In his explanation he refers to the relational frame that this group operated from: strong solidarity considerations were the salient relational frame of group membership which mattered most (see Siegwart Lindenberg, Chapter 3 in this volume). Wittek's interpretation:

> In correspondence with the high level of interdependence and solidarity, a strong reliance on [private] and public forms of control was found, with the former occurring significantly less and the latter significantly more often than one would expect. Obviously, public sanctioning provides a practical solution to the problem that [private] control efforts have a higher chance of being interpreted as negative control signals under conditions of strong solidarity. By making things public, the controller transfers a large part of the judgment about the legitimacy of the control effort to the group. This allows immediate feedback and reduces the chances of misinterpretations, but also puts more pressure on the target if the group considers the controller's claim as legitimate. Another side effect of a public sanction is that the controller can more easily show that it is not he, but the group that is the beneficiary of the sanction. (Wittek, 1999, p. 140)

In a later phase of Wittek's research, the context in which the management team operates has changed, especially in terms of the functional interdependencies. The researcher concludes that a relational frame with weak solidarity is now in operation. This results in approximately 55 per cent private actions and approximately 10 per cent public actions. Under this relational frame,

> Accepting advice and suggestions *in public* would immediately multiply the associated status loss by the number of peers present during such an event, so that the benefits of accepting the advice [. . .] would not outweigh the costs in terms of status loss. Nevertheless, this equation has a higher chance of resulting in a positive outcome when feedback is given bilaterally. [. . .] Therefore, the organizational context provided a setting in which private control attempts represented the least costly solution for both the controller and the target. (Ibid., p. 151)

Which relational frame is operational within TLC? TLC uses a frame of solidarity, not pure opportunism. But it is not pure strong solidarity as defined by Wittek and observed with the German management team in their first period. In his definition, in strong solidarity 'the salient goal is the realization of social and physical well-being of oneself *and* other actors in a *group'* (ibid., p. 53). This appears to be true also for TLC. Yet the description continues with 'a premium is put on redistribution and mutual sharing, that is, profits are distributed equally or according to need' and this does not appear to hold for TLC. The definition Wittek uses for weak solidarity also does not appear to apply. Weak solidarity is described as follows: 'the salient goal is the realization of a personal gain, but relational concerns are still present as a background goal and will therefore temper the unrestricted realization of profit. . . . Profits are distributed according to the principle of equity. Individuals are likely to keep individual accounts in order to trace their respective contributions and be able to come to a fair division of the profits' (ibid.). However, when we consider Lindenberg's description of the governance structure of an effective weak solidarity organization (Chapter 3 in this volume), we come to a different conclusion. TLC appears to be an effective weak solidarity organization as it appears to fulfil the criteria proposed by Lindenberg. Unfortunately, we do not have the space here for a more detailed analysis; this will be the subject of future publications.

In only the two direct trouble strategies – private and public – is a reaction of the other player possible, as he is not directly addressed in the other trouble strategies. The possible reactions of the other player can be characterized as follows (Table 10.4):

- makes repairs for past behaviour and changes behaviour;
- changes future behaviour;
- explains and is open to suggestions;
- wants to discuss a solution;
- continues behaviour;
- reacts hostilely;
- no reaction, often because he is not addressed directly.

The first three rows of the type of reaction signal an intention to want to continue the relationship, either at the same, or if possible a deeper, level (first two rows) or at a recalibrated level (third row). The reactions in the fourth and fifth rows signal ambivalence about the relationship and the last two rows signal loss of interest in the relationship.

The cases were analysed along these lines. The reactions of the other player were related to the first actions of the lead player (Table 10.5). In just

*Table 10.4    Reaction of the other player*

| Action of the lead player / Reaction of the other player | Private | Public |
|---|---|---|
| Makes repairs and changes behaviour | | |
| Changes future behaviour | | |
| Explains and is open to suggestions | | |
| Starts discussing solution | | |
| Continues behaviour | | |
| Reacts hostilely | | |
| No reaction | | |

*Table 10.5    Reaction of the other player related to action of lead player, for trouble, and trust and trouble, cases only*

| Action of the lead player / Reaction of the other player | Number of cases | | | | |
|---|---|---|---|---|---|
| | Privately (n = 62) | Publicly (n = 41) | Indirectly (n = 13) | Formally (n = 3) | No one (n = 15) |
| Makes repairs (n = 13) | 6 | 4 | 2 | — | 1 |
| Changes behaviour (n = 9) | 4 | 3 | 1 | — | 1 |
| Explains and open (n = 19) | 8 | 8 | 1 | — | 2 |
| Wants to discuss (n = 17) | 7 | 6 | 3 | — | 1 |
| Continues behaviour (n = 21) | 13 | 5 | 2 | — | 1 |
| Reacts hostilely (n = 13) | 8 | 4 | 1 | — | — |
| No reaction (n = 26) | 6 | 7 | 3 | 1 | 9 |
| Other, not coded (n = 16) | 10 | 4 | — | 2 | — |

under one-fifth of the cases, no reaction was given, in half of the cases this was because the other player was not addressed by the lead player and may therefore not have been aware of the troubling experience. In fact, if reacting hostilely or giving no reaction when spoken to directly (either privately or publicly) can be interpreted as signalling loss of interest in the relation-ship, then this happens in roughly one-fifth of the cases. However, not giving a reaction can also signal a silent acceptance of a point made.

In just over one-third of the cases in which the lead player addresses the other player directly (either privately or publicly), the other player responds in a way that can be read as wanting to continue the relationship: he makes repairs, changes his later behaviour or explains and is open to suggestions. In just over one-third of the cases in which the lead player addresses the other player directly (either privately or publicly), the other player responds in a way that can be read as being ambivalent about the relationship: he wants to discuss or continues his behaviour.

We also analysed whether the trouble was resolved and, if so, whether that happened immediately or at a later time. In roughly one-fifth of the cases where trouble was relevant, the trouble is resolved immediately; in almost one-third of the cases the trouble is resolved later. In this analysis a translation mistake created complications when the person involved did the coding. These participants interpreted the Dutch text as 'did you talk about the trouble to resolve it?', rather than 'in your mind is the trouble resolved?' Hence many participants answered with 'no resolution', even though in their minds the trouble was over, resolved. This is confirmed by relating res-olution of the trouble to the perceived impact on the relationship: in 50 per cent of the cases where 'no resolution' was coded, the impact on the rela-tionship was 'deepened' or 'restored'. When we reinterpret the cases with 'no resolution' and 'deepened' or 'restored' as 'resolution', just over three-quarters of the cases where trouble is relevant are resolved. This finding corresponds to the coding done independently by the researcher, which for this variable is sufficiently reliable as, during the interviews, data were col-lected about resolution of the trouble. Thus we appear able to conclude that, within TLC, trouble usually gets resolved. When looking at the types of action taken, we observe that, in nearly all of the cases that result in immediate resolution, the other person was spoken to directly, in private or in public.

**Impact on Relationship**

Both parties involved, the lead player and the other player, evaluate the impact of the event on the relationship, provided the latter has been aware of the troubling experience he has caused the lead player (Figure 10.1). If both parties conclude that a mishap or misunderstanding has occurred which need not happen again, the relationship will most likely be restored, if not deepened. If one or both parties conclude that a disagreement has surfaced which has not been resolved and may therefore lead to similar

| | | Lead Player | | | |
|---|---|---|---|---|---|
| | | Mishap | Misunderstanding | Disagreement | Distrust |
| Other Player | Mishap | RESTORE OR DEEPEN | | RECALIBRATE OR RUPTURE | |
| | Misunderstanding | | | | |
| | Disagreement | RECALIBRATE OR RUPTURE | | | |
| | Distrust | | | | |

*Figure 10.1   Evaluation of event and impact on relationship*

trouble in the future, the relationship will most likely be recalibrated, provided the parties involved have both shown an interest in continuing the relationship (or there was an initial ambivalence that turned into an interest in continuing). This recalibration may be limited to the specific dimension of the trustworthiness involved, or involve all dimensions. If one or both parties conclude that grounds for distrust have surfaced that have not been resolved satisfactorily, the relationship may well be ruptured.

One possible ground for relationship rupture, apart from the trouble that triggered this process, is that one of the parties involved behaved in a way that signalled loss of interest in the relationship. Distrust, however, need not always lead to relationship rupture. It can very well lead to relationship recalibration. This will be the case, for example, if the party who is seen as behaving in a untrustworthy manner has shown lack of competence, but good benevolence, dedication and integrity. The following categories were used for the evaluation of what happened.

- It was a mishap and won't happen again.
- It was a misunderstanding and won't happen again.
- We disagree and respect each other's position.
- We disagree on this and I have to take it into account in the future.
- I distrust the other in this respect and I have to take that into account in the future.

The categories used for the quality of the relationship (adapted from Lewicki and Bunker, 1996) are as follows:

- relationship is deepened;
- relationship is restored to previous level, or the event has no impact;
- relationship is recalibrated downwards, only for the specific dimension of trustworthiness involved;
- relationship is recalibrated downwards, for all dimensions of trustworthiness involved;
- relationship is ruptured.

It has been difficult to obtain valid information about the impact on the relationship from the perspective of the other player. We have good data for the evaluation of the lead player about what happened and the impact it has on the quality of the relationship, but data for the evaluation of the other player are missing in more than half of the cases. The lead player's evaluation of what has happened is related to his view on the quality of the relationship (Table 10.6).

As predicted in the theory developed above, a mishap and a misunderstanding lead to a restoration or deepening of the relationship. A disagreement that you have to take into account in the future leads to a recalibration on that specific dimension or has no impact on the relationship. The impact of distrust can usually be contained to a recalibration on the specific dimension, but relationship rupture and total recalibration also occur. The category 'the source of the trouble was wrong and has learned' was not initially foreseen and was added while coding the cases. The admission of being wrong and showing that you have learned not only allows for a restoration of the relationship, but can also lead to a deepening of the relationship. A similar phenomenon appears to occur with the category 'we disagree and respect each other's position'. Whereas a disagreement that you have to take account of in the future often leads to a recalibration on that dimension, there are also situations where you disagree, but can afford to just respect each other's position; you do not have to come to an agreement in order to function. Finally, in the trust and trouble cases the evaluation of what happened can also be 'the trust I put into the other was honoured'. This leads to a deepening of trust or the restoration of trust. Roughly two-thirds of the trouble cases had no negative impact on the relationship: the relationship was not affected, was restored or even deepened.

We asked the lead player to indicate the severity of the trouble, with a 1 for a very slight trouble event and a 10 for a very severe trouble event. We received such a grading for 77 per cent of the cases in which trouble was relevant. In some instances we also asked the other player to grade the trouble. We must stress that these grades are perceptions of those involved. For example, an employee in the finance department graded an incident where a management team member jokingly uttered a prejudice against finance

Table 10.6 *Evaluation of lead player about what happened, related to his view on quality of the relationship, for trouble, and trust and trouble, cases only*

| Quality of relationship | Number of cases | | | | | |
|---|---|---|---|---|---|---|
| | Deepen (n=29) | Restore or no impact (n=59) | Recalibrate, specific (n=18) | Recalibrate, all (n=4) | Rupture (n=2) | Unknown, not coded (n=22) |
| What happened: | | | | | | |
| Trust honoured (t&t cases; n=20) | 12 | 8 | — | — | — | — |
| Mishap (n=17) | 3 | 12 | — | — | — | 2 |
| Misunderstanding (n=11) | 8 | 3 | — | — | — | — |
| Source was wrong, learned (n=12) | 2 | 9 | — | — | — | 1 |
| Disagree, respect (n=4) | 1 | 3 | — | — | — | — |
| Disagree, take into account (n=21) | — | 11 | 7 | 1 | 1 | 1 |
| Distrust, take into account (n=21) | — | 6 | 11 | 3 | 1 | — |
| Other, unknown (n=28) | 3 | 7 | — | — | — | 18 |

people with a 10, while the management team member graded it with a 3. When asked about the high grade, the employee answered that this was the most severe trouble she experienced within TLC (which can be interpreted as a positive sign) and that it was not so much this one incident as the regularity and repetitiveness of similar incidents that made this a relatively severe trouble. Another example: during partner meetings two senior partners regularly have fierce arguments and debates. Both of them consistently grade these events as trouble severity 1, commenting that this is how they can behave towards each other as the relationship is so solid, based on respect and trust, that neither of them fears the confrontation.

Table 10.7 shows the relationship between the severity of the trouble and the lead player's perception of the quality of the relationship after the event. What is striking is the high frequency of deepening relationships with severe cases of trouble. In just over two-thirds of the cases where the relationship deepened after the trouble event, the trouble was rated with a severity of 7 or more. Most of these cases were coded as trust and trouble cases, rather than pure trouble cases. In all but one of these cases the other player was addressed directly; that is, voice was used. In all but four of these

*Table 10.7   Severity of trouble, related to lead player's view on quality of the relationship, for trouble, and trust and trouble, cases only*

| Quality of relationship | Number of cases | | | | | |
|---|---|---|---|---|---|---|
| | Deepen (n=29) | Restore (n=59) | Recalibrate, specific (n=18) | Recalibrate, all (n=4) | Rupture (n=2) | Unknown, not coded (n=22) |
| **Severity of trouble:** | | | | | | |
| 1 (n=11) | — | 10 | — | — | — | 1 |
| 2 (n=6) | 2 | 3 | — | — | — | 1 |
| 3 (n=5) | — | 4 | — | — | 1 | — |
| 4 (n=11) | 1 | 7 | 2 | 1 | — | — |
| 5 (n=6) | 3 | 2 | — | — | — | 1 |
| 6 (n=12) | 1 | 5 | 2 | 2 | — | 2 |
| 7 (n=18) | 3 | 8 | 5 | — | — | 2 |
| 8 (n=19) | 7 | 6 | 2 | — | — | 4 |
| 9 (n=5) | 3 | 1 | — | — | 1 | — |
| 10 (n=10) | 7 | 3 | — | — | — | — |
| **Other, unknown (n=31)** | 2 | 10 | 7 | 1 | — | 11 |

cases (that is, in four-fifths of the cases) the other player responded in the first instance in a constructive manner (making repairs, explaining, supporting, open for discussion). This serves to illustrate how severe trouble can trigger a process that can lead to a deepening of trust, provided that both players use voice and that they act in a constructive manner towards each other, signalling that they want to continue the relationship.

## CONCLUSIONS

The purpose of this chapter was to identify how people within an organization deal with trust and trouble. How is trust developed and maintained? How does trouble influence this process? We have done this by collecting and analysing empirical data through interviews and observations of the people working within the Dutch office of an international professional services firm. In analysing the results, we checked how useful the theory developed in the literature is in helping us understand the dynamics of trust and trouble. We found that, for most of the dimensions and angles we wanted to investigate, useful theoretical models exist, though some needed to be adapted for our purposes. Adaptations of existing models were especially relevant when analysing the dimensions of trustworthiness, effective actions for building trust and the relevant dimensions of trouble strategies. We believe these to be valuable contributions to the body of knowledge on this topic.

Furthermore, we found that this approach provides useful insights into the dynamics of trust and trouble at the micro level of an organization, in this case TLC. The Dutch office of TLC appears to be high trust. Most relationships appear to be good, if not strong. Apart from the two cases where the relationship was considered to be ruptured, I have not heard anyone say, 'I will never work with that person', or 'I will actively avoid having to work with that person', but that is also strongly against the culture. The high trust becomes apparent from the following observations.

- Relationships within TLC appear to develop beyond a pure cognition-based and functional stage.
- TLC is very explicit in its vision, mission, values and principles, thus enhancing value congruence. This not only reduces the chances of trouble due to unacceptable values and principles, but it also enhances the resolution of trouble when, inevitably, it does occur.
- Effective trust-building actions can be observed regularly within TLC. The main trust development strategy that TLC adopts as an institution is the intensive socialization process that newcomers into the organization are 'subjected' to.

- Voice is the dominant reaction when encountering trouble.
- Trouble usually gets resolved.
- Wherever possible, compliments are given in public and trouble is dealt with privately. Every opportunity to celebrate a success is taken, especially with newcomers. This helps build the trust others have in the newcomer.
- Severe trouble can trigger a process that can lead to a deepening of the trust provided that both players use voice and act in a constructive manner towards each other, signalling that they want to continue the relationship.

Further research can be formulated in three different directions to reduce the bias present and to complete the picture. Firstly, there is a bias inherent in the method of data collection. This bias consists of the fact that only cases that were told to the researcher in interviews or that were observed in public settings were recorded. The method of collecting trouble cases was taken from Wittek (1999) and Morrill (1995) and developed to include trust cases. Wittek also recognized the bias that this method only captures a fraction of all the relevant events. Respondents may focus their attention either on particularly serious issues or on relatively recent grievances. Moreover, the researcher did not have access to all meetings or private discussions. In the next phase of the research, we will correct for this bias by conducting a survey to inquire into the full range of possible trust and trouble strategies.

The second avenue for further research is aimed at extending the analysis from the micro level to the macro level. During the interviews and observations, data were collected about the organizational context: the norms, values, underlying assumptions, procedures, processes and structures. We will analyse how the organizational context affects the micro-level dynamics of trust and trouble. Finally, the research will be extended to other organizations.

## NOTES

1. A case is considered 'trust and trouble' when both are explicitly referred to.
2. Unfortunately, these words are so typically TLC that giving examples would give away the true identity of TLC to outsiders.

## REFERENCES

Argyris, C. (1970), *Intervention Theory and Method: A Behavioral Science View*, Reading, MA: Addison-Wesley.

Barney, J.B. and M.H. Hansen (1994), 'Trustworthiness as a source of competitive advantage', *Strategic Management Journal*, **15**, 175–90.

Boon, S.D. and J.G. Holmes (1991), 'The dynamics of interpersonal trust: resolving uncertainty in the face of risk', in R.A. Hinde and J. Groebel (eds), *Cooperation and Prosocial Behaviour*, Cambridge: Cambridge University Press, pp. 190–211.

Bradach, J.L. and R.G. Eccles (1989), 'Price, authority and trust: from ideal types to plural forms', *Annual Review of Sociology*, **15**, 97–118.

Deutsch, M. (1973), *The Resolution of Conflict: Constructive and Destructive Processes*, New Haven: Yale University Press.

Fukuyama, F. (1995), *Trust: The Social Virtues and the Creation of Prosperity*, New York: The Free Press.

Ghoshal, S. and C.A. Bartlett (1997), *The Individualized Corporation, Great Companies Are Defined by Purpose, Process and People*, New York: HarperPerennial.

Hardin, R. (1993), 'The street-level epistemology of trust', *Analyse & Kritik*, **14**, 152–76.

Hirschman, A.O. (1970), *Exit, Voice and Loyalty Responses to Decline in Firms Organizations and States*, Cambridge, MA: Harvard University Press.

Isaacs, W. (1999), *Dialogue and the Art of Thinking Together*, New York: Currency-Doubleday.

Lewicki, R.J. and B.B. Bunker (1996), 'Developing and maintaining trust in work relationships', in R.M. Kramer and T.R. Tyler (eds), *Trust in Organizations: Frontiers of Theory and Research*, Thousand Oaks: Sage, pp. 114–39.

Lewis, J.D. and A. Weigert (1985), 'Trust as a social reality', *Social Forces*, **63** (3), 967–84.

Luhmann, N. (1979), *Trust and Power*, Chicester: John Wiley & Sons.

Mayer, R.C., J.H. Davis and F.D. Schoorman (1995), 'An integrative model of organizational trust', *Academy of Management Review*, **20** (3), 703–34.

McAllister, D.J. (1995), 'Affect- and cognition-based trust as foundations for interpersonal cooperation in organizations', *Academy of Management Journal*, **38**(1), 24–59.

McAllister, D.J. (1997), 'The second face of trust: reflections on the dark side of interpersonal trust in organizations', *Research on Negotiation in Organizations*, **6**, 87–111.

Morrill, C. (1995), *The Executive Way, Conflict Management in Corporations*, Chicago: University of Chicago Press.

Nooteboom, B. (2000), 'Trust as a governance device', in M. Casson and A. Godley (eds), *Cultural Factors in Economic Growth*, Amsterdam: Elsevier.

Shaw, R.B. (1997), *Trust in the Balance, Building Successful Organizations on Results, Integrity and Concern*, San Francisco: Jossey-Bass.

Tyler, T.R. and R.M. Kramer (1996), 'Whither trust?', in R.M. Kramer and T.R. Tyler (eds), *Trust in Organizations: Frontiers of Theory and Research*, Thousand Oaks: Sage, pp. 1–15.

Wittek, R.P.M. (1999), 'Interdependence and Informal Control in Organizations', dissertation, University of Groningen.

Zand, D.E. (1972), 'Trust and managerial problem solving', *Administrative Science Quarterly*, **17** (2), 229–39.

Zand, D.E. (1997), *The Leadership Triad, Knowledge, Trust and Power*, New York: Oxford University Press.

Zucker, L.G. (1986), 'Production of trust: institutional sources of economic structure, 1840–1920', *Research in Organizational Behaviors*, **8**, 53–111.
Zucker, L.G., M.R. Darby, M.B. Brewer and Yusheng Peng (1996), 'Collaboration
structure and information dilemmas in biotechnology: organizational boundaries as trust production', in R.M. Kramer and T.R. Tyler (eds), *Trust in
Organizations: Frontiers of Theory and Research*, Thousand Oaks: Sage, pp.
90–113.

# 11 Conclusions

## Frédérique Six and Bart Nooteboom

## SURVEY OF RESULTS

In Chapter 1, we gave a survey of some of the fundamentals of trust: definitions, objects of trust ('trustees'), aspects of behaviour that one can have trust in, and conditions, foundations and sources of trust. We also summarized a theory of knowledge as a basis for the analysis of trust. We also briefly discussed the relation between trust in an organization and trust in the people in it. An important theme running through the book is the relation between trust and control. Often trust has to go beyond control, in what we called 'real' trust, but such 'real' trust is bounded by the potential use of control.

In Chapter 2, Bart Nooteboom gave a survey of the literature on the trust process. He highlighted the use of psychological 'frames' and decision heuristics that play a role in the attribution of intentions and competencies to participants in organizational processes, in the inference of trustworthiness, and stages in the process of 'trust production'.

In Chapter 3, Siegwart Lindenberg proposed several conditions that help create governance structures for facilitating frame stability and effective relational signalling, which in turn were argued to be important for trust development. He developed a theory in which individuals pursue goals under constraints and argued that in most organizations people operate under a 'weak solidarity' frame in which two master frames – the gain frame and the normative frame – keep each other in check. Here we encounter the issue of trust and control. People within organizations are constantly looking for signs in each other's behaviour about the stability of the other's frame. It is therefore important that governance structures help support the stability of the salient frame.

In Chapter 5, Henk de Vos and Rudi Wielers also argued that there is a limited set of master frames – in their terminology a 'complex' – from which people operate. They proposed that trust should be seen as part of the 'reciprocity complex'. They showed that trust in organizations can be analysed from an evolutionary perspective, how the 'reciprocity complex' can act as a source of resistance to market penetration and how this influences the behaviour of market participants. The analysis shows how trust can be viable under market conditions.

In the previous chapter, Chapter 4, Reinhard Bachmann also investigated governance and coordination, but from another perspective. He concluded his examination of the interplay of trust and power as coordination mechanisms within organizations with the statement that two distinct patterns of organizational control can be reconstructed, depending on the forms of trust and power and their specific combination. The first pattern is the strongly regulated organization where power primarily exists in the form of impersonal rules and procedures. This produces institutional and system trust. Personal trust and personal power are less important in this pattern. The second pattern is the more flexible organization where much depends on the individuals' idiosyncratic interests and the situational circumstances in which they make their decisions. Personal trust and personal power play an important role in this pattern.

Ana Cristina Costa's research in Chapter 6 showed how trust within teams is influenced by the composition of the teams and by work and organizational contextual factors. Three major conditions were identified that influence the level of trust within work teams: the quality of the interaction among team members, the level of interdependence and the degree of participation and influence in the organization.

Deanne den Hartog's research in Chapter 7 contributed to insight in the relationship between trust and leadership, showing that inspirational leadership is strongly related to different forms of trust in the leader. Trust in management is highly positively related to inspirational leadership as well as trust in the leader and perceived leader integrity, and less to transactional leadership. Inspirational leadership is related positively to trust in colleagues, but transactional leadership is not related to such trust.

In Chapter 8, Nathalie Lazaric described the experiences of a French steel company as it went through a significant change process of knowledge building and found that trust was crucial for success, notably for the tacit knowledge in the heads of the individuals to be made available for codification, for acceptance of the expert system and for continued support to keep the system up to date. She described how trust was built along every step of the change process.

Rafael Wittek's contribution in Chapter 9 employed relational signalling to analyse the way in which norm violations – here trust violations – are dealt with. His research found support for the multidimensional sanction hypothesis that sanctions are cognitively classified into at least two latent dimensions representing negative and positive relational signals. He also found support for the escalation hypothesis, which states that the willingness to allocate a sanction as well as the strength of the sanction are a function of the relational signalling character of the grievance. The third hypothesis, the group obligation hypothesis, was contradicted.

In Frédérique Six's research in Chapter 10, the case study of an organization showed many ways in which conditions influence trust: a combination of regularly observed effective trust-building actions, an intensive socialization process and the explicit formulation of vision, mission, values and principles. This led to high trust and (hence?) voice as the dominant response when encountering trouble, and a high degree of trouble resolution. Also severe trouble was seen to be able to trigger a process that can lead to a deepening of trust, provided that both players use voice and that they act in a constructive manner towards each other, signalling that they want to continue the relationship.

Implicit in our four-place predicate of trust – someone (trustor) trusts something or someone (trustee) with respect to something (competence, intentions), depending on the conditions – is the assumption that no one can be trusted in all respects under all conditions. There are valid reasons and occasions for distrust. The central issue in building trust appears to be not 'the more I can trust him the better it is', but 'how well do I know under which conditions I can trust him to do what?' (Gabarro, 1978). Thus it is best to take the other person's strengths and weaknesses as more or less given for the moment. The task, then, when building trust, is to get as realistic a picture as possible of the other person's likely behaviour under different conditions. One will probably have some influence in the sense that some parts of the other's behaviour can be negotiated. Relational signalling becomes a very important part of the interaction and interpretation of the interaction. This approach to the trust process puts an emphasis on the actions taken, communication skills and learning ability of the people involved and their psychological state of mind, as described by Nooteboom in Chapter 2. In the next section we develop this central issue into challenges for future research.

## AVENUES FOR FURTHER RESEARCH

The avenues for further research into the trust process are numerous. Following on the contributions in this volume, we highlight some below, without claiming that the list is complete. We also add suggestions made during the research seminar we organized in Rotterdam in May 2001, where most of the contributions in this volume were presented and discussed. First, we would like to suggest that, given the current status of research in this field, the focus should now be on further empirical testing of the many theories proposed and on the integration and synthesis of the many different approaches suggested. What is actually going on in organizations? What are good methodologies for researching this? Given the multifaceted phenomenon that the trust process is, it appears necessary to apply a multi-method approach in empirical research. In the literature, most authors define trust as a state, a belief, an expectation or a willingness. Methodologies that ask people about their willingness, belief or intention, such as (self-rating) surveys, get results that relate to this definition of trust. Other academics point to the importance of trusting behaviour and propose that it is your own trusting behaviour that is the best way to show your trustworthiness. Methodologies that are event-based, such as observations, the trust and trouble case analysis methodology, and the vignette methodology, may be better at capturing the dynamics and interaction of trust and how it develops. In this volume both approaches have been taken. It may be worth while to combine the two approaches within one organization in the future.

Second, as an important implication of the central issue stated above, an important research question is how we learn about the other person in a new relationship and how we continue to learn in an already established relationship. How do we observe and interpret the other person's behaviour? Which factors influence these processes? Theoretical indications were given in Chapters 2 and 3. Several of the contributions in this volume provided empirical studies of the trust process. Gabarro (1978) has done empirical research on the relationships that new executives build up with those who report directly to them. There is scope for much further empirical research on the question of 'how well one knows under which conditions one can trust someone to do what', the role of external market conditions and internal organizational conditions, such as organizational culture.

Related to this second avenue is the third: what are the roles of voice and the art of voice (Hirschman, 1970), information (Zand, 1972), learning about the other (Gabarro 1978) and relational signalling (Lindenberg, Wittek and Six in Chapters 3, 9 and 10 of the present volume) in building trust over time, given the assumptions of limits to trust and the inevitability of trouble? In several of the contributions parts of this puzzle were addressed, but much more work needs to be done to develop and integrate these concepts. In trust development, communication, information and relational signalling are important. How can these be put together in an integrative model? In dealing with trouble we are especially interested in the impact of trouble on the perceived trust quality of the relationship. The way in which the trouble is dealt with is shown by Six (Chapter 10) to be critical. Hirschman (1970) in his seminal essay uses the notion of the 'art of voice' to indicate that voice is not something that is straightforward to put into practice. If the central issue in trust development is as we propose, then learning about the other person becomes crucial. Viewing trouble events as opportunities to learn more about the other person appears to be a very constructive way of dealing with trouble. Viewing trouble as something to be avoided at all costs will make you act differently towards the other person. In the former case, you are more likely to suspend your judgment and inquire into the motives behind the other person's behaviour, hoping to learn more about him so that the limits to his trustworthiness may be revealed. In the latter case, it is more likely that sanctions aimed at punishing the other person are applied immediately. What are the critical elements in reacting to a trouble experience and how can this 'art of voice' be developed? Lindenberg and Nooteboom used the notion of 'framing', Lindenberg, Wittek and Six used the notion of 'relational signalling', and Nooteboom used the notion of 'attribution'. How are these notions related?

A fourth avenue for further research relates to the issue of trust processes over time. Nooteboom gave a theoretical discussion of stages in the trust process. How are these reflected in practice? As shown in Chapters 9 and 10, there are critical moments when someone perceives a violation of trust. This is a very fragile point: if the conditions are just wrong because of misunderstandings or the institutional environment is not conducive, the trouble or the disruption of the expectations can lead to an unravelling of trust. And if you just turn the knobs slightly on the conditions, it can lead to the deepening of trust. What are these critical conditions?

Fifth, what is the influence of the organizational context and which elements or patterns of elements are critical? What is the impact of the team or leadership? Relevant elements appear to be organizational culture, functional interdependencies, degree of ambiguity/uncertainty and the role of third parties. Den Hartog (in Chapter 7) points to the importance of the dynamics of trust and distrust between leaders and followers and the antecedents and consequences of such trust and distrust. What are the stages of development in trust in the leader and in generalized others? What is the relationship between leadership styles and forms of trust? What are the (possible consequences of the) leaders' violations of subordinates' trust and vice versa?

A sixth avenue for further research addresses the questions, can trust go too far, and when is trust counterproductive? The literature on social capital versus social liability deals with this issue. The social structure, or pattern of relationships, of an organization can generate social capital or social liability, and each in different degrees. However, there is controversy when social structure translates into social capital, and when it translates into social liability. For example, Nahapiet and Ghoshal (1998) argue that conditions for the development of social capital are: relationship stability and durability; that social capital increases with use; that there are high levels of mutual interdependence; and that there is a shared identity and a sense of sociological boundary. At the same time, other authors argue that social structure translates into social liability when current, strong relationships constrain the behaviour of actors, impeding their action and attainment of goals (Gabbay and Leenders, 1999); and too close relationships discourage social actors from taking risks that are connected to fundamental innovation (Bachmann, 1998). Other proponents of the view that 'strong links lead to social liability' are Burt (1997) and Granovetter (1973). The two positions appear to refer to similar conditions, for opposite results. We believe that this apparent contradiction can be resolved. One pointer may be that, if you look at counterproductive processes such as 'groupthink', the question should be raised whether trust is the problem or whether it is actually the lack of heterogeneity and too strong cohesion. Nooteboom (2002a) suggested a trade-off between, on the one hand, sufficient stability and perhaps a certain degree of exclusiveness in relations, for the sake of trust building, and on, the other hand, flexibility and variety for the sake of change and innovation. Empirical research is needed to investigate how this trade-off is made, and what the effects are on organizational performance, under different market conditions.

Related to this issue, a seventh question is how to end relationships. So far, most researchers have focused on the role of trust in building and maintaining relationships, but it can be argued that trust also plays an important role in ending a relationship. There are also 'voice' ways to end relationships (Nooteboom, 1999, 2002b). Business relationships are ended regularly, sometimes only for the sake of flexibility and change, and the previous partners (employee–employer, supplier–customer, alliance partners) part in many different ways. In an increasingly intertwined economic society there are productive and unproductive ways of parting that have, among others, reputational effects.

A final avenue is how to connect trust on the individual and on the organizational level. Nooteboom (in Chapter 2) and Bachmann (in Chapter 4) have each touched on the issue. Trust in people and trust in their organization are related in the roles that people play in their organization, organizational processes of motivation and monitoring, and organizational culture. How can one be sufficiently certain that different individuals, most of whom one has never met personally, will act in a predictable manner? More research on this is needed. How, more precisely, does the organizational context have its effect? How does that depend on external conditions, such as market pressures? How robust, for example, is trust between workers under threat of lay-offs? Individual behaviour is guided by the social context in which it operates. In psychology, the attraction–selection–attrition theory (Schneider *et al.*, 1998) states that organizations tend towards homogeneity of personality. Research on organizational culture shows that organizational members tend to share values and practices that make them behave in particular, predictable, ways. This is related to the notion of an organization as a 'focusing device', discussed in Chapter 1. If the organizational context encourages trusting and trustworthy behaviour, then most people may exhibit such behaviour, thus creating a pattern that we then call a high-trust organization.

# REFERENCES

Bachmann, R. (1998), 'Conclusion: Trust – Conceptual Aspects of a Complex Phenomenon', in C. Lane and R. Bachmann (eds), *Trust within and between Organizations: Conceptual Issues and Empirical Applications*, Oxford: Oxford University Press, pp. 298–322.

Burt, R.S. (1997), 'The contingent value of social capital', *Administrative Science Quarterly*, **42**, 339–65.

Gabarro, J.J. (1978), 'The development of trust, influence and expectations', in A.G. Athos and J.J. Gabarro, *Interpersonal Behavior, Communication and Understanding in Relationships*, Englewood Cliffs, NY: Prentice-Hall, pp. 290–303.

Gabbay, S.M. and R.Th.A.J. Leenders (1999), 'CSC: the structure of advantage and disadvantage', in R.Th.A.J. Leenders and S.M. Gabbay, *Corporate Social Capital and Liability*, Boston: Kluwer Academic Publishers, pp. 1–14.

Granovetter, M.S. (1973), 'The strengths of weak ties', *American Journal of Sociology*, **78** (6), 1360–80.

Hirschman, A.O. (1970), *Exit, Voice and Loyalty: Responses to Decline in Firms, Organizations and States*, Cambridge, MA: Harvard University Press.

Nahapiet, J. and S. Ghoshal (1998), 'Social capital, intellectual capital and the organizational advantage', *Academy of Management Review*, **23**, 242–66.

Nooteboom, B. (1999), *Inter-firm Alliances: Analysis and Design*, London: Routledge.

Nooteboom, B. (2002a), *Trust: Forms, Foundations, Functions, Failures and Figures*, Cheltenham, UK and Northampton, MA: Edward Elgar.

Nooteboom, B. (2002b), 'A balanced theory of sourcing, collaboration and networks', ERIM research paper, Rotterdam School of Management, Erasmus University Rotterdam.

Schneider, B., D.B. Smith, S. Taylor and J. Fleenor (1998), 'Personality and organizations: a test of the homogeneity of personality hypothesis', *Journal of Applied Psychology*, **83** (3), 462–70.

Zand, D.E. (1972), 'Trust and managerial problem solving', *Administrative Science Quarterly*, **17** (2), 229–39.

# Index

Printed and bound by CPI Group (UK) Ltd, Croydon, CR0 4YY

23/04/2025

14660956-0006